NIGHT

of a

MILLION

the inside story of Project Pearl

MIRACLES

Published by Open Doors International, Inc.
P.O. Box 27001
Santa Ana, CA 92799 USA

Library of Congress Cataloging-in-Publication Data
ISBN: 978-0-901644-10-7

Dedicated to the memory of Dr. Ed Neteland,
former ODI Executive Vice President,
who moved on to a better home
on December 3, 2006

〰

Contents

Cast of Characters vi

Acronyms viii

Prologue ix

1   The Vision 1

2   The Team 11

3   The Commitment 21

4   The Plan 31

5   The Preparations 41

6   The Tugboat 55

7   The Miracles 71

8   Paradise Regained 89

9   The Embarkation 103

10   The Needs in China 113

11   The Surprise 125

12   The Wait 137

13   Snake Bay 151

14   More than Conquerors 159

15   Welcome to the Party 171

16   The Promised Land 181

17   The Wet Bibles 193

18   More Precious than Gold 203

19   High Tide at Nine 215

20   China Today 219

Epilogue: Faith Steps to Accomplish the Impossible 227

Acknowledgments 233

Appendix: *Time* Magazine Story: Risky Rendezvous at Swatow . . . 237

Notes 240

Cast of Characters

Open Doors International (ODI) Management
Brother Andrew, Netherlands, President
Sealy Yates, USA, International Board Chairman
Dr. Ed Neteland, USA, Executive Vice President

Pearl Planning Team
Joseph Lee, Philippines, Asia Program Manager
Pablo, Canada, Asia Research Manager; Coordinator for Project
    Pearl
Keith Ritter, USA, Japan Director for Open Doors–Asia; Chaplain
    for the Project Pearl team
Dr. Jim Schmook, USA, Open Doors International Program
    Consultant
Doug Sutphen, USA, Open Doors Director for Asia
Captain Bill Tinsley, USA, CEO Sea Biosystems, Inc.

China Distribution Coordinators
Lili, Internal Distribution Coordinator
Chan
Mei-ling

China House Church Leaders
Mama and Papa Kwang (in Hong Kong)
John Chow
Matthew Lo
Enoch Ma
Peter Wang
Samuel Wu

Long-Term Crew Members on Tugboat *Michael*

Alastair Barr, UK
Cor Beukema, Netherlands
Michael Bruce, Australia
Terry Madison, Canada
Todd Miller, USA
Ronald Paras, Philippines
Bill Schwartz, USA
Jerry Simmons, USA
Douglas T. Sutphen Jr., USA

Short-Term Crew Members on Tugboat *Michael*

Art Babbington, Australia
Eddie Cairns, New Zealand
Bob Cole, Australia
John Everingham, Australia
Mark Houghton, New Zealand
Ivan Scott, New Zealand

Early Crew Not on the Final Delivery

Herman Boonstra, Netherlands
Faithful, Ghana
Terry Hickey, USA
John Kulisich, USA
Sonny Largado, Philippines
Godfrey O'Neale, Trinidad

Project Assistants

Dean Keaney, USA
Frank Phillips, USA
Lil Tinsley, USA

Note: In some cases, to protect identities only first names are given.

Acronyms

CIM   China Inland Mission. The missionary society founded by Hudson Taylor, today known as Overseas Missionary Fellowship (OMF).

ODI   Open Doors International. The international ministry, founded by Brother Andrew, whose mission is to encourage persecuted Christians.

PLA   Peoples' Liberation Army. China's military arm often called on to help in policing matters of national security.

PSB   Public Security Bureau. The national policing arm of China's Communist government.

TSPM   Three-Self Patriotic Movement. The Protestant arm of China's Religious Affairs Bureau, established in the early 1950s. The term *Three-Self* is based on the old missionary paradigm of indigenous churches: self-supporting, self-governing, and self-propagating. The TSPM is the registered Protestant Church of China. Many house churches oppose being registered for a number of reasons, mainly because of their belief in separation of church and state.

YWAM   Youth with a Mission

Prologue

In Shantou, China, a young Christian named Daniel Ng is on his knees. "Lord," he prays passionately, "I don't know why You have not answered my prayer for a Bible of my own, but You know. I promise You that I will give the rest of my life to distributing Your Word. Please send me a Bible."

⟩⟩⟩⟩⟩⟩

The candle flickers as it begins to burn out in a small room in Inner Mongolia. As she has done many times in the past, Sister Grace has worked most of the night hand copying from a borrowed Bible. She is exhausted yet exhilarated by the words she writes. Before taking a few hours to rest, she breathes an oft-repeated prayer: "God, what I desire most is a Bible of my own."

⟩⟩⟩⟩⟩⟩

In rural Zhejiang Province, dozens of villagers gather for a secret baptism at a secluded place along the riverbank. There is a bright full moon, and the reflections of a hundred lanterns dance on the water.

The local pastor speaks in a strong voice, quoting John 6:35 and 51: *"Then Jesus declared, 'I am the bread of life. He who comes to me will never go hungry, and he who believes in me will never be thirsty . . . I am the living bread that came down from heaven. If anyone eats of this bread, he will live forever.' "*

The pastor closes his Bible and carefully hands it to his assistant. Only the pastor has a Bible; during the Cultural Revolution era the local supply of Bibles was decimated. He speaks loudly yet compassionately, and his message is challenging: "Who among you is willing to eat this bread? Who among you is willing to give his life to Jesus? Let him come forward now! Let him put to death his old life and rise from these waters alive—a new creation in Christ Jesus!"

As people push forward, the pastor baptizes them "in the name of the Father, the Son, and the Holy Spirit."

Midway through the baptism, an eruption of bright lights and roaring vehicles pierces the quiet night. Army trucks are heading directly toward the people gathered at the river. They brake sharply and two dozen or more Chinese soldiers emerge suddenly onto the riverbank. Wielding their batons, the soldiers break up the gathering.

The unarmed villagers are helpless before them and neither the very old nor the very young are shown any mercy. The soldiers beat women and children along with the men. Anyone in their path receives a crack from a baton. And as people fall to the ground, the soldiers march on, oblivious to the fallen bodies beneath their feet.

Finally, the villagers who are still standing carry the wounded away. The pastor, however, is arrested, and his precious Bible is confiscated.

⚬⚬⚬

Brother Lee is riding his bicycle quickly down a rutted path in China's central Henan Province. He has made the twenty-kilometer trip many times before. It is his turn to study from Pastor Goh's Bible to prepare for another home Bible study with his friends. As his legs tirelessly pump the pedals, he prays, "Lord, as I've prayed every day for three years now, please may I have my own Bible!"

⚬⚬⚬

In the ancient capital city of Sian where the eastern end of the Silk Road originates, a young pastor is on his knees in prayer. His lips are moving but no sound comes out. Soon tears begin to flow and he stops his prayer to wipe his wet face.

"Are you praying for Bibles again, Wang?" asks his wife.

"Yes, my dear," replies Wang, continuing to wipe away the tears. "I promised God that I would deliver Bibles as far away as the mountains of Qinghai Province if He would send them to me."

⚬⚬⚬

In western China Sister Ling works as a young evangelist, having been commissioned to this ministry by her house church. They sent her out with a one-way train ticket and two weeks' worth of rice. Sister Ling loves her work, but it bothers her deeply that Christians without Bibles lack understanding and do unusual things. For example, today she's ministering to a group that carries around small vials of oil so they will be ready when the Bridegroom comes, like the five wise virgins in one of Jesus' stories.

This night after the meeting concludes, she pleads with her Lord for Bibles for His children. Her pleading continues for hours into the night until she senses that her prayer is heard and she can rest.

1

The Vision

The smile on Doug Sutphen's face was bigger than anyone could remember. With five friends and colleagues, Doug, the director for Brother Andrew's Open Doors ministry in Asia, had just arrived at the Dong Fang Hotel in Guangzhou, China.

His group's luggage included five trunks and seventeen suitcases full of Chinese New Testaments. With them now safely stowed in his hotel room, there wasn't much room left for anything or anyone else.

"Sam, you're a real actor," said Sealy Yates with a loud chuckle. "The cast on your broken leg sure was a bonus, diverting the officers' attention in the customs hall."

Sealy was a young up-and-coming lawyer and literary agent. He was also the board chairman of Open Doors International. Sam Jones, a man from South Asia and Doug's best friend, had overplayed his pain as he hobbled through the customs hall during the group's entry into Guangzhou, ostensibly to attend the biannual Trade Fair.

They were Open Doors Asia's final courier group of Project Rainbow, which brought thirty thousand New Testaments to needy Christians in southern China. Over the ten previous days, twenty other couriers had successfully carried two hard-side suitcases, weighing ninety-two pounds each, through the same customs hall. The total load of books for the project was two and a half tons. If discovered by the customs agents, any and all would have been confiscated.

"I thought it was hilarious, Sam," added Doug, "that you were able to get the customs officers to push those heavy trolleys through the building for you." He laughed deeply as the tension of the dramatic border crossing was now easing and he could relax a little.

Sam grinned, a fairly permanent expression on his friendly face.

"But I'm not leaving this room until all this 'bread' is delivered," continued Doug. "I don't want to give any unauthorized eyes a chance to see what's in these bags and trunks."

"Hey, I met Dr. Dale Kietzman downstairs, a few minutes ago," said Sealy, changing the subject. "He was quietly recounting for me that by the time he got his two heavy bags to the door of the customs hall, he had no more strength left to lift them. When the officer at the door pointed to his checkpoint table, it was way down at the end of the room. Dr. Dale said quietly to the two bags at his side on the floor, 'In the name of Jesus, rise!' The bags felt like feathers as he casually strolled down the room with one in each hand and his toothbrush in a small shoulder bag. After a successful short exchange with the officer, he rounded the corner of the customs hall and both heavy bags crashed to the floor. But he was through!" Everyone chuckled.

Over the next three days, other Open Doors couriers from a nearby hotel shared their border crossing experiences with this last team, who were taking their meals in their room until one by one the final bags of Chinese New Testaments were delivered. Carefully and quietly they were handed over to the Chinese contacts in charge of distribution, and thus thirty thousand New Testaments were soon in the hands of Chinese Christians who had pleaded for them.

Project Rainbow was Open Doors Asia's best effort yet and it seemed like a huge miracle. But very soon a message from Christian leaders in China came back to Doug, "They were not enough. We need one million Bibles!"

Manila
August 1980

Rain began to obscure the view through the front windshield as Doug Sutphen edged his car around the corner onto Balete Drive in Quezon City, Philippines. He quickly turned on the windshield wipers of his 1978 2.0 liter Ford Cortina. His staff referred to it as "the white stallion."

It's really unusual for it to be raining this early in the day, he thought. Rainy season in the Philippines usually produced only a light shower in the afternoons. Doug and his family had been in the Philippines for fifteen years now and were quite accustomed to the vagaries of the weather and its impact on traffic.

As the rain intensified, he turned up the wiper speed so he could see to navigate around the many potholes he knew were there, now obscured by pools of water.

While heading down E. Rodriguez Avenue, Doug thought about what he would say to his friend Bill Tinsley over breakfast. Doug's passion was China and he loved dreaming big dreams. This was going to be the most important meeting of the two friends anyone could imagine. It could even change history—especially the history of the church in China.

Bill lived with his wife, Lil, on a houseboat in Puerto Galera on Mindoro Island to the southwest of Manila. They called their place Paradise. Today they were in Manila for supplies and appointments.

Slowly Doug pulled up in front of his favorite restaurant on Quezon Boulevard. The new parking valet sized up this large *Americano* driver in the neatly pressed *polo barong* shirt and wondered if he was worth a tip comparable to his dimensions.

Doug had played linebacker on the University of Denver football team and was not just heavy, he was solid up and down his medium height. His light brown hair was thinning, and he had a rugged, square jaw, but his eyes were soft, and he had a quiet voice as well as a warm and ready smile.

As Doug enjoyed a cup of coffee at a table in a private corner, he soon saw his longtime friend approaching. They embraced with Doug's usual bear hug greeting. This trademark caused many Westerners to refer to Doug as a "big teddy bear." Because of his loving care and generosity, his Filipino staff called him *Tatay*. Literally it meant "father," but his American friends would translate it "Sugar Daddy."

"Hi, Bill! How ya doin'?"

"I'm doin' okay, Doug. Today I'm just trying to keep dry." Bill replied with a grin. He was a tall, tanned American with wavy, prematurely graying hair and a neatly trimmed goatee. His broad smile easily broke into a chuckle and then a loud guffaw.

Bill's life story was intertwined with the sea. He became disturbed by the poverty in the Philippines where he and Lil had lived for ten years. He knew the sea held the greatest potential for protein production, which could help with malnutrition problems in all of Asia. Soon Bill realized the major problem in the depletion of sea life in the Philippines, and elsewhere, was overfishing. Illegal fishing was also widespread: nets were used to catch undersized fish, and fish were killed with poison and blasted with explosives. His passion became ecological reconstruction of the marine environment. Bill dreamed of restoring and repopulating destroyed coral reefs with imported species from the remote reefs of the South China Sea. He and Lil chose to live at Puerto Galera with its dying coral reefs to work on a pilot venture he called Project Kema (named after the giant clam, an endangered species).

After their initial greetings and in response to Doug's questions, Bill updated him about Project Kema and his latest endeavors to get it underway. Currently he was monitoring the degraded health of the coral reefs and detecting the influence of man-made activities, with the objective of being proactive in addressing the challenges.

But then Bill said, "So what's so important, Doug, that you'd get me out this early? We usually do *lunch* at Alfredo's!" Bill was always very direct. His self-assured manner and strong personality made him a good conversationalist, and he didn't hesitate to say what he thought. He and Doug had been friends for fifteen years, starting back in Redondo Beach, California.

"We've got something really big coming up, and I need your help," Doug began.

"I'm in early retirement, Doug. I've done my big things and now Mom and I are just going to enjoy living in Paradise and working on Project Kema." Bill always referred to Lil as "Mom" when talking to others. When he talked directly to her, she was usually "Sweet Thing." Together they had three now-grown children.

"But tell me about it. You've aroused my curiosity." Bill took a long, slow sip of coffee.

"Not sure I can do that, Bill," Doug hesitated. "I've been reading a small book called *Principles of War,* and I'm very impressed with the need for secrecy and the element of surprise. This was also drummed into me during my years in the U.S. Marines. What's coming up is so big and so strategic, I can't tell anyone unless they're part of the inside team," Doug said without a hint of a smile on his face.

Bill let out one of his loud guffaws. "Come on, Doug. I've never known you to read a book. I've never even seen you read the newspaper!" Doug had suffered all his life with dyslexia and reading was difficult for him.

"I said a small book, didn't I? General Ray Miller gave it to me, and I've read it several times. But I must have your agreement of absolute confidentiality about what I'm going to share with you," Doug continued softly.

Bill paused for a minute before answering. "Okay, Doug. What's the big plan?"

Doug kept staring in his coffee. "What would you say about helping move a couple hundred tons of Chinese Bibles across the South China Sea to our brothers and sisters in China?"

"How many Bibles?" Bill asked slowly and deliberately, eyeing Doug as he spoke.

"One million," Doug replied with a grin.

"You're not serious!" Bill exploded.

"I'm very serious. Are you interested?"

"Of course, I'm interested."

"Let me ask you first," Doug continued, "do you think we can move this volume by sea?"

Bill thought for a moment, trying to quickly gauge the size of such a load. He couldn't calculate specifically but he knew, of course, that it was enormous. "Let me put it this way," he said finally, "I don't think you could move that large and heavy a load clandestinely by any other method."

"We've concluded that too."

"Who's the 'we' you're talking about?" Bill queried.

"Joseph and Pablo!" Doug responded, surprised he would even have to answer the question, since Bill was a friend of both men. Joseph Lee was the Chinese operations chief, and the other man, simply known as Pablo, headed the research department for Doug's Open Doors Asia team.

"I'm so pleased with the way these two guys worked together last year in Project Rainbow. In ten days, thirty thousand Chinese New Testaments were safely delivered into China using twenty-six couriers going to the Guangzhou Trade Fair. The couriers carried two suitcases weighing ninety-two pounds each. The six of us on the final team brought in seventeen suitcases and five trunks of books.

"Joseph coordinated the inside-China team and Pablo, the outside. That was the biggest and smoothest delivery we've made yet. It actually was a miracle! But it's not even begun to meet the Bible needs of the growing church in China."

"You're gonna need a *million* miracles, Doug, if you're thinking about a *million* Bibles for China," Bill concluded. "Do you realize how risky that is?"

"Yes, we do, Bill, but I have faith to believe it can happen and that we'll get our million miracles. You take your time and pray about it. If you sense the Lord leading you to join us, I'll fill you in later on the details."

New Manila
August 1980

Pablo sat at his mahogany desk and stared at the floor. His long face and dominant chin seemed frozen in a pensive mood. The sunshine reflecting off the highly polished terrazzo floor caught his attention and brought him back to reality. He surveyed the room, admiring the rich mahogany paneling. He'd never had an office like this. Earlier, the room had been the library; now the built-in mahogany shelves held *his* books.

The only challenge was that his office door was adjacent to the front entrance of this Spanish-styled building at 7 Bouganvilla Street in New Manila. Since he liked an "open door" policy, he was greeted by any and all who entered the building—often filling in for the receptionist when she was on break.

It had been only a year since Pablo joined the Asia team of Open Doors that Doug Sutphen directed. Pablo's first major project assignment was to coordinate, under Doug's leadership, the operations of Project Rainbow outside China.

He smiled as he remembered that first night of planning in a Hong Kong hotel room. He and Doug stayed up until the wee hours of the morning drawing circles with a Hong Kong five-dollar coin. They were making a program evaluation review technique (PERT) chart for the whole project. At four in the morning, Doug said, "Pablo, do you feel like some apple pie and ice cream?" Pablo chuckled. He knew that's what Doug wanted, and he was never one to turn down apple pie either—at any hour. And at that moment, he needed something to boost his energy.

After Project Rainbow, came the request for one million complete Chinese Bibles. The name chosen for this venture was Project Pearl—from the pearl of great price (Matthew 13:45–46). Again Doug came to him with the request to prepare a prospectus for Open Doors head office in Holland about this proposed undertaking—the biggest he would probably ever be involved in. He had few details of the final operational plan but he included all the scriptures and messages Open Doors had received from the leaders of a major house church network in southern China. One key scripture from the Chinese church leaders was from Psalm 104:27–28: *"These all look to you to give them their food at the proper time. When you give it to them, they gather it up; when you open your hand, they are satisfied with good things."*

The context of these verses is a description of the sea and the creatures in it as well as ships going to and fro. Bibles had long been given the code name "bread" in lands into which they had to be smuggled (Pablo preferred the term "unofficially delivered"), so the verses seemed appropriate for the proposed delivery of a million Bibles to China.

The Open Doors International Board, chaired by Sealy Yates, approved in principle the estimated twelve-million-dollar project in the spring of 1980 and worldwide fund-raising efforts began for Project Pearl. The operational plan was to be kept a secret—even within the Open Doors Asia team. Dr. Jim Schmook, a management consultant by profession, was the program consultant for Open Doors International and had been involved in long discussions with Doug about the project. He suggested much of the planning and procedures that needed to be in place.

Now Pablo was working on a preliminary research plan for accomplishing the project—including "things to avoid." He had made up a list of questions and requests for Joseph Lee, the Asia Program Manager, who was soon going to China. He was to visit the actual contacts who had requested the one million Bibles. Did they realize how many a million Bibles were? And how much space they took to store? Or what could happen if they were ever caught with even a portion of these Bibles? How did they suggest a million Bibles be delivered?

His concentration was broken with the familiar "Hi Pablo!" as Doug walked in the front entrance. "Can you come back to my office for a minute?"

They walked together through the front reception room and down the long paneled hallway. It skirted a central Spanish-style open courtyard garden. Doug's spacious and comfortable office was at the back of the building.

"I had breakfast with Bill Tinsley this morning," Doug began, once settled in one of the overstuffed chairs.

"How are Bill and Lil? I miss those guys since they moved to the province."

"They seem to be doing really well. But I actually went to ask him to join our team for Project Pearl."

"Great!" Pablo responded. "What did he say?" Pablo knew Bill would be a good asset for such a huge undertaking. He liked him and knew their personalities clicked.

"He's praying about it and will get back to me. But there's something I need to ask you."

Pablo nodded and waited.

"Will you be the coordinator for this project? You did so well on

Project Rainbow that I think you should handle this one too. Of course I'll be very much around and involved in the decision making. Project Pearl is my baby! I know this is taking you away from the main research task I hired you for, but what do you say?"

"Sure," Pablo shrugged. "I'd love to! Beth here in Manila and Timothy in Hong Kong can carry on with the research. They're both self-starters."

"Well, go get a one-peso coin and let's start working on a PERT chart right now. And you'd better call Dianne and tell her you won't be home for dinner."

China
August 1980

Lili looked carefully behind her to see if she was being followed. The beach she was headed toward was not far from her village of Dahao in southeastern China near Shantou. There was a lot at stake in every move she planned to make from this moment on and she had to be very cautious.

She skipped joyfully as she reflected on the meeting with her house church network leaders the night before. They told her that she was selected to be the internal distribution coordinator of a major Bible delivery—one million Bibles, in fact!

In her thirty-five years Lili had never seen at one time more than thirty thousand small New Testaments. Last year in Project Rainbow she had personally handled most of the fifty-five suitcases and five trunks brought in by couriers to the White Cloud Hotel and the Dong Fang Hotel in Guangzhou. The New Testaments had disappeared like morning fog because so many inside and outside the house church network wanted one. Many house church leaders in their network did not even get one. *But a million Bibles—how big a load would that be?*

No one else was walking on Hi Bean Road as she turned left and headed northeast toward the sea. First, she stood for a long time on the sandy beach of the fishing cove. It was part of a larger beach area known locally as Beishan. Then she sat on the sand praying silently for God to confirm that this was to be the place where the million Bibles should be delivered. So many brothers and sisters lived nearby. She could be assured of a lot of help.

An hour later, after receiving her answer, she headed off through the tree line toward home.

2

The Team

Bill Tinsley stroked his graying goatee as he pondered the decision that faced him. He reached for his Bible. It had been his guide every time he needed to make a decision. In fact his introduction to the faith came slowly during the time when he first started studying the Bible.

He prayed silently, "Lord, I need direction. I know Your Word well. I can find scripture to support almost anything, but I ask you to please lead me to a special word right now."

Bill opened his Bible randomly to chapters 13 to 15 of 1 Chronicles, which tell about King David moving the Ark of the Covenant. The Ark contained the tablets of the Ten Commandments carved in stone. They were God's instructions for His people. When David tried to move the Ark the wrong way, disaster struck. Moving the Ark the right way ended in success.

The Holy Spirit spoke to Bill twice through this passage. First, he was to be involved in the delivery of Bibles—God's instruction to men today. Second, the Bibles must be moved the right way. In the Bible story, only the Levites were qualified to move the Ark. So, Bill concluded, this Bible delivery should be accomplished only by committed Christians.

The next day Bill randomly opened his Bible again—this time to Psalm 29. He was impressed by verses 3 and 10:

The voice of the LORD is over the waters;
the God of glory thunders,
the LORD thunders over the mighty waters.
The LORD sits enthroned over the flood;
the LORD is enthroned as King forever.

Bill concluded that God was speaking about using the sea for Project Pearl.

On day three Bill's Bible opened at John 6:16-21. It was the story of Jesus walking on the water. This was further confirmation that the sea was the way to go but also with the nuance that Jesus had to be the true leader of the officers and crew.

Then, deliberately, Bill turned his Bible pages deep into the Old Testament to Deuteronomy 33:18–19:

> *Rejoice, Zebulun, in your going out,* [Bill's translation said *"on the sea"*]
> *and you, Issachar, in your tents.*
> *They will summon peoples ["foreigners"] to the mountain*
> *and there offer sacrifices of righteousness;*
> *they will feast on the abundance of the seas,*
> *on the treasures hidden in the sand.*

These were God's words spoken to Moses. In Bill's mind, however, the Bible delivery team was Zebulun, and Issachar represented the Chinese believers who had been praying for Bibles for years. They had made significant sacrifices for their faith, and this project had been their request. At the time, Bill did not even realize that the million Bibles were to arrive on a lovely, sandy beach.

Southern China
Late August 1980

Joseph Lee looked carefully to his right and left and then turned quickly down the dusty main street in Chaoyang. He was always apprehensive when traveling alone at night in unknown territory—especially inside China. Darkness hid his black hair and eyes and the prominent acne scars on his face. But even in the darkness, people who knew him would be able to sense his warm smile, kind eyes, and gentle spirit.

The directions given him were clear and he soon arrived at the appointed meeting place. Responding to his knock, Lili opened the door with a welcoming smile. Entering slowly, Joseph let his eyes adjust to the low light inside. Then Lili began introducing the five house church leaders: Matthew Lo, Enoch Ma, Peter Wang, John Chow, and Samuel Wu. Each one stood and gave Joseph a firm handshake. This was his first visit since Project Rainbow, and they wanted to assure him of their deep appreciation.

"Joseph, we had an all-night prayer and praise session after receiving those little New Testaments you sent," Matthew Lo began. "They were such a blessing to our groups."

"But they're all distributed now," John Chow chimed in, "and we desperately need a million more."

"Yes, I know," Joseph responded. "I've come specifically to ask you about this gigantic request you've made for one million Bibles all at one time, all at one place."

"Can they please include the Old Testament this time and be printed in simplified script?" Enoch Ma asked.

"Yes, we think this can be done. But my greatest concern is about the volume and weight. Do you know what a huge number of Bibles that is and how much space you'll need to store them?" Joseph looked around the large meeting room and quickly calculated. "You'll need about twenty rooms this size to hold them. And the weight will be more than two hundred tons."

No one spoke for a moment and then Peter Wang nodded. "Yes, we're aware this delivery will be huge and we're preparing depository space for those that need storing for a short time before personal distribution. We're much more worried about *your* safety in bringing them to us. Do you realize how dangerous this will be for *you?*"

"Yes, we know. But are you aware of what could happen if you get caught with this many Bibles from outside China—even a portion of them?" Joseph countered.

The man who looked the oldest, Samuel Wu, had not yet spoken. Now he stood up. "Brother Joseph," he began with a look of loving concern, "we have a well-known story here in China. A group of soldiers were ordered by their superior to arrest a Christian man. With the soldiers in hot pursuit, this child of God ducked into a deep, dark cave, praying hard all the time for the Lord's protection and deliverance. The soldiers were baffled by his sudden disappearance and then they came to the mouth of the cave where he was hiding. Over the entrance was a huge spider web—still intact—which convinced the soldiers he could not be in there and they withdrew.

"God can use even a spider in His providence to deliver His children from danger.

"Every one of us sitting around this room—except for Sister Lili and Brother Peter—has spent a long time in prison for our faith in Jesus. If you add up the total number of years we've been in jail, they total more than forty. And we're willing to *die* if it means a million brothers and sisters here in China can have a personal copy of God's Word!"

The other four men nodded vigorously in agreement.

A tear trickled down Joseph's face. He couldn't speak.

New Manila
Early September 1980

"I couldn't ask them any more of your questions, Pablo," Joseph said through more tears as he recounted the scene to the management team. They were all sitting around the table in Doug's comfortable conference room at the Bouganvilla Street office in New Manila.

It was quiet for a long time. The eight men also were unable to speak. To Doug's right was tall, thin Michael Bruce, an Australian. He was Doug's business and administration manager. Beside him was good-looking Terry Madison, the capable communicator who produced the monthly magazine, sporting a neatly trimmed dark beard; and then Keith Ritter from the Japan office. Keith was heavyset with a full white beard that nearly covered his quick and winning smile. He reminded most people of a saintly grandfather. Next to Keith was Frank Phillips, a middle-aged, early-retired American who managed the Hong Kong office. Beside him was Gary, the blonde, well-groomed director of Open Doors Australia. This was his first meeting with the management team. Joseph and Pablo completed the circle.

Doug was extremely proud of his team. He had worked hard

choosing and developing each of these men into the strong, unified group that they had become. He also prided himself on following the management advice of his boss, Dr. Ed Neteland: "Put men around you who are stronger than you in their respective fields. Be their leader but give them freedom to fly."

"It seems things are pretty definite on the inside," commented Doug, finally breaking the silence. "Now that we've had all the reports, I'd like to finalize our statement of goals for Project Pearl. Obviously, number one will have to be meeting the specific request of our contacts inside China. Pablo, would you please note these down for us?"

"I think we should expect this project to heighten general awareness in the church worldwide about the desperate need for Bibles in China today," Terry added.

Immediately Keith continued the thought: "And that awareness should then put pressure on China to print Bibles inside the country—with no strings attached—for believers who need them."

"I want our people in Australia to realize just how large the house church movement in China has become," Gary added.

"Let's also expect this project to be catalytic," Doug concluded. "I'd like to see hundreds of people and organizations worldwide responding by setting up Bible-delivery systems of their own for our family in China."

"Be careful how you say that word *catalytic* outside this room, Doug. Remember Michael!" Pablo chortled.

The group broke out into raucous laughter, and Michael shrunk down in his chair, his face getting red. Michael had used the term in his report at the last Asia planning conference. One of the Japanese pastors attending with Keith had raised his hand and asked innocently, "Why do we have to become 'Catholic'?"

Doug continued with a smile. "But the bottom line is to feed the huge revival now impacting the church in China. Pearl is not to become just another smuggling project. It's to be a love offensive to help our brothers and sisters in China pour God's love into their hurting nation of one billion people. And I want to see it completed no later than June next year."

The men looked at each other in shocked disbelief. That deadline was only nine months away.

Just then Alma, Doug's secretary, opened her door to the conference room. "Excuse me, Doug. You have a long-distance call," she said.

"It's probably Dr. Ed," Doug commented. "Take a break for a minute, guys."

The team was used to these interruptions in their management meetings. Telephone contact with the Philippines was difficult at the best of times and with the time zone differences from the United States and Holland, Doug always took long-distance calls whenever they came in.

"Pablo," Keith began, as some left for the *comfort room* (as the Filipinos call it), "I loved your comment that Project Rainbow should have been called Project Hernia!" Those who had been couriers nodded with a knowing smile while the others burst into laughter.

Keith was always an encourager. He created a great sense of team unity as he regularly praised each person's contributions. He also enjoyed a good laugh. He smiled as he continued, "And, Terry, you did a good job on our latest magazine. Your pictures are always great, of course. But I especially loved the story you titled, 'Why God?' Sue said the same thing."

"Thanks, Keith. It's always good to know somebody's reading my work," Terry chuckled.

Keith had been an associate pastor with Chuck Smith at Calvary Chapel in Costa Mesa, California. He felt a call to China in the mid-1970s and joined Open Doors Asia early in its formative stages. His first assignment was supervising Bible courier deliveries to China from the Hong Kong base on Cheung Chau Island. In 1980, his friends Frank and Ruby Phillips moved to Hong Kong to become the base managers. They worked from an office in a new building in Wanchai, allowing Keith and his wife, Sue, to pioneer an Open Doors base in Shinjuku, Tokyo.

Keith had become Doug's closest confidant and prayer partner.

Everyone appreciated his capable Bible-exposition skills, which he shared in a very loving spirit. He had a passion for finding allegories—especially in the Old Testament—relating to current events. When supervising the briefings of the twenty-six couriers in Project Rainbow at the New World Hotel in Hong Kong, he used Joshua 1:3, 9 as his challenge: *"I will give you every place where you set your foot . . . Have I not commanded you? Be strong and courageous. Do not be terrified; do not be discouraged, for the LORD your God will be with you wherever you go."* As the project unfolded, Keith saw parallels with chapter 2 of Joshua and then chapter 3—and all the way to chapter 6. By then he was absolutely convinced of the modern allegory. So when two suitcases, each containing five hundred New Testaments, were discovered at China's customs hall (later they were returned to Hong Kong and successfully taken in again by the final team), Keith saw this as Achan's sin, and great introspection followed. To Keith the final team entry for Project Rainbow was like the taking of Ai in Joshua 8.

The original request for one million Chinese Bibles was brought to Hong Kong by Mama and Papa Kwang—public names given by Open Doors Asia to protect their identity. They were house church network leaders in and around the Shantou area and had experienced a miraculous escape from Mainland China to British-controlled Hong Kong in 1978.

Mama Kwang was a heavyset, middle-aged woman with a soft, round face and brown sparkling eyes. She began preaching at age eighteen, although her official role in the eyes of the government was teaching school children. Soon she had developed a large and growing network of house churches in southeastern China. God performed many miracles among them. Once introduced to Westerners from outside, the group was labeled "Bapticostals."

Papa Kwang was a high school mathematics teacher. His black short hair and good looks made him seem younger than his wife. He and Mama had four children. Peter, their eldest, was martyred by Red Guards during the infamous Cultural Revolution. The others, Daniel, Joseph, and Mary, lived with them in Hong Kong.

Mama Kwang spent three separate terms in prison for leading the secret house church movement in her area. After each release from prison, she went right back to her ministry the following day.

During her third imprisonment, she saw a vision from the Lord. Thousands of missionaries from the West and the East were working side-by-side digging a trench. The trench became bigger and longer after much hard work. Then water started to flow into it. It became the River of Life. She saw it flow first through all parts of China and after that into the whole world. The workers were very happy and their singing filled heaven and earth.

Mama Kwang said to Doug, Keith, and Dr. Ed at the time of the one-million-Bibles request, "If a million Bibles could be taken into China at one time, it would be like the day the sun stood still for Joshua!" Immediately Keith read Joshua 10.

Doug's phone call was lengthy, so Keith began to talk to the team still seated around the table about the insights he had gleaned from Joshua. "Brothers, you all know how closely Project Rainbow paralleled Joshua 1 to 8. Mama Kwang says the accomplishment of Project Pearl will be like Joshua 10. I've been reading chapter 9 repeatedly about the Gibeonite deception. During this interim period between the two projects, I think we need to understand what this means."

Michael was the first to respond in his Aussie accent, "I think it must have something to do with the TSPM—China's official Protestant Church."

Keith nodded with a knowing smile.

At that moment, Doug came back into the room all smiles. "Brothers, Dr. Ed sends his greetings to you all!" he began. "Nothing but good news today. Ed says the donors of Open Doors are responding positively to the news of Project Pearl. The U.S. office alone is adding several field staff to enable more personnel to supervise and accomplish the fund-raising for the project.

"And the publishers have set a date for my book to be out this fall. I'll be code-named Brother David and now we're just arguing about the title. Dr. Ed wants me to piggyback it on Brother Andrew's book and call it *God's Smuggler to China*."

Everyone at the table either shook his head negatively or made a face. But Doug didn't wait long enough for a verbal reaction. "We'll discuss this later. More important right now, Dr. Jim Schmook has agreed to join our operations team for the project and is already gathering data, equipment, and other things he feels we'll need. Praise the Lord!

"Then when I got off the phone with Ed, Bill phoned to say he is willing to be part of the team. He wants to have lunch with me tomorrow while he's in Manila to explain how God directed him through the Scriptures.

"Let's stop right now and thank God for these wonderful answers to prayer."

Before the meeting ended, it was agreed that a special operations team of six would provide leadership for Project Pearl. The group would consist of Doug, Joseph, Keith, and Pablo from the Open Doors Asia management team, plus Bill Tinsley and Dr. Jim Schmook from outside. Their first planning meeting was set for December 8. It was agreed that the planning team would do nothing unless there was total unity among the six of them. And most important, the whole project needed to be covered in complete secrecy. Humanly speaking, it would succeed only with the element of surprise.

3

The Commitment

Doug lay flat on the couch in his office in New Manila. He talked for hours as Dan Wooding, an accomplished author of dozens of books, recorded his words and took copious notes. Doug was determined his book would be the best document to date about the development and growth of the house church movement in China. Dan's great sense of humor enabled him to deal with these long hours of dictation at unusual times of the day and night.

The deadline for completing Doug's autobiography was closing in, and the time for the Open Doors Planning Conference in Holland was also coming up soon. Dan worked furiously every night to meet the chapter deadlines.

Sara Bruce, Michael's wife, helped in research and writing too. And Elizabeth, one of the office secretaries, spent many hours typing and retyping the manuscript. There was further pressure to finish *God's Smuggler to China* when it was chosen as a book premium for a TV special in the United States to raise funds for Project Pearl.

Meanwhile, Terry and Pablo were in Hong Kong with TV producer-director Malcolm Neal, shooting scenes and testimonials from China ministry leaders for the TV special. Pablo was beginning to look a little shaggy as he had taken a personal vow not to shave until Project Pearl was completed.

Clean-cut Brother Andrew was in Hong Kong too. He stood in front of the clearly demarcated border of Hong Kong and China and shared, via the camera lens, the challenge of the request for one million Chinese Bibles. Then he and Terry Madison traveled together inside China for more on-location scene shooting. Terry left his movie camera with Lili, asking her to film Chinese believers worshiping in the house churches. These scenes were some of the earliest public footage ever of such activity.

The development plan for Project Pearl was well underway, but the tactical plan was far from formation. Doug's answer was always the same, "We're walking by faith. We believe in miracles."

China
November 1980

Lili smiled as she wandered down the narrow main road of Queshi, a village that was near her own. Her round face and almond eyes shone in the sunlight. The plans for the Bible project were getting larger as time went on, and her whole being was excited about serving God. She had commented about this earlier in the morning when talking to Mama Kwang on the phone. Though now living in Hong Kong, Mama Kwang was often the go-between for Project Pearl workers inside China. She realized Lili needed help.

"I think you need some good assistants for this task, Lili," Mama Kwang had said. "Please talk to Mei-ling and Chan. I sense the Holy Spirit saying they should be part of your team. Go with them to talk to Lao Zhao about where you could establish new depositories for large quantities of Bibles."

Lili knew Mei-ling and Chan well. They were both single, members of a nearby house church, and known for their wholehearted commitment to the Lord.

Lili had met Lao Zhao once, although just briefly. Most people just referred to him as "the old man." He was a Christian who lived in Yuxin and was the poorest person in town. After the Communist revolution, the cadres decided to make a positive example of him. Not knowing he was a Christian, they gave him the largest house in the village with a double ration of rice, even though he was single.

Lao Zhao used the large home for house church meetings and shared most of his food with believers who were hungry. When the cadres finally learned what he was doing, they angrily confiscated the house and put him in prison for several years. Now he lived in a small hut all alone. Lili looked forward to visiting him again.

Arriving at her first destination, Lili was greeted by the smiling faces of Chan and Mei-ling. Chan was a tall, handsome young man with an athletic build while Mei-ling was short, like Lili, but with an angelically beautiful face you could not forget. The trio sipped tea together as they discussed Mama Kwang's proposal.

After Lili prayed for God's direction, she explained that a plan was underway to deliver from outside China one million Chinese Bibles. Hearing this, Chan's and Mei-ling's eyes bulged. Then Lili explained that their job would be to supervise the distribution throughout all the provinces of China.

"It's wonderful and sounds simple enough," Chan said, "But how long are we committing to?"

"Well, we expect the distribution to go quickly," Lili responded. "Although it may take as long as one year, depending on how much we're watched by the local cadres."

Mei-ling changed the subject slightly and asked how much traveling she would be required to do.

"Quite a bit, Mei-ling. We'll be working with house church networks in just about every province of China," Lili responded. "I can't cover the whole country alone! You'll be helping the growth of the church in this country by serving the Lord in an unusual way. Mama Kwang has promised financial support for all three of us as well as covering all our travel expenses.

"But I must caution you. There's a very high risk involved. You know the authorities don't look kindly on those of us who distribute Bibles printed outside China."

Chan was the first to comment. "We were praying together about the need for Bibles even before you came, Lili. We're excited to be able to help in this great project."

Mei-ling nodded in agreement. "Just before you arrived, we were singing the chorus Mama Kwang wrote and taught us."

Lili knew the song and together the three sang it with hearts full of expectation:

Lord, send a Bible for that's Your gracious light,
True love and teaching and the Word of God.
We know for sure that Your Word will lead us on,
Brighten the path all through our journey home.

Then standing in a circle and joining hands, they prayed, asking God to help them in their important part of this great endeavor. After the last "amen," Lili said, "Mama Kwang wants us all to visit Lao Zhao before we do anything else."

It was only an hour's walk to the old man's little hut where they were warmly welcomed. His skin was saggy and wrinkled from age but his face communicated a pleasant youthfulness behind the long, straggly white beard. Quickly he started a fire to make tea. At the bridge crossing the delta river, Lili had purchased some fresh, hot, steaming *baodze*. China is famous for these tasty dumplings.

"The Lord told me I'd have visitors today," he said. The three young people looked at each other in wonderment. Over tea he retold in his weakening voice his oft-repeated story of prison miracles. Lao Zhao assumed that all visitors came to his home to hear about them.

"When they threw me into prison, I received watery soup without much nutrition. So one day when talking to the Lord, I suggested it would be nice to eat an egg. Four days later, though I had forgotten my prayer, I awoke and there in front of me was an egg on the floor. I picked it up to find it was real but I had no clue how it got there. I was so hungry I quickly devoured it. After so many days of drinking watery soup, it tasted delicious.

"When I awoke the next morning, there was another egg in the same place. That night I stayed awake to see who was bringing eggs into my room. About three o'clock in the morning, I heard a light scratching noise on the floor. I didn't move. A mouse was using his nose to push an egg through a hole in the wall and to the same spot where he had left the others. Then he sniffed around a bit and left.

"This went on for many days. One autumn day I was thinking it must be apple season outside. My mouth began to water just thinking about apples, so I prayed, 'Lord if you can bring me eggs, how about an apple?' And God used a different mouse to bring me the sweetest apples everyday through the fall. In the winter, a rat brought me sweet potatoes and nuts. God is so faithful!"

"Uncle, we came to ask your advice," Lili interrupted. "A group of brothers and sisters from outside China have agreed to bring us a very, very large shipment of Bibles for our growing churches. Mama Kwang wants to know what you recommend for local storage possibilities."

Lao Zhao paused, stroked his straggly beard, and then a twinkle came to his eyes. "A fellow believer has a barn not far from here in Mianbe, which can be one of the depositories. I'll show you before you head home. Don't worry about security. Even at my age, I can still keep a secret! And I'll also check with my niece in Hexi about their large *godown* [storage warehouse]."

As they parted ways later that afternoon, the old man commented, "God is faithful and He will also provide the Bibles we need for our fast-growing churches. Trust Him, young people, and do not doubt!"

As the three young people walked home, they talked softly among themselves with great excitement. They knew that God, our Provider, was about to perform another miracle.

"Let's gather trusted friends for three days of prayer and fasting for the planning meetings in Manila," Lili suggested.

Manila
Monday, December 8, 1980

The six men of the "inner circle" sat around the living room of Doug's suite in the Philippine Plaza Hotel. They were excited because the time had come to get serious about planning Project Pearl.

Doug began with some worship choruses. He thoroughly enjoyed singing and always included his favorites. Then he said, "I've asked Pablo to be the coordinator of this project, so he'll also be our recording secretary for the meetings. And I've asked Keith to be our chaplain.

Since his bad back limits him physically, he has volunteered to lead all spiritual aspects of this effort. He wants to be intimately involved with what we do right to the end—including the delivery. He'll lead the prayer efforts on-site. I've also asked him to lead our first devotional time this morning."

Keith looked around the room and began, "Yes, brothers. I think I'm more excited than you are. I want to see the day when the sun stands still—or maybe for us it'll be the moon!" he chuckled. "Anyway, turn in your Bibles to Ephesians chapter 1. We're going to read the prayer of the apostle Paul from verses 15 to 23. I suggest we read it around the circle verse-by-verse. Pablo, you start, then Jim, Bill, Joseph, Doug, and me."

After the reading Keith commented, "I believe the Lord has directed me to this passage in Ephesians 1, with a focus on verses 19 and 20. Paul is talking here about God's great power. And he goes on to say, '*That power is like the working of his mighty strength, which he exerted in Christ when he raised him from the dead . . .*' My simple conclusion is this. If we're going to achieve anything with Project Pearl, it will only be accomplished in God's power—that power that He used in raising Jesus from the tomb. Yes, we must do our part in planning and preparing, but let us *never* think that this is *our* project and *we* will do it. Project Pearl belongs to God and it will be accomplished only in His strength and power. The beautiful thing is that we are His co-workers. We will get to stand still and see the power of God at work!"

The five others nodded enthusiastically as Keith shared. A circle of prayer followed.

After prayer, Doug stood beside the easel with the thick pad of white paper and new colored markers. "Thanks, Keith. It always amazes me how God speaks to you and through you.

"Brothers, God can speak to all of us. As we meet over the next months, be sure to share any scriptures or messages that God gives you. Bill, I'll ask you to share tomorrow morning what God showed you in the Scriptures about your involvement.

"Again, I can't reiterate enough the need for secrecy. Frankly I'd appreciate it if you'd not share anything discussed here today with the rest of the Open Doors Asia staff—and not even with your wives."

"Sorry, Doug," Keith responded quickly. "Don't tell me anything that you don't want Sue to know. We keep no secrets from each other!" The others in the circle nodded in agreement.

"Well, you guys know what I mean," Doug replied with an anguished expression. "Share with your wives on a need-to-know basis. We must practice daily the discipline of secrecy. I'm going to be tough on this right to the end, and some of you may not like it."

He continued, "We're so thankful to have Dr. Jim Schmook on our team. He has a navy background and is also a hobby sailor. That gives you at least one other person who knows something about the sea, Bill!" Bill gave one of his knowing smiles and nodded.

"Jim's our ODI program consultant. He's taken time off from his personal management consulting work to help us. I've asked him to bring all of his gifts to the table and share whatever the Lord puts on his heart. Jim, you're first on the agenda today."

Jim walked to the front of the small room with a shy smile and a can of cola in his hand. His short hair made him look like a navy man. Wearing jeans, deck shoes, and a crisply ironed, short-sleeved sport shirt, he had a youthful appearance that belied his many years of experience.

"Well, Doug, all I can say is that I love your big vision," he started. "Ever since I first heard of this project, I've been eager to play a part. So I'm as excited as you guys to be in on this. After my first courier trip to China two years ago, I've been burdened by the need for Bibles in that country.

"On that trip, we were asked to leave the Bibles in a park not far from our hotel. The hotel was bugged, so we couldn't discuss anything while in the room. As we studied the Bible and prayed, 2 Corinthians 4:7 suddenly popped into my mind: '*But we have this treasure in jars of clay . . .*' I didn't know what to do about it and decided to go to the park for some reconnaissance.

"We did a complete walk-by of the park, looking for a good spot to hide the Bibles for pickup. I sat down on a low stone wall, trying to figure out what to do. I looked to my right and there, not thirty feet from me, was a series of large urns. They were decorative items, and I knew immediately that the Bibles would fit in them. We returned to the room and that night we hid the Bibles in the 'jars of clay.' Our contacts were told of the location and picked up the Bibles later that same night.

"I was delighted to read in Pablo's project proposal that this time the believers in China suggest the sea as a delivery method. I've already secured eight sets of high quality walkie-talkies for the delivery—however we do it.

"What I'm suggesting we do to start our planning is to look at unsuccessful, as well as successful, clandestine projects involving foreigners and learn lessons from them. The one I'm prepared to share about first is the Bay of Pigs invasion in Cuba twenty years ago. The U.S. military has now released a document of lessons learned. I'd like to list them for you and then discuss them together."

Jim began to write quickly on the easel pad:

Lessons Learned from
the Bay of Pigs Invasion

1. No one seriously studied whether it was even possible to overthrow Castro in the first place. They underestimated Castro's strength and popular support.

2. The organizers were victims of *groupthink:* Fifty of the presumably smartest and most experienced people planned the operation, although later many claimed they were never in favor from the beginning.

3. President Kennedy, as military leader, did not have accurate information—partially because he stifled protest and potential resistance.

4. For information, the CIA relied on Cuban exiles who claimed to have special inside knowledge. They were not aware of many things, such as the offshore reefs.

5. The U.S. leadership was unaware of the impact of a decision once the mission was underway (i.e., JFK's refusal to send air support once the invasion team was pinned down on the shore).
6. There was poor government interagency coordination.
7. There was a lack of contingency planning.
8. Everyone underestimated the consequences of failure.

For an hour the group wrestled with relevant applications for Project Pearl. It was a thought-provoking experience and developed even further the camaraderie of these committed men working together for the first time. Every conclusion was prayed over. One of Doug's strengths in leading meetings was communicating that time was less important than the issue being dealt with, so he made sure that time was taken to talk to the Lord in depth and to come to clear conclusions.

Finally Dr. Jim said, "I would rather compare our upcoming project to the Entebbe, Uganda, raid by the Israelis four years ago. It's an example of how we *do* want to operate. I'm sure you remember that in Operation Thunderbolt one hundred Air France hostages held by Idi Amin's government were rescued in ninety minutes at the Entebbe airport. The Israelis pulled it off because they were completely prepared for the mission. And we must be too. We have a lot of homework to do before we're ready to go."

"I'd rather go by air too," commented Pablo. "The *Manila Times* reports that there may be a 'devil's triangle' in the South China Sea. Between May last year and February this year, three Chinese vessels have mysteriously disappeared without a trace. Even Beijing is trying to offer a scientific explanation for the losses, suggesting that the flushing effects of ocean currents converging with circular warm streams cause a huge whirlpool."

"We'll just have to trust the Lord even more," said Bill with a smile.

In the afternoon, Dr. Jim led a planning exercise known as O-M-R, which required detailed outlining of outcomes, methods, and resources.

The biggest issue at hand was the method. As the discussion developed throughout the afternoon, it was soon obvious that the weight and volume of the delivery ruled out using any type of airplane. Some favored using a large motorized military landing barge, which could push right up onto the shoreline. If the sand was wet and packed enough, they could even use a forklift—or a small crane—to off-load the heavy cargo.

Bill countered that this would be noisy and create too much confusion.

Then Dr. Jim mentioned that he had friends in a Washington, D.C., think tank who had agreed to prepare for him a proposal for this type of delivery of such a cargo—though they did not know which country was being targeted or the type of cargo. He passed out photocopies of the detailed diagrams they had provided.

"This is extremely sophisticated," he started, "and may not be too practical for us. But let me explain it. The plan calls for a very powerful fishing boat to pull large fifty-gallon metal barrels underwater on long metal towlines. There are enough lines and barrels to hold two hundred tons of cargo—all underwater so no one can see them.

"Once we arrive at the destination, a pulley arrangement for the lines allows us to pull the barrels onto shore one at a time." A long discussion followed about the pros and cons of such an endeavor. It was agreed that the cons outweighed the pros—especially since the men were not yet sure who would be the crew and how they would get the needed boat.

Before the day ended, a number of approaches were discussed using different types of vessels and equipment. They discussed using a local fishing boat, a submarine, and a cargo vessel. Each proposal was carefully recorded on the easel board and analyzed in detail. The relevant factors included:

- being seaworthy enough to cross the China Sea;
- capability of depositing the cargo quietly onto the beach;
- simplicity for delivery inside China with minimum packaging.

These factors, when applied to the huge weight and volume of one million Bibles, staggered the minds of all six men.

4

The Plan

The next day Bill shared in the morning devotional time how God led him through the Scriptures to join the project. Then he went on to explain his strong conclusion that they needed an all-Christian crew who were just as committed as the inner circle.

Joseph affirmed this vigorously. As the program manager for the Asia region, working with the contacts inside China, he had the most at stake.

Dr. Jim agreed to contact ministries that worked with ships and seamen to find Christian crew members for the project.

Doug said, "You all know by now my favorite topics are secrecy and the element of surprise. Jim has another exercise for us to ensure a successful mission."

At the easel again, Jim began to write the group's concepts about what it would take for Project Pearl to be successful:

Elements of Success
1. Common, everyday appearance (vessels normally seen in the area)
2. Surprise—usual, expected approach, with last-minute diversion
3. Adequate number of receivers
4. Adequate system for immediate movement to protected areas
5. Adequate plan for total distribution
6. Willingness and ability of recipients to handle entire load
7. Adequate size of beach landing area
8. Clear approach lanes to the beach
9. Good team communication
10. Time to modify, brief, and replan, if necessary
11. Coordinated information from the three aspects of the project

"There was a good amount of discussion about some of the 'elements of success,' such as what would constitute an adequate number of receivers and an adequate size of beach landing area. When they began to talk more about delivery methods, Bill said, "I prayed a lot about this—especially last night—and my firm belief is that the plan must be as simple as possible. As we've agreed earlier, we must be able to unload quickly and quietly. Also, the packaging material must be kept to a minimum. Using crates or large containers would leave too much debris after the delivery.

"Here's a plan I think will work with the fewest negatives involved. Lil and I noticed plenty of tugboats around Shantou's harbor when we made our exploratory visit to the area two months ago. I suggest we acquire a tugboat that will tow a barge containing the books. On board the two vessels, we'll have small boats to tow the cargo to shore on arrival."

"Very interesting, Captain," said Doug. "Keep talkin'."

"First, let me focus on the tug. It'll need a powerful engine—say, a thousand horsepower—to tow more than two hundred tons for any distance in the open sea. It'll need a high bow for ocean travel, and the bigger problem with a tug is space for sleeping and feeding a large crew. Normally they have six men on an oceangoing tug. I estimate we'd need about twenty guys for this method. It'll be a challenge to find a tug with that capacity."

"Why don't we just have one built that way?" asked Pablo.

"What year did you say you wanted to do this project?" countered Bill with a gentle smile. "Any contractor would want to have at least six months to build a tugboat. And typhoon season will be on us by next June."

"Let Bill finish his proposal, interjected Doug, and then we'll analyze it step-by-step."

"The barge is the biggest challenge of all," Bill said. "We'll need to get it as close to shore as possible, so we'll probably need to arrive at high tide on a sandy beach with not many rocks. I'm suggesting we can quickly build a large aquarium barge here in the Philippines that will be like no other in existence. It would be designed to carry aquariums on its deck, of course, and could profile two large marine aquariums on the foredeck. The main deck—which would normally carry marine aquariums also—will be exactly the measurements to fit the Chinese Bibles packaged in blocks.

"I suggest the blocks be waterproof-wrapped and heat-sealed, then loaded by a crane onto the barge deck. We'll have electric side doors that can be lowered. Usually barge doors are on the bow and aft. But the most unusual aspect is this: We'll install tanks below deck that can take on water like a submarine or a dry dock. So the barge can then be lowered just enough for water to cover the deck. Then the blocks of Bibles will drop out the side doors like slices of bread when you open the end of a packaged loaf. Small boats can tow the floating blocks to shore. They'll be tied to each other and towed in a line. Afterward, we pump out the water, the barge returns to normal position, and we head home. I figure twenty men could accomplish this kind of delivery in about one hour's time. That's ignoring Murphy's Law."

It was a magical moment. Everyone thought through the process silently. Then the questions began to fly. The rest of the day was spent answering them and walking through an analysis of every step. A special concern of Jim's was whether the waterproofed blocks would actually float.

After prayer, the team felt it was obvious Bill's plan had been inspired by God. Everyone agreed to it, assuming, of course, that it would be developed in much greater detail and fine-tuned before it was implemented.

Bill shivered as Doug concluded the day by saying, "I'd like to see this completed in about seven months!"

⌒≫⌒≪⌒

After devotions together on the morning of the third day, the inner circle began detailing "things to be done" and who would be responsible for each task.

First, it was agreed they could not expect to rent or charter vessels to accomplish this bold, clandestine project. They would need to be purchased. This presented its own set of problems regarding the licensing of officers and crew.

Then Doug moved to security issues and the cover needed for such an audacious plan. "Captain Bill has agreed to use his Sea Bio-Systems Company as our cover and legally registered corporation. We will outfit the tugboat and the barge to appear to be a marine oceanography operation. If anyone asks about the cargo, we're just transporting books for a client to make some money for our cause.

"And speaking of the books, it looks as if Thomas Nelson Publishers in Nashville, Tennessee, is our choice of printers. Pablo and I have already checked out other printers in Japan, Korea, and Southeast Asia for price quotations. Most of them want a long time to print this many books. I'll also check with the United Bible Society's head office in New York about using their printing plates for the Chinese simplified script Union Version edition.

"Nelson has access to two press locations. If these presses run night and day, they could have the Bibles delivered anywhere on the U.S. continent by the end of February. Each Bible will weigh about half a pound and the estimated total weight will be more than two hundred tons. Nelson will charge only one point twenty-five million dollars plus shipping!"

The men looked at each as the magnitude of what they were committing to do was sinking in.

Doug continued, "I have to go back to Nelson to finalize the deal, but as of now, each book will be five and a half inches high, three and a half inches wide, and three-quarters of an inch thick."

Bill quickly calculated the total load at over ten thousand cubic feet. "That's the size of a large two-story house in America!" he exclaimed.

Then Dr. Jim offered: "I'll help Doug locate a U.S. packaging and logistics company to prepare the boxes of books into whatever block forms we finally decide we need."

"There's one aspect of these Bibles I think we've overlooked," interjected Joseph, "the size and weight of the boxes for the end delivery. Though they may have big plans inside China to use vehicles, the majority of these boxes of Bibles will probably be carried at some point by classic over-the-shoulder Chinese bamboo poles. I think we should have no more than ninety copies of the Bibles to a box. That'll make each box come out at forty-five pounds—or twenty kilos—two of which can be carried by a shoulder pole or even with a sling over the back of a strong bicycle."

"Good point, Joseph," Bill agreed. "That means there'll be exactly—let's see—yes, if we make two-ton blocks, there would be ninety-six boxes and thus there would have to be 116 blocks. That'll actually require 2,240 extra books printed, Doug. And once we have that cardboard box size, we can plan the barge's exact deck space."

"I'll get that to you right away," Doug promised. "I'm also assigning Pablo to work with you, Bill, in locating an adequate tugboat and choosing a local builder for the aquarium barge."

Captain Bill nodded and then added, "In any time lapses during the immediate schedule, I'll prepare living space down in Paradise for the crew members to come and train there as soon as possible."

"It should be obvious," added Joseph, "but we need to expand our suitcase courier program over the next seven months as a diversionary tactic. That'll put a lot of pressure on Frank in Hong Kong and Keith in Japan."

"I like that," Doug confirmed.

Dr. Jim led in a final run-through of the delivery plan in reverse so as not to overlook any details. Everyone agreed the group needed even more research data before they could make any final tactical decisions for the actual delivery, so they asked Joseph to visit the appointed location in China once more. He was to take panoramic photos of the beach from as far into the water as he could get at low tide. He also needed to check the sand quality on the bottom of the cove, the beach sand at high and low tide, the depth of the water at high tide, as well as any underwater obstructions.

Additionally, it was important to know what type of vessels passed the area during a typical day and night. Were they all cargo ships or were there tugboats and barges? What about naval patrols and local fishermen? Finally, he was to assess what the local people who lived nearby did in the early evening just after dark. He was also to meet with Lili and her team again to encourage them in their distribution process planning. Would they be willing to assist by flashing a light when the vessels approached the beach?

Also the group discussed the type of small boats they should use for towing the lines of blocks to shore. They decided that two fiberglass Boston Whalers would be an asset for the project—especially good if a quick getaway was necessary. Whalers were known to do fifty miles an hour even in the roughest water. This was significant because Shantou, where the landing was planned, is the southern port city of the Chinese navy.

Bill agreed to travel to California to order the smaller boats and all the nautical and oceanography equipment the team would need.

"Finally," Doug commented, "we need officially to establish our command system. I've already asked Joseph and Pablo to coordinate the project from our organizational standpoint: Joseph inside China and Pablo outside China. But I think Bill should be the captain in charge of the practical carrying out of the project. Jim has already volunteered to be first mate."

Everyone but Bill nodded in agreement; then he responded slowly, "Well, I don't have a commercial seaman's license currently, but I'll agree on the basis that when we're sailing, I *am* the captain and the final authority. I've already lost one man on an earlier expedition and I hope you'll understand if I become very hyper about safety at sea. I also welcome Jim to the bridge as first mate. And I'd like Pablo to be the second mate. He's the one who'll oversee the crew members and be the financial and radio officer on the ship. The three of us will also head the three watches on the bridge when the vessel sails.

"Doug, you'll be the commodore. We'll make sure there's room for you and Keith, our chaplain, to have appropriate quarters on the tug."

Everyone noted his homework assignments, and a second meeting was scheduled for February 2-4 in Manila.

"Don't forget our secrecy agreement," Doug reminded them again.

Southern California
Sunday, December 28, 1980

"Good to see you again, Captain," said Keith at the Los Angeles airport luggage carousel. Keith and Sue were home from Japan for Christmas. Bill was coming in to purchase the marine equipment.

"It's good to see you folks too. How long have you been waiting?"

"Not long," Keith said with his usual warm smile. "By the way, what are your plans?"

Bill replied, "My first priority is to locate a dealer for Boston Whalers. Then I need to buy some diving equipment and many other smaller items."

"We can look up the whaler dealership in the phone book," said Sue. "But first we want to take you out to dinner. Have you heard of the Chart House Restaurant?"

"No, I haven't been in these parts for years."

Keith headed their vehicle along the beach road toward the southern bay area where Bill and Lil had lived for more than twenty years prior to their Philippines experience. The Chart House Restaurant was near the old pier in Redondo Beach, an area that brought back many memories for Captain Bill. The room was decorated with a nautical motif and all the table covers were laminated sea charts.

They were taken to a table by the window, and it wasn't long before they were enjoying dinner while discussing the project. Bill told Keith and Sue that he planned to visit Dr. Jim and Kaye to work out details for packaging of the Bibles.

Sue was the first to notice. "Look at the sea chart on our table!" she exclaimed. The men moved plates and glasses from the dimly lit tabletop and were amazed to find a sea chart of the Philippines. Right under Captain Bill's water glass was Puerto Galera, Mindoro, his Paradise home base.

"That's got to be more than a coincidence!" Captain Bill exclaimed.

As they finished the meal and Keith sensed Captain Bill's jet lag, he said, "I know a little hotel near here where you'll be very comfortable."

In the morning, Bill woke up early and went for a walk. As it turned out, the Boston Whaler dealership was not far from the hotel. After breakfast he headed for the store as soon as it opened.

When he walked in the showroom, he was surprised to see Bob Mistra, an old acquaintance. "Hi, I'm Bill Tinsley," he said. "Do you remember me?"

Bob had been a part-time diver at Pacific Marineland when Bill worked there more than twenty-five years earlier. Now Bob owned the Boston Whaler dealership. He looked closely at Bill and then said, "I sure remember your name, but, maybe it's your graying hair, you just don't look the same!"

Bill chuckled, "That's what twenty-five years will do!"

Together they talked of old times, recollecting names of diving buddies. Then Bill explained that he wanted to buy some equipment.

"Tell you what," Bob said before Captain Bill could even ask, "I'll give you a straight 30 percent discount on everything, and on some items I can do even better!"

Bill breathed a thank-you prayer praising God for all the "coincidences" that had occurred since his arrival in the United States.

Over the next several days, he purchased diving gear, two high-speed Boston Whalers, and three rubber Zodiac boats—usually referred to simply as Z-boats—with smaller outboard motors. The two Boston Whalers were the twenty-two-foot Outrage model with 235 horsepower outboard engines. In addition, he bought oceanography gear, the cover for the big project. By the time he finished, Captain Bill had spent more than one hundred thousand dollars, even with the discounts. With God's provision, it was all paid for by the time he headed back to Asia a week later.

New Manila
Monday, January 5, 1981

As usual, on the first workday of the year, Doug called a day of prayer for the entire Open Doors Asia staff at the Manga Road Guest House. He and Judy with Douglas Junior lived upstairs over the guest rooms.

Doug began his devotional thoughts for the new year. "God has directed me to share with you about Nehemiah's rebuilding the wall of Jerusalem. It took them just fifty-two days. First Nehemiah prayed; then he did his research. He made a strategic plan based on the research and carried it through, undistracted by much criticism and many threats.

"Somehow, I sense this process is also related to Project Pearl. But the Spirit is telling me that for us it's two times the fifty-two days they took to rebuild the wall."

Pablo was startled. He opened his Day Timer and began to count. One hundred and four days from today ended on the eve of Easter Sunday, April 19. He thought back to their first meeting and Keith's devotions from Ephesians 1:19–20. *"That power . . . he exerted in Christ when he raised him from the dead . . ."* Easter Sunday, God's power, and the mission! He hadn't put it all together before. He was so energized he did not hear another word of Doug's devotional.

As soon as possible Pablo corralled the inner circle, minus Captain Bill and Dr. Jim, into the private Project Pearl office upstairs and excitedly shared the insight. Doug's timing would place the delivery right at Easter time—the time when we celebrate the power of God when he raised Christ from the dead, as Keith had noted in his earlier devotions.

"It's all beginning to fit together," Keith exploded with delight. "God wants to bless His Chinese children with His Word at Easter time this year!"

✿

"Do you realize the pressure this puts on me?" Bill asked Pablo the next week when he returned from the States. They talked over a grilled chicken lunch at Alfredo's on Tomas Morato Street. "One hundred and four days—now ninety-six days—is *really* going to require a miracle! We haven't even ordered the barge construction. And no crew members have arrived so far to be trained. For all I know, we don't even have a crew selected yet."

"Well, we claim we're expecting a *million* miracles," said Pablo. "So these will just have to be another two of them!"

"At least I have the detailed architectural drawings for the barge," Captain Bill responded. "I finished them on the plane coming home. I firmly believe the Holy Spirit gave me the concept and design."

Bill added, "I suggest we go to the offices of EEI Engineering this afternoon. They gave the best quotation on the construction bids. We'll need to see if they can advance their time frame for its completion, which is usually one hundred and twenty days, up to the end of March."

Pablo added, "And tomorrow we'd better finalize a quick and detailed plan for the tug search. We need to compose a tugboat 'want ad' for the newspapers."

5

The Preparations

Todd Miller was a muscular young man with a ready smile, straight black hair, and an affable personality. His role as a field representative for Open Doors USA in Georgia also involved raising funds for Project Pearl. He was surprised one day when the phone rang and Doug Sutphen said softly, "Todd, pack your bags! Your boss, Dr. Ed, has given permission for you to come to Chicago with me."

Now, for the first time, Todd found himself having coffee at O'Hare Airport with the man now known publicly as Brother David.

They hit it off well from the beginning. Doug was an easy conversationalist. He asked many questions and listened carefully when people answered. He explained as much as he felt he could share about the project with Todd, who responded very positively.

"Thanks, Todd, for helping me with Project Pearl," Doug said. Then he stopped talking and looked around to be sure no one was listening. "There are some special assignments here in the States I'd like you to supervise. What do you say?"

"Sure, Doug," Todd replied. "I'm excited about this whole adventure. I've wanted to see God do miraculous things. And from what I hear from you, there're going to be a *million* miracles!"

Doug smiled and nodded. He glanced around again with an air of paranoia. "Our big challenge right now is to find people who can package the 'shipment' we're going to make, and I want you to be the ongoing liaison with them. First, we'll go to a logistics company here in the Chicago area that ships for the military. They handle various kinds of equipment from very large cargo to top-secret shipments."

When Doug and Todd met with the logistics company, things didn't go very well. The management was dumbfounded by their request, and they asked for more information than Doug was prepared to give.

First, Doug presented the challenge to them: boxes to be waterproof-packaged on a large scale in such a way as to float partially above the water in the open seas. They reacted by saying this was beyond their experience and asked if it was even possible to do such a thing. Obviously they were suspicious that Doug's intentions might not have been legitimate.

Doug and Todd met with other companies, but they were repeatedly turned away. Too hot and too challenging was the rationale for everyone refusing their business. For whatever reason, those best equipped to take on the challenge wanted no part of it.

∞∞∞

"Where do we go from here, Doug?" asked a discouraged Todd.

God will help us find a solution, Todd," Doug replied. "I've been talking on the phone extensively with Dr. Jim. We think that we'll have to do the packaging ourselves, probably somewhere on the West Coast."

To Todd this did not seem like a feasible option. *How can we possibly do it successfully, when we've been turned down by those much more qualified in logistics?* thought Todd.

Doug continued, "While we wait for a solution to the packaging challenge, let's go to Nashville and talk to the printers and get a definite commitment for the million Bibles.

At O'Hare Airport, Todd watched Doug talking to one of the scruffiest characters he had seen in a long time. It was like a scene from an espionage movie. The unkempt, greasy-looking man surreptitiously handed Doug a bag, and Doug carefully slipped him a very large wad of cash.

"Todd, we've got to be careful with these," whispered Doug. "They're two pairs of infrared night goggles. I think we might need them. But no one else should ever see these except the crew."

The door to the conference room at Thomas Nelson Bible Publishers was locked. Doug insisted that only the top management hear what he was going to say. A select, small team sat around the table. All of them knew Brother Andrew and were strong supporters of the ministry of Open Doors.

After demanding their agreement to secrecy, Doug confided in them the whole operational plan. They were stunned.

"So," Doug concluded, "we'll need one million Bibles printed at one time even though, as you say, it's never been done before. We'll off-load the Bibles from the barge and float them on the water to the shore. Yes, it's untested, as you say, but we believe it's possible. With God all things are possible."

"But, Doug," Sam Moore, one of the owners of the company challenged, "not only is the delivery method risky, do you realize how much it will cost to print them? If you can't pay for these Bibles, I don't know enough Chinese people who would want to buy one. And we're not sure we can complete the printing according to your timetable. You didn't give us these details when your Dr. Ed Neteland asked for a price quotation."

"At the time the need for secrecy was uppermost in my mind," said Doug. "I couldn't take a chance on revealing the true nature of the project. But I have faith God will provide the finances as well as the delivery."

By the time the meeting concluded, Doug had persuaded them to agree to the plan. Thomas Nelson Publishers would print and bind one million Chinese Bibles in conjunction with Royal Publishers in Nashville. They would be delivered by truck to a specified address on the West Coast. The shipments would begin on February 18 and continue until March 6.

Philippines
January 21, 1981

"Well, what do you think, Captain?" Pablo asked as they poked around the smelly engine room with a flashlight. They were inspecting a tugboat in Cagayan de Oro, a northern city of the southern Philippine island of Mindanao.

After closely checking the two eight-cylinder diesel engines, Bill replied, "These are real fuel burners. That's probably the reason they want to sell it. It'll mean bigger fuel tanks than we want for the distances we're planning."

The tug was smaller than prescribed and was built for towing on the inland seas. It was not a true seagoing vessel, but they were getting desperate in their search.

"Do you think we could use it?" Pablo pushed Bill for an answer. "It's the best we've seen so far. And you know how many we've looked at."

"I think if we raise the freeboard on the bow and build a flying bridge along with the larger fuel tanks, then maybe we could make it."

"How long do you think that would take?"

Captain Bill thought for a moment. "If we get it into a shipyard right away and we push them, I think they could do it in thirty days. But then we'd also have to add the redesign of the fo'c'sle for sleeping sixteen men."

"We'd better get on with it then; we're way behind schedule," Pablo concluded. Later, on the plane flying back to Manila, Captain Bill detailed the alterations that would be needed. This tugboat was a big compromise but time was running out.

There were eighty-seven days left to Pearl.

China
January 1981

Joseph jostled along in the antique Chinese bus. His simple clothing helped him blend in with all the other passengers. The bus was so packed with people that one person's chickens had to be tied to the roof rack. The eight-hour ride from Guangzhou to Shantou was a long, dusty, bouncy one. Looking out the window, Joseph prayed silently for those he saw along the road. So many people. *Lord, may they have an opportunity to come to know You.*

After eight hours, he happily stepped off the bus in Shantou and headed for the nearest hotel. He looked forward to a refreshing shower. Joseph marveled at the old buildings in this city. Most of the larger ones were European-style, fronted by tall round pillars. Shantou, located on the delta at the mouth of the Han River on China's southeast coast, was soon to become a FEZ (Free Economic Zone) and the port bustled with activity. Large cranes dominated the harbor skyline beside the piles of coal and the sand dunes to the south.

Early the next morning, Joseph timed his departure from the hotel perfectly to catch the first morning ferry across the harbor to the south. Dozens of people were in the parks and along the waterfront doing their tai chi exercises. He noticed an old fort with thick walls and protruding canons at the entrance of the harbor. Young boys were already flying dragon kites from the top of its walls. Other youngsters fished with small nets beside the fort.

The smell of the sea air invigorated him as he watched the sun peep over the distant horizon. Joseph knew this assignment was crucial to the success of Project Pearl. He double-checked his shoulder bag to be sure he had everything necessary.

At the ferry terminal on the south side of the bay, he hired a pedicab to take him three miles farther east. He would walk the last mile so as not to raise any suspicions about his intended destination. At Gezhou, Joseph saw Lili waiting at the side of the road with her bicycle. Without so much as an eye-contact greeting, the two fell in step together.

After a few minutes of silence, Lili spoke as she walked alongside Joseph, pushing her bicycle: "Brother Joseph, we had three days of prayer and fasting last month during your planning meetings in Manila. While we prayed, the Lord impressed on us a Scripture passage for you. It is Ephesians 1, verses 19 and 20."

Manila
Monday, February 2, 1981

"That's exactly what we read and focused on during our first planning meeting together!" Keith burst out, amazed and smiling from ear to ear.

There was a significant pause before Joseph nodded and added, "I doubled-checked with her about the reference and that was definitely it! There's no way she or the others could have known we were reading that passage together."

The six men of the inner circle were back together—this time at the Philippine Village Hotel in Manila. This place held memories for them, because this was where Doug and Brother Andrew had organized and held the Love China conference in 1975. Several hundred delegates had come from Asia and around the world to focus on the billion people of China: to learn, pray, and share their experiences. At the front of the hall they had hung an enlarged photograph of Chinese Communist soldiers on the march. Above it was written: "Lord Jesus, through us let the people feel your love."

Brother Willis, a Welshman converted in the Welsh revival of 1904, came to Love China to talk about prayer. As the meetings went on, he was not seen. The conference organizers asked his wife where he was. Brother Willis was on his knees, with his elbows on a chair seat, praying for fourteen hours a day for China.

Eventually his turn came to speak. You could hear a pin drop. "An intercessor," he said, "is a person who prays and weeps in the secret place of prayer until God stoops down and dries his tears." He finished his talk with these amazing words: "What does your prayer cost you? Are you satisfied with your prayer life? Pay the price. May I remind you of the words King David uttered three thousand years ago? *'I will not sacrifice to the Lord my God burnt offerings that cost me nothing.'*"

Brother Willis's talk was remarkable, but not half as remarkable as what he did next when the conference ended. He said to Doug, "Come with me to a point where we can look into China." So they went to the Hong Kong–China border at Lo Wu. At the time, China was a totally closed country. Many thought the church had died. Mao Zedong had plunged the country into chaos during the Cultural Revolution. Millions died—many by suicide.

The two men looked out over the rice paddies. Then Brother

Willis dropped his bombshell: "God has shown me this past week that China will soon open up. Get ready!"

Within a year both Premier Zhou Enlai, and Chairman Mao Ze-dong were cold in their graves. Two years later, a new leader threw open the doors. China began to open up to the West.

ⵥⵥⵥ

Exhilaration was in the air as the six men met in Manila.

"Doug!" Dr. Jim was excited. "You asked us to share what the Lord showed us individually from the Scriptures. This rarely happens to me, but let me read you what the Lord directed me to in Psalm 77:19:

'Your path led through the sea,
your way through the mighty waters,
though your footprints were not seen.'

"I'm claiming this as a promise! There'll be no tracks to follow after we leave a million Bibles on the beach in China. It sure relieves my detection concerns," Jim concluded, his eyes gleaming.

Doug nodded and smiled broadly.

Then Captain Bill added, "And now read Psalm 29:3 and 10."

"Hey, guys," said Doug. "I know you're all excited. I am too. But let's take these one at a time. Pablo, please note for the record that the Lord gave our co-workers in China Ephesians 1:19–20, the same verses we studied at the Philippine Plaza Hotel in December. That's amazing! Make a note of Dr. Jim's and Bill's Scripture references too.

"Thank you, brothers, for sharing what the Lord is saying to each of you personally. Already we can see God at work in our little team. We'll have more time in the next two days to hear from the rest of you.

"Let me begin with what I planned to share this morning. The Lord spoke clearly to me on the plane on my way to a special meeting with ODI leadership in Holland last month. I was reading in my regular Bible study program in Exodus chapter 14, about the Israelis at the Red Sea after leaving Egypt. Turn there in your Bibles. Let's read verses 10 to 22."

The men read one verse per person around the circle. "I want to highlight verses 19 and 20," Doug continued.

> *Then the angel of God, who had been traveling in front of Israel's army, withdrew and went behind them. The pillar of cloud also moved from in front and stood behind them, coming between the armies of Egypt and Israel. Throughout the night the cloud brought darkness to the one side and light to the other side; so neither went near the other all night long.*

"I want to ask the Lord to separate the two groups: the Chinese believers—along with us—and the Chinese authorities with light and darkness so that neither goes near the other all night long. We also want to go in and come out without losing a man or even being discovered in any way!"

The prayer circle time that followed was intense. The men wept as they thanked God for His goodness and petitioned for His protective presence.

As they began the business part of their meeting, Doug outlined the plan for the day. "Let's talk about our agenda," he said. "We'll meet here until evening dinner. Then we'll watch a movie that Pablo, Bill, and I saw in Hong Kong. It's called *Sea Wolves: The Last Charge of the Calcutta Light Horse.* It's based on a true story about some old military guys called out of retirement to destroy three Nazi German ships. Watching a movie will at least give us a break and still help us focus on some sea concepts."

Captain Bill laughed loudly, surprised by how Doug wanted every minute of their time together to be profitable. The others just smiled at each other. They were not surprised that Doug had thought of a movie that would fit so well into their time together. They marveled at his memory and ability to keep so many details in his head.

Joseph was first to report when they got down to business. He showed an enlarged, taped-together, three-frame composite photo of the appointed beach southeast of Shantou harbor. Everyone stared in awe and expectation at the photograph.

"Beishan is the name of the very large bay in the area," Joseph explained. "At the northwest end of Beishan is a smaller fishing cove, which the locals call Dawandu. It literally means in English, 'big bent belly.' The sandy beach of Dawandu is what you're looking at in this photo."

"Since we just read about an angel," Doug said, "let's call this 'Michael Beach.' And Joseph, I want to get this enlarged even more. We'll make it the first item we place on the wall in my private 'war room' at the house. We'll dedicate the room to this and other Project Pearl materials and keep it locked."

Then Joseph shared the important, detailed information he and Lili had gathered on his recent trip. Most significant was the fact there was a small lighthouse just to the northwest of the fishing cove. At 9:00 p.m. every evening the shift of soldiers on duty changed. The new shift began with dinner and during this time they paid no attention to what was going on around them.

Next Doug reported, "The Bibles are being printed in the U.S. right now and should be ready on schedule. Let's move on to Bill's report on the barge."

"Well, the aquarium barge is presently under construction at the EEI shipyard down in Batangas City. It'll be one hundred feet long and thirty-seven feet wide. And she'll weigh three hundred and fifty gross tons.

"Normally they take one hundred and twenty days to construct a barge, but they're adding extra workers to finish ours by the end of March. We got away with a small down payment but we'll have to have the balance of the two hundred thousand dollars before we can take command. EEI will also help us register her in the Philippines.

"She'll have two ten-inch gate valves. Once opened, they should allow the barge to sink until the deck is three feet under water. She can still, however, maintain her stability in that state. By present calculations, our cargo should float free."

"Will it work?" asked Keith.

"We won't be absolutely sure until we test it after construction," Captain Bill replied. "It's different from any barge ever built."

"Pablo, can you report on the search for a tug?" asked Doug.

"Not much to report actually. The only ones we've located are all relics. This is an urgent matter for prayer," Pablo said.

"And were you successful in contacts for a crew?" Doug turned to Dr. Jim.

"No luck! There are many problems. First, a seaman's license is his livelihood. It's asking a lot to risk it on a questionably legal operation," was Jim's discouraging reply. "Besides that, there's the problem of having to reveal too much information before a seaman can intelligently make a commitment. Then we have a security risk. But I believe we can find enough good men in Open Doors offices around the world to make up a crew," Jim concluded.

Much discussion followed about using men who weren't trained as seamen. Finally, Captain Bill finally blurted, "Okay, I'll agree to use an amateur crew on one condition. I want to have thirty days of concentrated training with them before the voyage."

"That sounds great," Doug replied. "We can put together a special boot camp for training."

Excitement ran high as the men talked of learning seamanship, navigation, diving, and other related skills of the sea.

Then Dr. Jim handed out copies of *Mariner's Notebook,* which he had brought for everyone from the United States.

That night the men watched the *Sea Wolves* movie, a dramatic true story of espionage against the Nazi German naval fleet in neutral Goa, eastern India. The movie has a tense and suspenseful ending because the protagonists purposely used an old fishing scow that unfortunately also had worn-out engines.

At breakfast early the next morning, Captain Bill commented, "Shows you we'd better have good equipment! No junk for this project. I've already lost one man at sea on a ship that lost its engine. I'm not prepared to lose another man."

Day two began with devotions as usual. Doug directed the group to Jeremiah 33:3: *"Call to me and I will answer you and tell you great and unsearchable things you do not know."* He explained how this verse had meant so much to him many times in the past. Also it was one of the verses discussed at the recent ODI meetings in Holland under Dr. Ed's leadership.

He said, "We don't know the answers to all the questions we're both fielding and creating, but God does, and His promise is to let us know if we ask Him. We have to be totally dependent on God for Project Pearl. Let's ask Him for the answers we need. Remember, what's impossible with man is always possible with God.

"Pablo's done some research on the history of the Bible in China recently. Tell us about it briefly."

"Robert Morrison, who translated the Bible into Chinese, arrived in China from Scotland in 1807," Pablo started. "During his long journey, the steamship captain jeered, 'You think you can change these people who have been steeped in their own culture and religion for four thousand years?' Morrison replied, 'I cannot, but God can!'

"About six years into the secret project, his translation assistant, A-ko, questioned his faith. 'Don't you see that our land and the hearts of our people are utterly closed to you and your religion?'

"Morrison replied, 'Yes, but it is written, *"Is not my word like a fire? says the Lord; and like a hammer that breaks the rock in pieces?"* This Bible is the one thing that can burn gates of brass and penetrate walls. I can't preach to the people, but I can secretly translate and circulate this book with the confidence that its divine message will operate with divine power!'

"It took many years and much personal sacrifice, but by 1823 the first complete Chinese Bibles were finally printed. And A-ko was his first convert.

"In my research I learned that the first major Bible Society project for China in the mid-nineteenth century was printing one million

Bibles. They had to be smuggled into the country in small quantities at a time, since foreigners and their ideas were suspect and kept out at all costs.

"So Project Pearl is simply following in a long line of those who lived and walked by faith. We can't do it, but God can!"

A warm and sincere prayer time followed as urgent needs—especially for a tugboat—were laid before the throne room.

The planning part of the meeting began with listing the problems to avoid. Again they were written on the easel pad:

Problems to Avoid

Endangering our friends inside

International incident

Being detained or loss of life

Being <u>seen</u> or <u>heard</u> by Communists

Detection of cargo contents

Looking "out of the ordinary"

Loss of Bibles en route

Loss of Bibles when off-loading

Long time on the beach

Creating difficult unloading for friends inside

After this, discussion turned to the crew and crew assignments. "We'll need twenty guys," Captain Bill reiterated. "There'll be a cabin for two on the barge, so we'll have to sleep eighteen on the tug. Usually the captain's quarters has a bunk bed so we'll need a fo'c'sle that'll sleep sixteen. There are six of us right here to start the crew list."

As they discussed other potential crew members, Captain Bill shared that his personal assistant, Ronald, would be a good choice. He was a Filipino medical university student who had dropped out for a term for personal health reasons.

Doug decided he could spare two more staff—Terry Madison and Michael Bruce—and suggested his son, Douglas Junior, would make a good crew member.

Jim chimed in, "I know a great guy in Phoenix, Jerry Simmons, and I also recommend Todd Miller, who's already helping Doug."

"Well, that's half my crew," said Bill. "Jim, you only need to find us eight more."

Before the meeting concluded, Doug displayed one pair of the infrared, night vision goggles to the group. "Just don't ask me how much I had to pay for these." He traced the number seventeen in the air with his finger.

There were seventy-four days left to Pearl.

6

The Tugboat

The Bell 47J Ranger helicopter's blades began slowly rotating: *thwack, thwack, thwack.* Doug settled into his passenger seat behind the pilot. Pablo was already strapped in the rear seat beside him. They adjusted their headsets so they could hear the control tower from Manila's domestic airport give takeoff permission as well as talk to the pilot. Soon they were rising above the hot, sprawling city. Doug found his first ride in a chopper exhilarating. He scarcely noticed the oppressive humidity.

The pilot pointed out some landmarks below. He didn't have to mention the old American cemetery with its acres of neatly arranged rows of pristine white marble crosses and Stars of David set in well-trimmed, lush green grass. It was a memorial to those who had died in the Philippines in World War II. Both men had visited there with American guests and family many times but had never noticed its beauty from the air.

The chopper skimmed over the miles of palm trees and the occasional small village of bamboo huts with roofs of nipa thatch.

"Look, there's Lake Taal just beyond Tagaytay!" the pilot shouted in his headset.

"Wow!" Doug yelled as they flew toward Volcano Island set in the middle of the large freshwater lake; then they went right over the open mouth of the crater with its smaller salt water Crater Lake inside containing a small island known as Vulcan Point.

"Amazing!" This trip was turning out to be more fun than imagined.

Doug and Pablo were on their way to Paradise to meet with Captain Bill about the project. Driving to Bill's place would have meant a hot, slow, three-hour trip to Batangas City. And then they'd have had to be at the pier well before noon to catch the once-a-day ferry crossing the Verde Island Passage to Puerto Galera on Mindoro Island. The ferry didn't return to Batangas City until the next day. Then they'd have that very long, hot, and tiresome drive back to Manila, dodging oxen, horses, and water buffalo that shared the paved road with the wide variety of vehicles. In the chopper it would take only half an hour each way, and the pilot would even wait for them. They would be home for dinner and in their own beds that same night.

Soon they descended to a clearing on the west beach at Puerto Galera, named by the Spanish colonialists "Port of Galleons" because it was a natural protective bay. That alone made it important, but now tourists had discovered its coral reefs, white sandy beaches, and friendly people. By landing on the west shore, they avoided the numerous hawkers at the village pier selling everything from leis of *sampaguita* flowers to peanuts and cigarettes.

Bill and his Hawaiian-born wife, Lil, lived on a houseboat anchored near the shore on the east side of the large bay. They had also leased some land for seven years and this allowed them to build a narrow pier for walking from shore to their houseboat.

"I can understand why Bill lives here!" Doug said as he glanced around the bay. The sunshine, the green coconut palms, the white sand, and the azure sky were worthy of a painting—or at least a postcard.

After agreeing on a departure time with the pilot, they climbed into a long, narrow, canoe-like native pump boat to make the short crossing to Bill's houseboat. This was the part of the trip Doug enjoyed the least. The vessel was motorized and had outriggers on each side, but Doug's large frame filled the seat making him fearful of capsizing. In the Philippines, these boats were called *bancas*.

The trip took only ten minutes and soon they were pulling up alongside the dingy float. It was connected to the rear deck of Bill and Lil's houseboat, which faced west so they could enjoy the spectacular sunsets each evening.

"Welcome to Paradise, brothers," Bill called out as the *banca* operator cut his engine and glided alongside the houseboat. Bill grabbed the mooring line and tethered the vessel.

"Hi, Bill! How ya doin'?" Doug asked smiling broadly. He walked up the short ramp from the dingy float to the rear deck and embraced Bill and Lil with his usual bear hug greeting.

Soon they were sitting in comfortable deck chairs with a glass of cool *calamansi* juice in hand looking west over the bay. "This is an unbelievably beautiful place, Bill," Doug started. "I'd love to bring Judy down sometime—especially in that helicopter over there."

"So, what's so important, Doug, that you'd chopper down here? I'm sure this is not just a social visit," Bill queried. "Your budget must be improving!" he added, grinning.

Doug ignored the dig and responded, "Pablo and I've been looking over the detailed project PERT chart and I'm alarmed that we're falling behind in several areas—especially in finding a tugboat. Also I want to see the boot camp you're constructing for crew training as well as hear your report on progress with the barge construction."

"Well, you can see the crew's bunkhouse is all framed in over there on the shore," Bill responded. "We've just got to do the electrical work and put in the bunk beds."

"You should see the box aquariums he's building for the barge and for towing practice," Pablo added.

"That's encouraging," Doug nodded. "I received a telex from Jim yesterday. He's been successful in lining up some more potential crew members. They'll be here very soon. What about the barge? We think we saw it as we flew over the shipyard coming here."

"EEI keeps assuring me that it'll be completed on time, but the way they're goin', I have my doubts." Bill set his empty glass down on the coffee table and leaned forward as he spoke. "I think we're going to have to assign someone to ride herd right on site."

"I've been thinking . . ." Doug paused. "Frank Phillips, our Hong Kong director, worked in the aerospace industry. I'll ask him if he's willing to come over and supervise."

Bill nodded and continued, "The tugboat is our biggest challenge."

He gestured toward Pablo. "The two of us have been to Taiwan and Hong Kong with no luck. I really thought we'd find one here in the Philippines. I still believe that! But nothing we've looked at so far is close to what we need. We've been to Cebu and Mindanao as well as Manila. I don't want to take just anything and be sorry later."

"And we've advertised everywhere possible," Pablo added.

"Keep looking and I'll send out a prayer alert," Doug concluded. "Carefully worded, of course! We still need to operate with secrecy if we're going to be successful."

Before long Doug had discussed with Bill everything that was on his mind. He finished his juice and handed the glass to Lil with a thank you, then gave Bill and Lil a farewell hug.

As Pablo hugged Bill farewell, he said, "I'll be back next week to check on the barge."

"Give my love to Judy and Dianne!" Lil shouted as the *banca* noisily headed out. "And bring them with you next time. I could use some good female company down here."

China
February 1981

Chan and Matthew Lo pushed onto a bench in the third-class railway car. They were on their way to China's interior Henan Province, a twenty-hour train trip. Lili and Mei-ling had seen them off at the railway station. Chan felt an unusual twinge at leaving Mei-ling. They had worked so much together over the past weeks and he was realizing how much he enjoyed her company.

Matthew, an itinerant evangelist from Shantou who had spent the past twelve years in a "reform by labor" camp, had invited Chan to join him on this trip. As a Project Pearl distribution coordinator, Chan could talk with house church network leaders in Henan about the delivery of the much needed Bibles.

Lying in the center of China, straddling the Yellow River, Henan is the cradle of China's five-thousand-year-old civilization. From the eleventh century B.C. to 1127 A.D., more than ten dynasties set up their capitals successively in Henan. The result was a plethora of ancient relics and ruins spread throughout the province of thirty-one cities and ninety-nine counties. In 1981 the capital was Zhengzhou and the provincial population was seventy million.

Canadian Presbyterian missionaries opened this area to the gospel. Best known among them is Jonathan Goforth. He and his wife, Rosalind, began missionary work in North Henan in 1888. During their service there, five of their eleven children died, and they experienced many other hardships.

In 1900, during the Boxer Rebellion, the Goforths had to flee for miles across China. Jonathan was attacked and injured with a sword, but they both survived and escaped to safety. After their return to China in 1901, Jonathan was inspired by reports of the Welsh revival and the stirring Korean revival. During a visit to the northeast of China, he experienced the Manchurian revival. This transformed his life and ministry. From then on he was primarily an evangelist and revivalist, not a stationary missionary.

Jonathan Goforth did not see his prayers for revival in Henan answered. But God did answer those prayers. In the late 1970s and early 1980s, church growth exploded throughout the province, and there were more than one million who had committed their lives to Christ. Now Matthew Lo was en route to encourage believers there and to continue preaching the gospel.

People were crammed around them on the train as Mathew and Chan talked quietly together. Two soldiers stood in the crowded aisle and a family of three occupied the opposite seat. They all stared at Matthew, a small man dressed in a drab, shabby Mao suit of dark blue. His hair was still dark but beginning to thin. His craggy face revealed the hard years he had experienced. Everyone stared at him so intently that Chan wondered if something was wrong.

One of the soldiers could restrain himself no longer. He leaned forward and said, "Old man, tell us why you seem so happy."

Matthew, a master at getting people to talk, replied with a smile and a question, "What do you think? Tell me what would be the happiest thing that could ever happen to you, and I'll tell you whether that has happened to me."

He addressed his question to all who were listening, and the suggestions came quickly. The young wife sitting opposite said, "A big house would make me the happiest person in the world."

The younger man on the other side of Matthew said, "No, I just want to be loved by a beautiful, wonderful woman."

Another said, "I'd like a passport to America," and one of the soldiers shouted, "If I had the power to command the People's Liberation Army, I would be the happiest man in the world."

A broad grin spread across Matthew's face at all these comments. They asked, "Do you have any of these? Is that why you're so happy?"

"Yes," Matthew replied. "I have all of them and more." They drew back aghast. He smiled again and they hung on his every word.

"Let me see now," he said impishly, "I have a mansion so large an emperor would be green with envy. I am loved devotedly by the most beautiful person in the world. I have perfect freedom to go wherever I wish. And I happen to be a very close friend of the most powerful man on earth."

He continued, "In fact I have received all this from one person. His name is Jesus Christ."

Chan was surprised that the listeners showed no change of expression at the mention of Jesus. There was only insatiable curiosity.

Matthew talked for many hours. He pulled out his tattered Bible and went through it book by book. Chan kept dozing off, but Matthew continued, his eager audience listening intently as he talked through the night.

Late the next afternoon they reached their destination. Matthew shook hands warmly with everyone. He and Chan stepped out of the train into the frosty air.

"*Ni hao* [Hello]," shouted a smiling young man approaching them on the railway platform. He introduced himself as Wang and he whispered softly, "God has answered my prayers in sending you." Then he led them out to the front of the station and pointed to three rusty bicycles.

"Our transport," he said cheerfully. "It's a five-hour ride to my village."

Australasia
Mid-February 1981

The publication of *God's Smuggler to China* in 1980 required Doug to make an author's promotion tour of Australia and New Zealand. He was so engrossed in Project Pearl he didn't want to use up the time, but he gave it his best.

Doug—or Brother David—was well received and raised one hundred thousand dollars for Project Pearl. By the time he finished in New Zealand, he was antsy to be home on the job. The last night there he had a meeting with the Open Doors New Zealand Board of Directors in the country director's home.

"Brothers," he began, "I'm sure you all know that we've received a request for one million Bibles for China. We need your help."

Doug swore them to secrecy and then laid out the plan for Project Pearl. "The barge is being built, and the Bibles are now being printed, but we need a good tugboat. We've looked all over but, so far, have found nothing suitable."

The board agreed to go to serious prayer—even all night if required. As they prayed, one person repeatedly said, "The Lord keeps impressing the city of Singapore on my mind."

After more time praying together, board member Eddie Cairns said, "Stop praying. God's given me a vision. I saw a large tugboat propped up on four stays. It had a rusty red bottom and was under an overhanging tree."

Then the group prayed, "Lord, where in Singapore is the tugboat?" The answer came: "Two miles from the airport."

⁂

That night the news media were highlighting the fact that all international flights in and out of Australia were cancelled. Doug's flight connection was scheduled via Sydney.

Early the next morning, the Open Doors New Zealand director took Doug to the Auckland airport and was able to find him one seat left on a flight to Manila via Singapore. The connections were not good, so Doug would have to spend a night in Singapore. As Doug took his seat, he began to reflect on the meeting with the New Zealand board. The Lord seemed to be telling them that the tugboat was in Singapore. And now, miraculously, he was en route to the Garden City where a river runs through the middle of the lush, green, island city-state not far from the airport. There were strong possibilities Eddie's vision could be realized there.

When the plane landed at Paya Lebar Airport, Doug collected his luggage quickly and headed to the taxi queue. "Take me where they make boats!" Doug commanded the quiet, unassuming taxi driver.

"What kind of boat are you looking for?" asked the driver.

"A tugboat. And it should be only about two miles from here."

As they drove along the highway, Doug looked across the river. There he saw a tall pastel-striped building with an enclosed area surrounded by a fence. Off to the left stood some tall, green, overhanging trees. Down below on the waterfront, up on four-legged cradles, was not one but two black tugboats with rusty red bottoms.

It was after five o'clock and the gates were locked. The night watchmen told Doug that these two tugs had been built for an Indonesian company that went bankrupt. Thus they were not completely finished inside, but one was still for sale.

Securing the address of the owners, Doug went to his hotel but could hardly sleep. The next day he flew to Manila and phoned Captain Bill and Pablo right away. "Pack your bags," he told them. "You're going to Singapore with me tonight. I found a tugboat!"

Singapore
Friday, February 20, 1981

"Well, what do you think of it?" asked Doug looking at the captain expectantly.

"It's a beauty!" Captain Bill replied honestly.

"Will it do the job?" queried Doug.

Bill looked Doug straight in the eye. "It's not my ideal, but it meets what I specified as a minimum in our first meeting, remember? I said it needed a high bow to take the big ocean waves. It would also need to be about one hundred feet long and have a thousand horse-power engine."

"It's one hundred and twenty-eight gross tons and ninety-six feet long. It has a nine hundred horsepower, single screw engine," ex-claimed Doug proudly. "But you haven't answered my question. Will it do the job?"

"Of course, it'll do the job," Captain Bill responded.

The three men inspected the tug again closely. The engine was new, clean, and large. There was enough room in the crew's quarters down in the fo'c'sle to build eight bunk beds to sleep sixteen men. Above it was a small galley with an adjacent mess hall containing a fixed dining table with bench seating for ten—twelve if you squeezed. Next door were adequate toilet and shower facilities. There were two separate sleeping quarters behind the bridge that each had built-in double bunks—one for the captain and his first mate and the other for the commodore and the chaplain. The bridge was elaborate. In addition to a classic helm and compass system, it came with hydraulic steering and marine radios as well as remote engine controls right beside the helm.

"Pablo, we've got only one hundred thousand dollars in the bank but let's go make an offer to the owners," said Doug.

Henan, China

While Matthew finally rested, Chan and Wang talked late into the night about the Bible needs in Henan Province. Together, they made a detailed plan for distribution if loads of the books were available.

The next night the peaceful atmosphere was shattered. Someone had arrived in the village saying that the Public Security Bureau (PSB) was looking for an evangelist and his companion.

"I knew it," said Matthew. "It was that quiet young man on the train who has informed on us."

Matthew, Chan, and Wang mounted their bicycles again and quickly pedaled away from the village over deeply rutted roads in the black of night.

After four hours of pedaling they reached another bus terminal. A bus was leaving for one of the major cities of Henan Province, but the driver claimed there was no room. They pleaded with him until he finally relented. Short elderly Matthew Lo and tall young Chan boarded and settled in the narrow aisle.

It was an eight-hour ride and all the seats were taken. Matthew just stretched out lengthwise along the aisle and promptly went to sleep, waking only when they reached the city outskirts in the morning. Chan dozed while sitting on the floor with his long legs tucked under one of the seats. They did not realize at the time the miracle God had worked for their escape.

Later, however, Wang wrote a letter to Chan. As Wang was cycling back to his village, he met a car of the PSB. It had run out of gas barely one mile from the bus station. He could tell by the heat of the engine that they had not been stopped long. If the car had been functioning properly, it would surely have overtaken the bus.

As Wang cycled past the stranded car with its three frustrated occupants, he could see that one of them was the young man he remembered had stared at Matthew and Chan on the train platform. He was the one who had traveled with them in the same railway car.

Wang added that a few weeks later he was sitting in a house church meeting in a nearby city. A Christian youth told that he was the gas pump attendant on duty that night when a local PSB car drove in. The driver told him to fill up the tank and hurry!

Through the open car window the young attendant heard them talking about arresting an evangelist and his companion who had just arrived by train. The attendant stopped filling the tank. It was less than a quarter full.

Singapore
Saturday, February 21, 1981
"You men need to sharpen your pencils!"

The Chinese owners of Robin Shipyard (PTE) Ltd. looked at each other nonplussed. This quiet outburst from Doug had come in response to the owners' first request of one million Singapore dollars for the tugboat. The Singapore dollar at the time was worth two to one U.S. dollar, making the tugboat price a half million U.S. dollars.

Though not familiar with the expression, the owners guessed quickly that Doug was not happy with the price. "Of course that includes all the safety equipment required by the American Board of Shipping," they added.

Doug was resolute, so the owners withdrew to an anteroom only to reappear with the question, "What are the payment terms you are offering?"

"We'll pay one hundred thousand dollars up front and the rest on delivery."

Again they withdrew to the anteroom and whispered intensely to one another.

At last they emerged with a smile. "Here's our final deal. You deposit up front your one hundred thousand dollars. We will outfit the tug to your specifications with all the necessary safety equipment as well as radar, sonar, autopilot, VHF radio, and satellite navigation. In thirty days—March twenty-third—you will pay the balance of three hundred and eighty thousand U.S. dollars and take delivery or forfeit your deposit."

Doug had not counted in the cost of outfitting in his original thinking about the tugboat's price. "What do you mean forfeit our deposit?" Doug questioned with raised eyebrows.

"Well, we have to use that much money to outfit the vessel. We'll also need some of your officers around to give direction to the outfitting."

Doug took a deep breath and looked at Pablo. "Do you have faith to believe God could provide three hundred and eighty thousand dollars in thirty days?" Doug asked.

"I do if you do," Pablo replied with a dry smile. Doug was the one with the gift of faith. "Anyway, if we don't get this tug, we don't have a project."

They both signed on the dotted line.

There were fifty-six days left to Pearl.

Paradise
Late February 1981

"This is Bill Schwartz, Alastair Barr, and Cor Beukema," said Lil as she introduced the three new crew arrivals to her husband. All of the young men looked to be in their early thirties. "Cor's a Dutchman, Bill's an American working in the Middle East, and Alastair's a Scot," she explained. Cor, tall and muscular, had short-cropped, light-brown hair. Bill was most easily distinguished by his shock of unruly white-blonde hair. And Alastair was a shorter man with dark wavy hair and an easy smile. They had spent the better part of the day making the arduous trip overland by car from Manila to Paradise in Puerto Galera.

"I'm sure glad to see you guys," said Captain Bill. "We've got a lot of work ahead of us."

"We know only a very little bit of what this is all about," said Bill Schwartz. "Dr. Jim was very mysterious when he asked each one of us if we would volunteer. He said he couldn't tell us much and he didn't." Bill was a key player on Open Doors' ministry team based on the island of Cypress.

"Jim said we could still opt out after we ken what's goin' on here," added Alastair in his thick Scottish brogue. He had worked for several years for Open Doors UK.

Captain Bill explained the entire project, then asked, "So how about it? Are you in or out?"

"We were in before you even explain it," said Cor. "The Lord has spoken to each of us very direct about this." They proceeded to fill Captain Bill in on their faith stories.

"Have any of you had experience with boats?" he asked.

"I haven't," said Bill Schwartz. "But I've always been interested."

"Just a wee," added Alastair. "But I've worked repairin' motor cars and I'm a trained electrician."

"I'm willing to do whatever you ask me to do," said Cor. "But I never worked on a *big* boat before."

"Okay, then let's get to work and see what we can do."

First, the three men helped Captain Bill complete the hastily built bunkhouse for the remaining crew who'd be coming for training in Paradise. They all worked with energy, tackling first the things they knew best how to do. Alastair was able to quickly install the electrical wiring. Bill welded the bunk bed frames together, while Cor helped everywhere with his amazing strength. Captain Bill thought the new crew looked very promising. This was the first sign that made him think this project just might work.

"We're going to have one big problem," said Captain Bill to Bill Schwartz. "We're both named Bill!" They both laughed, and Captain Bill added, "So from now on you're Bill and I'm Captain Bill—or just Captain. That should eliminate any confusion."

"Sounds good to me," Bill agreed.

Captain Bill spent substantial amounts of time on long-distance calls with Jim regarding the packaging of the blocks of Bibles. The original design just didn't cut it and appeared to be a major stumbling block for the project. Dr. Jim was concerned that the blocks were too big and heavy and when loaded might crush the bottom boxes in each block. Based on other research data, he also continued to question whether the blocks would actually float.

"I suggest we halve each block and double the number," Captain Bill offered. "That means there'll be 232 one-ton blocks."

"I'll test the first one we make in the water," concluded Jim.

There were forty-nine days left to Pearl.

Henan, China

Chan finished his planning for Bible deliveries in Henan Province, and Matthew felt he had spent as much time there as was practical for a well-known itinerant evangelist on the run—an "undesirable." Just as they were ready to leave the house where they were staying, however, there was a knock on the door. To their horror it was the local

Communist party cadre. He was the boss of this community for the central Communist party.

"Which of you is the evangelist, Matthew?" the cadre demanded.

To protect Chan, Matthew quickly stepped forward and said, "I am."

"Will you come and pray for my eight-year-old son? He's very sick, and the doctor doesn't know what the problem is."

Amid sighs of relief from others in the room, Matthew replied, "Why have you come to me? What makes you think I can help?"

"Because I've heard you are in touch with a God of real power," the cadre answered simply.

Matthew persisted, "Why do you think I should be willing to ask God to heal your son? After all, you've not shown much liking for Christians yourself."

Chan could feel tension rising in the room. Was Matthew going too far? This cadre was powerful. One word from him and they would be spending the next few months in jail.

Speaking with great emotion, the party boss declared, "All my life I've been taught to hate—to hate tradition, to hate capitalism, to hate the West. Always the cry is 'Hate, hate, hate.' I know I've accomplished nothing. And I know China has gone nowhere. I know that hate only kills. But I still feel love—love for my son—and I know that without that little love I bear for him, and he for me, I'm dead. Christians are supposed to worship a God of love. Maybe this loving God will take pity on my sick son."

A shocked silence filled the room. No one had heard the cadre speak so frankly before.

Matthew responded gently, "We do worship a God of love, and He's the One who has given you the love you have for your son. But you don't have to ask me to pray for your son. Why not speak to God yourself about him?"

"Will he listen to me?" gasped the incredulous cadre.

"Of course," replied Matthew. "Now you pray and we will pray with you, too."

Haltingly the distraught father put together a fragmented prayer.

"God, since You are love, save my son, and free him to live a life of love!"

Everyone echoed "Amen," and hurried after him to go observe his son. Of course, they need not have had any anxiety. When they arrived at the house, the boy was completely well, and two more people were united in love to the Lord Jesus Christ.

On the train going home, Chan and Matthew discussed the results of their trip. They talked softly to make sure no one informed on them. Chan's objectives had been met, and Matthew had seen more than fifty people come to the Lord in a remote village. He had also founded a new house church.

Matthew Lo talked excitedly about his next trip to Anhui Province the following weekend.

"Aren't you going to rest?" asked Chan.

"Rest is for the next world!" Matthew said.

7

The Miracles

Keith was in Manila for management team meetings and his exuberance could not be contained. He asked Doug for permission to speak right at the beginning of the meetings.

"I stopped in Hong Kong on my way here and met with Mama and Papa Kwang," Keith smiled broadly. "Mama Kwang had just received a phone call from Lili. The house churches in her area held another three-day meeting of prayer and fasting while our second Project Pearl planning session was going on here in Manila last month. Here's the surprise: They said the Lord gave them a Scripture passage for us while they were praying: Exodus 14:19 and 20. That's exactly the reference Doug shared with us in our devotional time together! This gives me goose bumps!" he said, rubbing his large, hairy arm.

"Is goose bumps a gift of the Spirit?" Pablo teased.

Keith grinned and continued as though uninterrupted, "My brothers, God is in Project Pearl and He wants us to know it."

The management team members all nodded with growing conviction.

San Francisco, California
February 26, 1981

Jerry Simmons scratched his head of prematurely graying hair. He surveyed the warehouse where thirty-six people were hard at work under his supervision. Piles of clear plastic, banding materials, heavy plastic tarps, and hundreds of pounds of polypropylene rope cluttered the area. The scruffy looking workers made him smile.

Dr. Jim had organized this packaging process since no commercial company would touch the project of waterproofing a million books. He had contacted churches in the area, offering a two-week work project to college-age youths who wished to earn some money. On the first workday a large group of long-haired, hippy-looking street people showed up. Many were new believers, quite excited about their newfound faith. Jim and Jerry gave them the standard lecture on the secrecy of the project, without explaining anything about the delivery method.

One of the young men wryly commented, "If this is a secret project, why are all the pallets from the printers labeled 'Chinese Bibles'?"

God protect us from ourselves, Jim prayed silently.

The process that Jerry was now supervising was straightforward. First, the plastic-wrapped cardboard boxes were piled two deep, four wide and six high to form a block. This block was then wrapped in clear heavy plastic and duct taped tight. Banders were then used to add strapping around the blocks both ways to give them some strength and stability. Then the heavy blue plastic tarp material was folded around the blocks and welded tight on all sides and corners and taped. Finally, the black polypropylene ropes were tied around in four places vertically and three places horizontally to give more strength as well as a method for a crane to lift and load the blocks. All this would have to be done 232 times!

When the first block was finished, Jim and Jerry took the one-ton monster on a truck to San Francisco Bay. With the help of a rented crane, they dropped it in the water. Not only were they amazed at how sturdy and waterproof it was, but the biggest surprise was it floated with eight inches of freeboard. Even with a man standing on the block in the water, it continued to float with two and a half inches above the water's surface. Captain Bill had been right all along.

Now Jerry was counting the days to completion so he could head off to the Philippines and join the crew at the training center in Paradise.

"Jerry, we have a huge problem!" Sean's voice broke into Jerry's thoughts. "The bander won't work anymore!"

As Jerry examined the banding machine, he noticed immediately that the serrated teeth on the flywheel that tightened the strap were all worn off. No wonder it wasn't working. His first thought was, *Where on earth at this hour can we find another bander?* Thirty-six people stood staring at him waiting for a solution. Their work was finished without the bander.

"Let me pray over this thing," said Sean. Jerry was amazed at the faith of this young believer as well as others like him in the group who held hands in a circle and earnestly prayed.

"Father," Sean began as he held up the broken bander, "You know the predicament we're in. This is Your project and this is Your Word for needy brothers and sisters in China. And now this bander has stopped functioning. I pray in the powerful name of Jesus that You will make this thing work again. Not just for us but for Your glory and Your people in China. Amen."

The thirty-six men went right back to work without any hesitation or verbal direction. It was as if they knew that the bander was now in good working order. Jerry didn't hear a word from anyone until coffee break.

"How's the bander working?" he finally queried, with some hesitation.

"Actually, it's working better than it ever did!" several of the men announced triumphantly.

Manila
Friday, February 27, 1981

Michael Bruce, the Open Doors Asia business manager wiped the perspiration from his face. For many hours he'd been working to clear through Philippine customs the huge crate of marine equipment Captain Bill had purchased in the United States. Fortunately, the two large Boston Whalers looked very used, which helped considerably. But the complicated bureaucracy and red tape for so much equipment was exhausting and seemingly endless.

The Philippine customs officers could not believe the low prices declared for the equipment in the crate, especially when the shipping bill alone was almost eight thousand dollars. The whalers did look used but the two 235-horsepower outboards were not even out of their original boxes. Then there were three rubber Z-boats, each with its outboard motor.

"This will take a miracle," mumbled Michael to himself.

New Manila
Tuesday, March 10, 1981

Doug and Pablo, now darkly tanned and bearded, were studying the PERT chart again in Doug's office, calculating what had yet to be completed for the project to be on time. Things were not looking good.

"I've just been talking to Dr. Ed," said Doug. "It's unbelievable but the funds for Project Pearl have seemingly stopped coming in. No Open Doors base has any current funds for the project. Dr. Ed says the board's getting very worried about the lack of finances. So, apart from the three hundred eighty thousand dollars we need in two weeks to pay for the tugboat, what else are we missing?" asked Doug with a wrinkled brow.

"Well, Captain Bill says the next important thing before we can sail is the matter of registration for the tugboat as well as licensing for the officers and crew," said Pablo.

"Explain this again to me, please," Doug sighed.

"All ocean vessels must be registered in some country. All of these ships are also required to have licensed officers. Even the crew must have a basic seaman's license. Most countries—like here in the Philippines—insist that their crews be licensed nationals. We're proposing to use an international crew on the tug, so we must register under a flag of convenience."

"A flag of what?"

"A flag of convenience. If we register with a Third World country, such as Panama or Liberia, it is called registration under a flag of convenience. These countries make a lot of money this way, since it costs thousands of dollars a year for registration of a large cargo or container vessel."

"Will we still have to have licensed officers and crew?" asked Doug.

"Sure, and that's a bigger problem. Earlier this week, I went to the Panama Embassy in Singapore. They're the only flag of convenience country with offices in our region. I explained our marine oceanography operations but got a very frosty reception. The headman there, Mr. Sanchez, said that if we could produce the money, they might be inclined to register the tugboat. But no way would they register our crew or give waivers on our officers. Looks like we're at a dead end again."

Doug leaned back in the oversized lounge chair. He looked weary and frustrated. "Well, all I know is that God wants us to complete Project Pearl. I know He can do it, so let's not lose faith in Him no matter what obstacles we face. Here's what I want you to do . . ."

"Doug, I'm sorry to break in like this, but I have Pastor Chuck Smith on the phone," Keith announced excitedly, sticking his head in the side door to the office. Since the time Keith had joined Doug in Open Doors Asia, he had kept in touch with Pastor Chuck Smith at Calvary Chapel in Costa Mesa, California. "Can I tell him about Project Pearl and our financial need for the tugboat?"

Doug grimaced and paused a long time. "Keith, you know how secret this project is. I don't want any more people to know about this." After an awkward pause, he continued, "So tell him, but don't tell him!"

Keith nodded with a knowing smile and went back to his phone conversation, explaining to his pastor friend the financial need for a "vehicle" for Project Pearl and that the final payment deadline was only two weeks away.

After Keith had closed the door again, Doug fretted and stewed for some time. "How are we going to keep the element of surprise if everybody knows about this project?" he asked aloud, not expecting Pablo to answer.

Keith entered the room again. "Doug, Pastor Chuck wants us both to come to California to meet with him personally about Project Pearl right away."

It appeared that Doug hardly heard what Keith had said; he just nodded and continued his conversation with Pablo. "I know that money talks here in Asia, so when are you going back to Singapore?"

"This weekend after I visit Captain Bill down in Paradise."

"Doug," Keith said, more emphatically this time. "Did you hear what I said? I have a good feeling about this. Chuck wouldn't ask us to come if he wasn't excited about the project."

Doug smiled at Keith, "I hope you're right. We could certainly use his help." Then he turned back to Pablo. "On Monday I want you to go back to the Panama Embassy first thing in the morning and take cold cash—lots of it—to show Mr. Sanchez we can easily pay for the ship's registration and anything else needed. And we'll have a prayer meeting every day until this issue is resolved."

As Pablo headed out the office door, Doug called out, "By the way, we've decided on a name for our new tugboat—*Michael,* after the guardian angel of Israel who fought on behalf of God's people." Then he added a little glumly, "We're going to need all the angelic help we can get too!"

Pablo turned to Doug with a smile. "Then you'll probably name our barge, *Gabriel.*"

"No. She's feminine, so *Gabriella.*"

There were thirty-nine days left to Pearl.

Costa Mesa, California
Friday, March 13, 1981

Pastor Chuck Smith shook hands with Doug, Keith, Dr. Jim, and Dr. Ed. His broad smile put them at ease as he welcomed them and invited them to sit down in his comfortable office at Calvary Chapel in Costa Mesa.

After the greetings and small talk, he said, "Obviously, I need some more background on this project before considering any involvement."

Doug began the long story of the Bible need in China, the success of Project Rainbow, and the subsequent request for one million Chinese Bibles. "We believe God has directed us very specifically," he continued, "and I'm going to ask Dr. Jim to brief you on the technical plans of the mission. Of course, there's a lot of information that is secret, but he has discernment as to how much he can safely reveal."

Jim launched into a detailed presentation about the tug and barge as well as the loading and off-loading plans.

When he finished, Pastor Chuck asked, "Well, Doug, how much money is needed to purchase the tug? And how much are you asking us to provide?

Jim was thinking, *Don't go too far, Doug! Just ask for something reasonable, something Chuck can do without too much of a burden on him, something we can get within a few days at most, like fifty thousand dollars.*

Doug replied without hesitation, "Pastor Chuck, we need three hundred eighty thousand dollars!"

Jim just about fell over. *Now we've blown it entirely! We asked for way too much.*

Pastor Chuck did not even flinch. He paused for a moment and said, "I need to think and pray about what I've just heard. And I'll need to talk to my board. You go back to your hotel room. I'll call you when I have an answer."

Santa Ana, California
Friday, March 13, 1981

The air was thick with tension as Dr. Ed Neteland called to order the evening meeting of the Open Doors senior management team and the Open Doors USA board. He opened in prayer. Sealy Yates was also present, representing the ODI board. Doug had been asked to come and update the group on progress in the Project Pearl plan. But in reality the meeting was called because funds for the project were short worldwide. Since there was no strategic plan for project fundraising, financial resources had fallen way behind in every area. The board had a fiduciary responsibility, which often brought decisions to that crisis intersection of faith and practicality. Their hearts were behind the project, but their heads were telling them to be cautious. As members of the board, they did in fact feel deeply responsible for taking on debt that might cause trouble for ODI. The treasurer in the group was alarmed that Doug would jeopardize one hundred thousand dollars of the ministry's money for a tugboat, when there was no hope of funds for the final payment.

Doug had decided to allow the drama of the evening to play out naturally. He gave his report and answered early questions about the progress of the delivery plan. Most things were now right on schedule, he said. He did not want to share his deep concerns about the completion of the barge and the licensing of the crew. He was still walking by faith. Then he went on to describe how he and Pablo had signed a contract in Singapore on February 21 for tugboat *Michael,* which was being outfitted to meet international sea travel safety standards.

Tell us the details of the contract," Dr. Ed encouraged Doug.

"Well," Doug started, "we had only one hundred thousand dollars in the bank. We agreed to use this as a down payment, which we will forfeit if we do not pay the balance of three hundred eighty thousand dollars in thirty days."

"But how could you do that, Doug, when there is no hope of receiving that much money—especially now with just ten days to go?" asked the treasurer.

Doug looked at the treasurer and answered, "Because I have faith in God, and God is faithful." He paused and then went on, "An hour before this meeting, Pastor Chuck Smith at Calvary Chapel called me to say we can come by his office tomorrow morning to pick up a check for three hundred eighty thousand dollars."

Everyone around the table gasped and sat for a moment with mouths open, then shouts of "Hallelujah!" pierced the air. Worried faces broke out into broad, happy smiles.

Despite the report of this miracle, Doug received only a tentative green light to proceed with the project. As one attendee remembers, it wasn't a warm, fuzzy feeling of full support.

Singapore
Monday, March 16, 1981

Four men sat around a breakfast table in the Bali Hut coffee shop, located behind one of the marble-covered support posts in the small lobby of the Seaview Hotel near the East Coast Parkway. A sign on the wall read: "Singapore's Friendliest Hotel." Observers may have wondered why the heads of this small group were bowed so long and to whom were they talking.

Before their prayer time, Dr. Jim briefed the men on the recent meeting with Pastor Chuck Smith and the subsequent Open Doors USA board and senior management meeting. He added, "Pablo, we'll be praying all morning until you return with good news about registration. And I'll also be praying that enough funds come in to the USA office to pay for the shipment of Bibles from San Francisco to Hong Kong. Dr. Ed just informed me there's no project money at the moment."

Jim had arrived in Singapore the previous night. As first mate on tugboat *Michael,* he was to work on installing and checking the electronic equipment for the vessel. Before the trip, he had secured a crew for the maiden cruise from Singapore to Captain Bill's Paradise in Mindoro, Philippines. Some of the men were already in training at the Paradise camp and others were awaiting the go-ahead to fly directly to Singapore.

"We'll stay here in the hotel this mornin' and pray too," Alastair was speaking for himself and Cor. They were in Singapore to work on all the logistical matters in getting *Michael* seaworthy and prepared for a crew of twenty. Alastair would become the chief engineer.

"We saw God answer prayer with the shipment of the wee boats from the States, and we believe He'll solve this problem too," added Alastair.

"By the way, how did that happen?" asked Pablo. He had been so involved in the Singapore operations, he missed the excitement of the shipment's arrival in Paradise.

"It was crazy," Cor said. "We went to Manila with the five-man crew on Captain Bill's *Windsong* ship. Michael had been working hard to clear the paperwork through customs. We waited a long, long time but finally were able to load the big crate and head back to Puerto Galera."

"We arrived back at half past two in the mornin'," Alastair

continued the story. "Ten of us worked hard all night unloadin' the boats and gear. Even Lil worked with us all night long.

"We brought some of the navigational equipment from the crate with us yesterday here to Singapore. The other crew members are back in Paradise completin' their training and breakin' in the wee boats. They're just waitin' to hear your go-ahead for the shakedown cruise."

We're a long way from that point, thought Pablo. He said, "We need a lot of prayer, a lot of money, and a lot more miracles." Then he picked up his briefcase loaded with the operations cash and headed out the front door of the Seaview Hotel onto Marine Parade Road. There it was easy to hail one of the ubiquitous blue taxicabs for the short ride to the Panama Embassy in the Hong Leong building at Raffles Quay.

⌀〰〰⌀

After a *buenos dias* greeting, Pablo nervously opened his briefcase and, as instructed, placed a stack of cash on the desk of Mr. Sanchez, the senior official in the office of the Panama Marine Authority.

"Well, I can tell you really *do* want to be registered," commented Mr. Sanchez with a wide grin. "It looks like you might have enough there."

His change of attitude from the last meeting astounded Pablo. "And if it isn't enough, I can get more," Pablo added.

"Well, let's see," Sanchez said. "First, there's the one time enrollment fee, based on a graded scale. For a ninety-six-foot tugboat, that'll be just one thousand U.S. dollars. Then there's the government fee charged at twenty cents U.S. per net ton with a 20 percent surtax." He quickly calculated on his sheet and said, "That's only thirty dollars and seventy-two cents."

"Finally," he continued, "there's the annual tax of ten cents U.S. per net ton . . . plus other charges. We'll round that off to . . . one hundred dollars."

Pablo counted out 1,131 dollars, pushed the amount toward him, and said, "Receipt, please."

"Your registration papers made out to Sea Bio-Systems will be your receipt," Sanchez said slyly as he placed the cash in his desk drawer.

"What about the other issue?" Pablo asked cautiously. "We need you to waive the officers' licenses for just the first year."

"Well, that's a different matter," he replied. "Tell me more about your oceanography operations."

Pablo breathed a prayer of thanks that he had spent so much time recently with Captain Bill. He could almost mimic Bill's spiel word for word.

As he finished explaining Captain Bill's vision and his personal experiences with the sea, diving, and coral reefs, Sanchez asked, "And how many crew members will there be?"

"Exactly fourteen in addition to the captain, the first mate, and the chief engineer. They've been at our base camp in the Philippines training and will be here in Singapore within the week."

"Okay. In light of your captain's significant experience and since your crew has received training, we can waive the officers' licenses for just the first year. And that will be another five hundred dollars. But all seventeen of your crew and officers must secure an Ordinary Seaman's license here at the Panama Marine Authority office. There's a very stringent medical exam that each must pass. And the licenses will cost one hundred dollars each. We'll even open on Saturday to expedite these licenses for you."

"There may be a few extra crew members joining us later in Hong Kong," Pablo added sheepishly.

"No problem," said Mr. Sanchez. "Just go to our office there and they can go through the same process to acquire their seaman's license."

Pablo held in his exuberance until he was outdoors on Raffles Quay. There he jumped and yelled, "Yes! Thank You, Lord!"

Singapore
Saturday, March 21, 1981

Seventeen men from a variety of backgrounds sat around the circumference of the top-story conference room of the Seaview Hotel in

Singapore. Doug made sure the door was locked and then stood in the middle of the room mentally preparing his briefing and message. There was a lot of buzz in the group. Some were old friends and others were new acquaintances. One group was laughing with Keith, who was all smiles.

The crew members of tugboat *Michael* had all just had their medical exams for their seaman's licenses. Though Keith usually carried a cane, he had left it in his hotel room for the medical exam, and he had passed the test with flying colors, in spite of his twelve pills a day for a heart condition.

Now they were gathered to receive final instructions before their first hands-on experience as a crew. Each of these men had signed on to the project with an agreement to secrecy and a document absolving Open Doors from responsibility in case of imprisonment, death, or injury. Tomorrow tugboat *Michael* would sail to the Philippines on its shakedown cruise.

Doug smiled broadly as he began. "Men, this is an important meeting, and we have much to be thankful for. Project Pearl has already seen numerous miracles. In addition to the fact that *you* all are here, we also own a registered tugboat." Again he rehearsed for them the amazing story of how tugboat *Michael* was located as well as its purchase price details.

"Just twenty-eight days ago, Pablo and I signed the purchase agreement here in Singapore with no idea of where the money would come from. It's due on Monday. Two weeks ago, I still didn't know where it was coming from and I must admit, that was a big test of my faith.

"If you don't know already, Pastor Chuck Smith of Calvary Chapel had a church board meeting. God led them to pay the entire three-hundred-eighty-thousand-dollar balance owed on tugboat *Michael*. A telegraphic transfer arrived here yesterday. And that's why you're now here and—more importantly—why we can sail tomorrow."

The group broke out into cat whistles, applause, and loud "Hallelujahs."

"Pablo tells me you all have your Ordinary Seaman papers completed and issued. That includes even Keith and me. That's another miracle!" Keith was not the only one with health problems. Doug had already experienced several heart attacks and was considerably overweight.

"One million Chinese Bibles are printed, packaged, and en route in twenty-five shipping containers to Hong Kong for loading onto *Gabriella*.

"Michael and Terry will fly home tomorrow to look after the office in Manila, but they'll join us on the ship in Hong Kong before we head out to China. Also, Jerry Simmons, Sealy Yates, and the other crew joining later will acquire their Ordinary Seaman licenses while we're in Hong Kong.

"Before I share with you what's on my heart, I want Captain Bill and then First Mate Dr. Jim, our ex-Navy man, to brief you on some important matters."

Captain Bill stood and stroked his goatee. "We haven't had near as much time for training as I originally wished, but everything is a go back in Paradise. We have the two whalers and three Zs ready, as well as a few of the aquarium tanks that will be both our cover and part of our practice equipment.

"You guys who haven't been to Paradise yet will love these Boston Whalers. They're twenty-two-foot "Outrage" models with two hundred and thirty-five horsepower outboard, six-cylinder engines. They drink two gallons of gas per mile from an eighty-gallon tank but will travel up to fifty miles an hour—even on the roughest seas! They're also considered almost unsinkable by design.

"I sent Cor to EEI where the aquarium barge is being built to help expedite the process. It's way behind schedule. Not Cor's fault. I've re-designed the barge—again—to try to speed things up.

"During that time we witnessed another miracle. Cor accidentally fell down a ten-foot hole in the barge but landed on his feet. No broken bones. Just paint all over him.

The crew broke out into cheers and whistles. John slapped Cor on the back and said, "That's my partner for ya!"

"Frank Phillips from Open Doors Hong Kong came over to EEI in Batangas to take Cor's place after he left for Singapore," Bill continued. "I'm hoping Frank is able to push the process along while we're en route back to the Philippines.

"Now the next big step is our seven-day shakedown cruise. Yesterday we had our sea trials for tugboat *Michael* and all went well. Today was a very busy day getting all the fuel we need as well as final provisions. I also acquired all the detailed sea charts we'll need for the total project. Everything on the bridge is ready to go. We just didn't have time to hook up the autopilot. But we'll do that later.

"We'll leave at noon tomorrow. I want you all to report for duty at 8:00 a.m. sharp. I will be as patient as possible in your training, but remember, when we're sailing, I'm a no-nonsense captain.

"You will form three watches for the bridge and the engine room. Tomorrow morning your watch and duties will be posted on the bridge. Keith, our chaplain, will be on the prayer watch. He wants to spend as much time as possible praying on the firefighting tower thirty-five feet in the air."

When Captain Bill noticed the concerned looks of the men, he added, "I've asked him to strap on a safety belt while up there when we're sailing.

"I'll be bridge officer for Alpha Watch from eight to twelve in the evening and in the morning. First Mate Jim will be bridge officer for Bravo Watch from twelve to four both night and afternoon. And Second Mate Pablo will be bridge officer for Charlie Watch from four to eight in the afternoon and morning.

"A big challenge is that we don't have an official cook. I'll be assigning people to work on specific meals. Please be willing to help in this area. It's for the good and the morale of the whole crew and the project."

The crew looked at each other with broad smiles and nodded in amused agreement.

"First Mate Jim is helping me with some of the administrative details, so Jim, over to you."

Jim began by thanking the men for their positive responses to his request for crew members for this project. As usual, he was dressed in deck shoes and jeans, but the normally well-pressed, short-sleeve shirt was looking a little soggy. He had been working all day in the wheel-house of the tugboat in Singapore's notorious humidity. Among other things, in the private cupboard of Captain Bill's quarters, he had carefully hidden the infrared night goggles and the multiple sets of walkie-talkies to be used on the delivery night.

"I want you to know I've learned a lot about God's faithfulness already in this project," Jim continued. "Pastor Chuck Smith's response showed me that you have to be willing to think big, and ask big, if you really need something. Then you have to wait and let the individual decide how much of the total he is able and willing to give.

"I was truly impressed with Doug's chutzpah and with Pastor Chuck's willingness to listen and to help."

Jim paused and glanced down at his list of administrative items. "Let me talk first about the bridge. It's action central when the tug is sailing, so let's be sure to keep it an area with a significant amount of discipline. If you're not on duty, you must ask the bridge officer's permission to enter. I want to discourage any loitering there.

"Second, we need to talk about daytime sleepers. There'll be as many as fourteen men sleeping down in the fo'c'sle. With some of you on night watch, it means there'll always be men trying to sleep during the day. Please respect their need for rest. It'll be hard enough to sleep there anytime with the engine pounding in the room next door.

"Third, don't be afraid to ask questions. You're not expected to know everything. We will not underestimate your intelligence nor will we overestimate the amount of knowledge you have about ships and navigating. We'll learn many things together.

"Don't try to be a hero. If you're sick or can't stand your watch or are overly tired, ask for help!

"When Captain Bill thinks it's appropriate, he'll give you all a fire drill, a man-overboard drill, and an abandon-ship drill. We do *not* want to leave anyone behind!

"Let me conclude with a scripture my father gave me for this mission. Joshua 1:9: '*Have I not commanded you? Be strong and courageous.*

Do not be terrified; do not be discouraged, for the LORD *your God will be with you wherever you go.'*"

"Thanks, Jim," said Doug, as he took the floor again. "We sure appreciate you being part of the project leadership team and the operations team."

Then as he looked around the room at each of the crew, he said, "Men, as we embark on this project's seagoing operation, I feel you need to be aware of the background behind what you're getting into. You could learn this best by reading my book, but we can't take it aboard since there's to be nothing that identifies Open Doors on this tugboat. Remember, you're on a marine oceanography mission and working for Sea Bio-Systems. So for those who haven't read my book, let me summarize.

"God definitely called me to China. It's become my consuming passion. No believers in the world have suffered as much as the Chinese Christians. Their worst period of time was the recent Cultural Revolution that ended in 1976. Believers were imprisoned, tortured, and some even martyred. Bibles were burned by the thousands.

"A few high-profile missiologists declared the Chinese church dead because of the Cultural Revolution. But we know differently. Out of the ashes of the fire has come a purified church that is growing quickly. We're convinced there are at least ten million believers in China today and the numbers are growing daily.

"Now Deng Xiaoping, the restored Chinese leader, is declaring a new Four Modernizations period. There's expected to be more openness in the country than ever before. In spite of growing openness, Bibles are still unavailable for the exploding church growth. That's why we have to respond to this request for one million Bibles.

"Brother Andrew believes in only *personalized* delivery of Bibles and spiritual materials. We will not dump these Bibles just anywhere. We'll deliver them personally to believers who will distribute them personally.

"Though this is an exciting project, it's not a game. It's a spiritual battle. Satan does not want these Bibles to get into the hands of Chinese people. And this battle will be won only with spiritual weapons.

Please be much in prayer as you undertake your role in this project. Prayer groups all over the world are deep in intercession right now for Project Pearl. That's why I believe we *will be* victorious."

At that moment, for no plausible reason, Doug pulled an aerosol breath freshener from his pocket. He opened his mouth wide and sprayed in two long shots. This mundane act in the midst of such serious words struck the whole group as extremely funny and everyone laughed loudly. It was an opportunity to release the tension that had been building, as the reality and imminence of the mission was sinking in through what the men had been hearing that evening. Doug smiled and carried on as though nothing had happened.

"You're going to get tired of my repetition. But this is a secret mission. It will succeed only with the element of surprise. So please be aware of security and secrecy. Now that we're owners of vehicles, the challenges will increase. Always be on guard!

"Tomorrow is Sunday. As soon as we're in international waters, we'll share in the Lord's Supper together on the tug. Now go to bed and get some good rest. It may be your last opportunity to sleep soundly for awhile."

There were twenty-eight days left to Pearl.

8

Paradise Regained

Freshly painted tugboat *Michael* sparkled in the sunshine. The lower-level hull and the specially constructed bow wings—designed for tugboat pushing—were painted the traditional black. The long, low towing stern was also black, with the ship's name and country of registry clearly painted in white on the metal transom. The stern deck was green, covered in only two places by one-foot-wide towline guides. These were painted black and solidly attached to the metal gunwales on both sides. They allowed the tug's metal-cable towline to move freely over top of them as directions changed, without negatively impacting or getting caught on any cargo below on the stern deck.

Two levels of housing, including the upper wheelhouse, gleamed pristine white, as did the tall foremast and firefighting tower. On the rear deck of the wheelhouse was a white pivoting davit for lowering the wooden lifeboat, perched on the starboard side.

Immediately behind the mast was the engine room exhaust stack, painted a light green. Red life buoys, attached around the second story of the white wheelhouse, added another colorful touch.

A brand-new Panama flag flew proudly from the flagpole at the back of the bridge-level rear deck. The flag has red, blue, and white quadrants, the two white quadrants adorned with a blue and red star. The predominantly red and white Singapore flag flew high on the impressive, white foremast.

The name *Michael* was embossed right into the metal hull on both sides of the high bow and was painted white to stand out from the black hull.

Joseph Lee was first to man the helm, with Captain Bill and Jim on the bridge, as the tug sailed out of Singapore into the South China Sea. With nothing to tow, the vessel could easily cruise at more than ten knots. But that also made it more difficult to steer straight. Looking behind the ship, Joseph realized that their wake was a continuing figure S.

"It's okay, Joseph." Captain Bill smiled. "You'll get the hang of it soon."

The crew on the bridge learned how to use the radar system, satellite navigation, and the VHF radio for ship-to-shore and ship-to-ship communication as well as for emergency calls.

One by one, Jim and Captain Bill trained the novice crew to be helmsmen. "No, no, you turn toward the compass error," Captain repeated frequently.

Because of the excitement and great weather the first day, most off-duty crew members hung around the open stern deck or the upper deck area above the wheelhouse, enjoying the scenery as they left the beautiful city of Singapore.

Pablo sat on the front edge of the high bow with his legs dangling over the sides above the bow wings, his back propped against the T-bar bollard with both arms hooked around the T-bars. He loved the smell of the ocean and especially the tropical beauty of Singapore. After the tensions and pressures of the past four weeks, he wished this moment could last forever, but soon the impressive city's skyline was just a dot on the horizon.

"All hands report to the wheelhouse," shouted Chaplain Keith as he rounded up the off-duty crew members. As they crowded into the small bridge area, they noticed the sign on the bulletin board:

ALPHA WATCH: Captain Bill
Joseph L
Terry H
Todd M—Engine Room
Ronald P—Engine Room

BRAVO WATCH: Jim Schmook
Bill S
Douglas S Sr.
Cor B—Engine Room
Godfrey O—Engine Room
CHARLIE WATCH: Pablo
John K
Douglas S Jr.
Alastair B—Chief Engineer
Sonny L—Engine Room

"As we begin this maiden voyage of tugboat *Michael,* we want to thank the Lord for His goodness to us," Keith began, once all the men were assembled. "And we want to identify with our Lord Jesus in the sacrament He left for us to remember Him. Serve it to each other as a symbol of the way we will serve each other throughout this trip and this project."

The men passed the emblems of bread and wine to each other.

"The body of Jesus, broken for you . . . the blood of Jesus shed for you!"

Gezhou, China

The courtyard at the back of Samuel Wu's tiny home was packed full of smiling faces. It was dark, and as believers arrived for the house church meeting, they entered the courtyard single file after security scrutiny by Samuel's two young adult daughters, Rachel and Leah. Their mother had died of cancer just two years earlier, and they were now committed to helping their father in his ministry. One coal oil lantern hung from the outside rafters of the house to provide enough light for people to maneuver through the crowded backyard space.

Once Samuel was convinced that everyone was present, he walked to the back door of his little house and out into the courtyard. The scene made him smile. It did not seem very long ago that the group of believers was small enough to fit inside his home. Now they were so numerous they were crowding each other in the spacious courtyard. The sight made him smile but also caused a tear or two to roll down the deep lines of his wrinkled face. *Thank you, Lord, that You are building Your church as You promised!*

He smiled again as he noted the anticipation evident on each face. Somehow the crowd could sense that this meeting was to be very special. Perhaps it was due to the unusual presence of Lili and Mei-ling.

Samuel's two daughters kept watch outside for any sign of PSB officers approaching this illegal gathering as Samuel began to address the people. "Brothers and Sisters, I suggest we don't sing aloud tonight because we are even more concerned than usual about security for this meeting. I will open in prayer asking God's blessing and protection and then Lili and Mei-ling from our sister fellowships in Dahao and Queshi will share with you tonight. It is most important that you keep the things they will share a secret."

After prayer, Lili thanked Pastor Samuel for his introduction and asked to borrow his Bible. His seemed to be the only one in the entire group. She had a small Project Rainbow New Testament in the pocket of her Mao suit, but tonight she planned to read from the Old Testament.

"I want to read to you from a psalm of David," Lili began, "Psalm 119, the longest chapter in the Bible. In this psalm David assures us that God's Word is eternal and stands firm in the heavens. It is sweeter than honey. It makes us wise and gives us peace. God's Word also provides a light for our pathway just like that lantern over there in the corner of the courtyard.

"Let me read you verses 105–112:

Your word is a lamp to my feet and a light for my path. I have taken an oath and confirmed it, that I will follow your righteous laws. I have suffered much; preserve my life, O LORD, according to your word. Accept, O LORD, the willing praise of my mouth, and teach me your laws. Though I constantly take my life in my hands, I will not forget your law. The wicked have set a snare for me, but I

*have not strayed from your precepts. Your statutes are my heritage
forever; they are the joy of my heart. My heart is set on keeping your
decrees to the very end.*

"I know you all want to put God's Word into practice every day
and walk in that light. Some brothers from the West have promised
to secretly bring us many copies of God's Word for the church here in
China. There will be one for each of you. But we'll need your help
with storage and distribution of the books to others when they arrive.
All I can ask is that you be prepared to help just like the believers in
my fellowship in Dahao."

Mei-ling stepped forward and added, "We already have the
promise of help from twelve hundred other brothers and sisters in
the fellowships of Queshi, Yuxin, Mianbe, and Hexi. They will have
farther to travel than you to pick up Bibles and take them away with
them."

Lili continued, "All we can tell you now is that the delivery will
be at the Dawandu fishing cove of Beishan beach—very near here.
Pastor Samuel's daughters, Rachel and Leah, will let you know the
date and time once it has been agreed on. Bring bicycles, pedicabs—
any form of transportation you can get your hands on—and your
bamboo poles for carrying the boxes.

"Please tell no one else about this other than trusted brothers and
sisters who may also want to assist us. It'll be very risky to be involved
in any way. You could be imprisoned or even lose your life for helping."

Samuel Wu walked slowly to the front, "Now, how many of you
can we count on to help out?"

Every hand in the group was in the air.

On Board Ship
"Who in the world cooked tonight?" asked Captain Bill after the
evening meal of the second day. Earlier he had given the entire crew a
safety drill on life rafts, life jackets, fire extinguishers, and emergency
procedures.

"Well, I think it was a community effort," Pablo replied apologetically.

"That was terrible! The one way to destroy morale on a sea voyage is bad food. I guess I'll also have to be the cook from now on," concluded Captain, with a disgusted look on his face.

"It's a good thing he didn't have breakfast here this morning," said Terry Hickey after Captain Bill returned to his quarters. "Godfrey made the porridge. He thought the left tap was hot water. He didn't know it's the salt water tap!"

The crew sitting around the dining table in the galley groaned from the memory of the salty porridge.

Ronald had made the evening meal. He said it was a chicken casserole. But the chicken was chopped so fine it was impossible to find any.

In the morning Captain Bill was true to his word. As the crew on Pablo's watch finished at 8:00 a.m. and descended to the galley and the mess hall, they were drawn by the appealing odor of garlic rice. It tasted even better than it smelled. Something about the salt air of the sea enhances a sailor's appetite—especially after working at night. Captain had to make at least four large pots of rice for the hungry seamen. It was the last time a number of them would eat for awhile because it wasn't long before small squalls caused the boat to roll and took away the desire for food. Sonny became so seasick that, when he wasn't on duty in the engine room, he stayed on the stern deck.

Terry Hickey resigned his watch because he always felt ill up in the wheelhouse. Chaplain Keith took his place on Alpha Watch. But Terry was fine down at ocean level in the galley. He began to serve others by cleaning the toilets and washing the crew's clothes. Then after Captain Bill gave him lessons, he became a hardworking, first-class ship's cook. The crew affectionately dubbed him Mother Hickey. He worked hard to keep morale high.

As he had promised, Captain continued to help Terry with the cooking. One night he made a succulent beef stew and another time, sweet and sour pork. Ronald later redeemed himself with a good meal of chop suey and rice.

❦

"Captain, number one generator is down and I can't find the problem," crackled Alastair's Scottish accent over the ship's intercom from the engine room.

"What else can go wrong?" muttered Captain Bill. First the radar stopped working, then the satellite navigator quit—a black box on the wall that read out latitude and longitude whenever a satellite passed overhead. The only method left for navigation was dead reckoning, using the ship's compass. At least *it* kept working.

Next the battery charger for the emergency batteries burned out. The refrigeration in the galley stopped working and now—a generator.

All new vessels go through shakedown cruises to uncover problems, but this cruise was finding more than its share. Add to this a few days of rough seas, and the once inexperienced crew learned their routines very quickly. During the trip, Captain gave the much needed safety lectures as well as fire drills.

Then after 170 hours of sailing, *Michael* arrived safely and dropped anchor in Batangas Bay. Captain Bill's dead reckoning navigational skills had been amazing.

Once in the Philippines, Doug, Keith, and Jim disembarked quickly to get to Manila and the United States, where administrative duties awaited them. Captain was eager to get home to Lil. He cleared Philippine customs in a hurry, planning to check on the barge construction at EEI before crossing the Verde Island Passage and anchoring in Paradise to resume crew and project training.

Only twenty days left to Pearl.

Shantou, China
March 1981

Lili and Mei-ling walked together slowly down the waterfront sidewalk of Shantou's central park. Young boys were fishing at the water's edge with homemade throw-nets. Plenty of people were around but they seemed intent on their own destinations and did not even notice the two young ladies.

Across the little bridge at the eastern end of the seashore corridor, they could make out the figure of a tall young man on his way toward them. Mei-ling's heart began to flutter as it became clear the young man was Chan. He fell in step with them without even a greeting but he could hardly conceal his joy—first at seeing Mei-ling again, and second in sharing his report from Henan Province.

"I think the brothers in Henan would take the whole million Bibles if they could be transferred there successfully," concluded Chan in a soft voice as he described the journey he had made with Matthew Lo.

"Well," countered Lili, "we could distribute a million right here in Guangdong Province also. I'm amazed at how fast the churches are growing and how desperate they are for Bibles. I'm soon going to visit Inner Mongolia with Enoch Ma to see if everything is set up there. Chan, I'd like you to join Matthew again in Anhui Province and assess their situation. Mei-ling will visit church leaders in Zhejiang Province. That should be the end of any traveling we need to do until the actual delivery."

Mei-ling looked shyly at Chan and said, "We've arranged for about two thousand brothers and sisters to meet at the Dawandu fishing cove of Beishan beach. They're excited to help with a quick distribution plan. Some have bicycles, pedicabs, and other small vehicles."

"But what's more exciting," added Lili softly, "is that Peter Wang's fellowships in Chaoyang have contacts that can get us a fleet of vehicles, which will make the depository transfers very fast. Chan, I'll ask you to be the coordinator of that aspect with Peter."

She quickly continued, "Our distribution lines to Guangzhou, Beijing, and Shanghai—even to inland provinces—are all ready. But we're going to have to be very careful. Yesterday a sister visited me and reported that one of the local TSPM pastors has already heard rumors about some Bible smuggling happening soon in this area. There must be a Judas in one of our fellowships. From now on, we'd better meet here in the open or at Lao Zhao's. And Mama Kwang says we must organize more prayer meetings. Satan is already doing his best to try to stop this project."

Batangas, Philippines
Sunday, March 29, 1981

"Oh, no! It's a long way from launching," Captain Bill exclaimed as he and Pablo toured the barge *Gabriella* with Frank Phillips. "Why isn't it ready?"

"I've tried," was Frank's simple reply. He had even become good friends with EEI's project manager, Commander Jimenez, which is important in Philippine culture. But try as he might, it was difficult to speed up the process of construction on the barge at the EEI shipyard in Batangas. There seemed to be only one speed at which everyone worked—slow.

"They have some important questions about the towing chain bridle that I can't answer," added Frank. He had worked in the aerospace industry in the United States, but this was new territory for him.

"Well, all I can do is ask Cor and John to come and assist you in pushing this project along," Captain said.

When Captain Bill talked with Cor about it, he nodded at the request and asked with a grin, "Has the meal menu changed? Last time I ate for breakfast fish with rice. For lunch it was rice with fish, then dinner was fish with rice again!"

"Let me ask Commander Jimenez if their technicians can also look at the problem with our radar on *Michael*," added Captain Bill, "once he's finished his rice and fish!"

❦

Each of the crew decided that Paradise was well named. It was an idyllic, sunny, quiet cove in the Puerto Galera bay. *Michael,* the large tugboat, seemed out of place among the numerous small sailboats in this delightful, scenic haven. Lil's tasty cooking was the icing on the cake. She took Mother Hickey under her wing, and his repertoire of delicious menus increased significantly.

Cor wrote home to his wife, Gerri, that he was now living in Paradise. He said that it was beautiful with lots of trees and fresh fruit. And it was so warm he walked around dressed almost like Adam and Eve!

Pablo and Captain Bill were enjoying morning coffee on the front porch of the Tinsley's houseboat. Though the weather was exquisite, Captain was discouraged.

"You can't deny that everything has gone according to schedule up to now," Pablo argued.

"But there are so many problems I don't think we can continue to keep up," Captain Bill countered.

"I understand what you're saying, but we must try everything possible to meet the schedule."

"You're right. I just feel such constant pressure and tension. Everything seems to fall on my shoulders!"

"Well, let's forget the barge and tug just for today and focus only on Paradise training. What's needed?" Pablo asked.

"I've already constructed wooden boxes to simulate the size of the one-ton Bible blocks. We need to have the crew tow them around as we will on the night of the Pearl delivery. Ultimately, they'll need to work in the dark at night without lights to sharpen their night vision.

"Our initial plan is to use the Boston Whalers. I want you, Pablo, to skipper whaler number one and Bill Schwartz to skipper whaler number two—starting today. The two of you will be the only ones to handle these fast boats. That'll also require keeping them gassed and serviced. Then when we lift and stow them on *Gabriella,* you'll be responsible for that aspect too.

"But I want the other guys to enjoy their time here," Captain continued. "I'd like to start off today with some scuba lessons, so they all can experience the pleasures of diving over these incredible coral reefs. And while I'm doing that, you can help install our new ham radio rig on *Michael*'s bridge—the ICOM we bought last month in Hong Kong, remember?"

Pablo nodded.

"Tom, an American doctor living on his yacht here in Puerto Galera, has promised to help erect a good antenna for us. He made one on his yacht that works well. You can go pick him up with the whaler."

"Great, I'll get started," said Pablo. "Once the radio's up and running, maybe I can contact Dean Keaney at our base station in Manila and arrange to talk with my wife. I haven't been home for what seems like months."

⁕

"Pablo, wake up," Lil said in as loud a voice as she could without waking up everyone else. "Bill's not back yet in the whaler. It's one o'clock in the morning, and I'm beginning to get worried. It's not like him to be gone this long and not contact me."

"Okay, I'll take the other whaler and see if I can find him," Pablo responded trying to shake off his sleepiness. Bill Schwartz and Cor woke up and wanted to go along.

The three set out to the east across the Verde Passage at top speed. It was a warm, calm night, and the whaler flew. First they went to the Batangas pier to see if anyone had seen Captain Bill, but it was deserted. It was upsetting when the lone official of the Batangas Coastguard said no one could be reached by radio until morning, so they wouldn't start searching before daylight.

The three hunters scanned the ocean waters as they slowly headed north to the EEI shipyard to see if Captain might be there. There had been some talk of *Gabriella* being launched soon. When Captain Bill was nowhere to be found and no drifting boat was seen in the darkness of the Verde Passage, the three gave up the search and headed back to Paradise, very worried about the fate of their captain. It was four o'clock in the morning.

⁕

The next morning both whalers were tied up in Paradise, and everyone breathed a deep sigh of relief. Captain Bill had taken Tom, his American doctor friend, to Batangas but was unaware that the whaler he chose had not been refueled. They ran out of gas. Over lunch, Captain shared the drama with the whole crew.

"Tom thought we would drift toward the beach," Captain Bill

said. "It was one o'clock in the afternoon and the heat was terrific. We were both in shorts with no shirts. The tropical sun bore down on us mercilessly.

"Instead of drifting toward shore, we traveled in a semicircle around the bay never more than a mile offshore at any time. At one point I put on my diving mask and fins and attempted to tow the boat, but the waves were too strong to make headway.

"Finally after eight hours of drifting, we came to shore at a large shipyard. It was night and we stayed just long enough to borrow some tools so I could be sure that the problem was only lack of fuel.

"I suggested to Tom that we drift farther along the coast and we'd come to EEI where the barge was being built. I knew we'd get help and gas there. While drifting, we heard the sound of another whaler. Then we saw the running lights. It was Pablo, Bill, and Cor. But you guys were going about thirty knots and over the roar of your engine, you couldn't hear or see us. We were only about two hundred yards away.

"Well, we made it to EEI. We gassed up and were back here about five in the morning.

"But I have to tell you, I did a lot of thinking while drifting. I've been very discouraged with all the recent problems as well as the responsibilities. The Lord reminded me that this project is His and it will be through His abilities, not mine, that success will be achieved.

"So let's all get back to work!"

◦⁓◦

The crew bonded during the long days of training in Paradise. Even though the men learned to scuba dive, there was precious little time to do any. But the camaraderie at mealtimes and other group-sharing sessions kept morale and anticipation high.

Projects abounded and created themselves. When towing the wooden frame replicas of the Bible blocks, the whalers exerted so much power, the tow lines repeatedly broke because of the high friction with so much of the block under the water. Captain began to realize that it was not power that was needed for the towing, but consistent slow movement. The Z-boats turned out to be just the right craft for the job. At full power they would initially just barely move the blocks but once movement began, the blocks would slowly continue along in the desired directions and no tow lines broke. So another project emerged: construct t-shaped tow bars and attach them to the rear wooden bottom platforms of the three Z-boats. And daily practice of the towing exercise continued.

Then it became necessary to create platforms with adjacent davits for stowing and launching the Z-boats on and off *Michael.* Bill Schwartz's ability to weld was again put to good use. This launching project was repeated ad nauseum until all three Z-boats could be launched and manned within three minutes of Captain Bill's order.

When not in use, the two Boston Whalers would be stowed on each side of the stern deckhouse of *Gabriella.* There were two symmetrical and distinctive looking davits built to aid the whalers in and out of the ocean, powered by hand-operated winches.

Every night the crew would join together in a devotional time. Bill Schwartz played the guitar well and led in worship. Alternate nights, Godfrey from Trinidad would play and lead. Keith had assigned Todd to be resident chaplain when he was away, and Todd took his responsibilities seriously. Each evening there were significant Bible studies and discussions that concluded the workday on a spiritual note.

Then the word finally came that *Gabriella* was ready to be launched. Captain ordered the crew to pack up all the gear, load the gas tanks and oceanography equipment on the tug's stern deck, and prepare to move across the straits to Batangas. He kissed Lil good-bye and hurriedly headed *Michael* out of beautiful Puerto Galera with two Boston Whalers in tow.

Only thirteen days left until Pearl.

9

The Embarkation

Gabriella was finally launched. Though way behind schedule and costing considerably more than originally agreed, she was structurally sound and floating. Her boxy hull and deck were freshly painted a striking royal blue. The cabin on the stern deck and the safety equipment on its roof were pure white. The davits for the Boston Whalers on each side of the stern deck stood like two blue sentinels.

Gabriella had been constructed on land high above the tide line. Rollers were placed under the hull to move her to the water. The deadweight of the hull was more than one hundred tons, so it took at least fifty men to keep the rollers straight. Two cranes provided the motive power. She was stubborn and refused to move easily, but by two in the morning, she slipped into the water with a tremendous splash.

But problems on *Michael* continued to attract more attention.

⟨✎⟩

"I'm sorry, Captain," said Alastair, the chief engineer. "I've checked everythin' but nothin' seems to work."

"You've checked all the diodes?" Captain Bill asked.

"Aye, checked and double-checked," came the emphatic reply.

The second generator on the tug had now quit. Only emergency lighting from the battery bank still operated. Since the ship was anchored just offshore from the EEI shipyard in the open bay, they were literally stranded. Without the generators, they could not even haul up the anchor.

"Pablo, we've got to do something quick," Captain shouted. "The EEI electricians have been out to check the generators and weren't able to find the problem. We're anchored here with almost all the crew aboard, due to leave in two days. And the barge's internal plumbing and machinery are yet to be completed."

"I'll get on it, Captain. You work on *Gabriella*," answered Pablo.

"Okay, but first I want to pray with the crew. This is becoming too much!" And with that Captain Bill blatted in his loudest voice, "All hands on deck! Tell anyone in the galley, mess hall, and fo'c'sle to come out here on the stern deck. All hands on deck!"

The crew came running, thinking there was an emergency. The last member to arrive was Joseph and he was in a panic. Holding out his hands, he kept repeating, "Where's the deck? Where's the deck?"

Captain laughed. "You're standing on it, Joseph!" Joseph's face turned three shades of red as all the crew joined in the joke.

"I don't mind working with a green crew like you guys," Captain Bill said. "You've all come a long way in the past weeks. But I *do* get upset when Satan tries to sabotage us. He's a defeated foe but he never gives up. Please join hands with me as we ask our Father to put an end to the devil's tactics against us."

The circle of prayer lasted for some time as thirteen men took their eyes off their immediate problems and pleaded with their Lord for His assistance in counteracting the challenges they were facing. They sensed that heaven came right down on that deck.

∽∞∾

Pablo navigated the Boston Whaler through the darkness up to the Keppel boatyard wharf and tied up the lines. He and Doug began the long walk down the pier to the front office. Doug, Keith, and Jim had rejoined the crew, which now numbered sixteen in Batangas. Michael Bruce, Terry Madison, and possibly Sealy Yates would join later in Hong Kong, bringing the number of crew members to nineteen, one or two short of Captain Bill's ideal number.

The Keppel boatyard right next door to EEI had sent out their tugboat to supply power to *Michael*'s anchor winch. Then they offered to sell and install an external deck generator as an emergency measure. It would cost fifteen thousand dollars.

The cash was in an envelope tucked away in Pablo's cargo pants pocket as he and Doug walked silently for several minutes in the dark. Then Doug asked, "What do you think of this project so far, Pablo?"

"I've never been involved in anything this big, Doug. It's amazing!"

"This is only the beginning," Doug continued. "I believe God has much bigger projects for us in the days ahead!"

This one is almost more than I can handle, thought Pablo. *I don't really want to see anything bigger!*

The two men paid the bill and walked back down the pier to the whaler for the short ride back to the tug. The next day there was plenty of power on the tugboat and all the equipment was working again. Bill Schwartz and Chief Engineer Alastair built a plywood house around the stern deck generator, but Captain was not totally happy with this temporary construction, and the basic electrical problem was still unresolved.

෴

"We're right on schedule and we've got to leave today. The twenty-five containers with the million Chinese Bibles are now in Hong Kong waiting to be loaded." Doug was chairing a meeting of the inner planning circle of six on the roof deck above the wheelhouse. Getting there involved a good ladder climb but was quite private from the rest of the ship. That small deck was topped with a green vinyl weather covering.

"Everything's been so rushed and we're a ragged bunch," Captain Bill complained. "We've got what looks like an outhouse on the stern deck and we haven't towed or tested the barge even once. After the mess EEI made of her plumbing and machinery, I don't even know if she'll sink when we want her to or whether she'll come back up when we want her to. Right now, she's anchored in a shallow basin where testing is impossible. Let's tow her to Paradise, test her overnight, and then leave for Hong Kong first thing in the morning."

"Jerry's been checking and says everything on the barge is working fine, Captain. To meet our schedule, we have to leave *today*," Doug replied with more intensity.

The four others in the circle said nothing as this seemed to be an issue just between the captain and the commodore. Certainly, logic said it would be wise to test the barge at least once, not to mention the possible impact of Murphy's Law. But keeping on schedule was also critical.

"Well, I disagree," said Captain Bill. "But then," he added after stroking his goatee for a few seconds, "we're not putting the crew or the tug in any immediate danger, even though the crew has not had any practice with the barge. And I agreed in the beginning to take orders on nonsafety issues, regardless of the circumstances.

"Let me hold a training session this afternoon on tug-towing. Then we'll stow the Boston Whalers on the barge, fuel up the vessels, and get all the water and supplies on board we'll need. We can depart tonight at eleven-thirty for Hong Kong. At seven knots, we'll be there right on time."

⌒⟋⟍⟋

"It looks like she's towing well," Captain said as he relieved Pablo of his watch at 8:00 a.m. the next morning. The first hookup with the barge had been made in the dark the previous night.

The departing Charlie crew prayed for the arriving Alpha crew, a custom implemented by the chaplain at crew watch changes. Then the Charlie crew went off to bed.

"*Gabriella, Gabriella,* this is tug *Michael,*" Captain Bill shouted into the mike of the CB radio. He was calling Jerry, Cor, and Godfrey, who were riding in the barge to accomplish some of the remaining work assignments Captain had given them. The barge had its own generator power and welding machine.

"Tug *Michael,* this is *Gabriella.* Good morning. Over." Jerry's voice sounded crisp and clear over the speaker.

"How's everything riding back there, Jerry? Over."

"Everything's dandy here. We all had a good sleep and we're gettin' ready to begin work in a little while. Over."

"Have you got enough food? Over."

"Yup."

"Well, keep in touch throughout the day—especially if you need anything. Over and out."

In the next moment, a call came from Alastair down below in the engine room. "Captain, the startin' compressor has developed a knock."

"Do you have parts to fix it?" asked Captain Bill.

"Aye, I think so."

"Well, we'd better do it now."

Just at that moment, Doug arrived on the bridge. "How's it goin', Captain?"

"You'll be happy to know we've averaged eight knots since leaving the Philippines." *Gabriella* had no cargo weight on her yet.

"Well, praise the Lord!" Doug replied with a grin. "Looks like we *will* make it on time."

∽⚓∾

While sailing, Pablo thoroughly enjoyed the ship's routine. There was a rhythm to life, with the four-hour watch and then eight hours off. On the bridge his crew was quite capable of following Captain Bill's compass course instructions, reading the radar, and keeping a general lookout. They especially enjoyed their watch schedule because they saw every sunset and every sunrise.

Captain had briefed the crews who worked on the bridge, explaining that towing vessels are given the right-of-way in every situation. The tug was flying its towing flags and at night displayed the special towing lights on the foremast in addition to the regular running lights that any oceangoing vessel must have.

The most intriguing part of the watch was navigating and plotting location, direction, and speed on the sea charts located on the map table—a small countertop at the back of the bridge. From there it was easy to read the satellite navigator and plot the longitude and latitude fix on the sea charts each time a satellite passed over. Then calculations could be made from the previously marked fixes.

At dusk on the second day of the voyage, Douglas Junior was at the helm. John Kulisich, manning the radar, suddenly shouted, "Pablo, there's a freighter coming quickly at a forty-five degree angle on our port side. She doesn't appear to be slowing down, and my projection is a collision course!"

Pablo jumped to the port window and aimed the binoculars to the southwest. Sure enough a large freighter was heading toward *Michael* at a good clip. He didn't need the binoculars to see it.

"Ronald, quick! Run down to the mess hall and ask Captain what we should do," Pablo ordered.

Captain Bill was enjoying dinner with a group of about ten other crew members. He was also in the middle of a long story. Ronald, the gentle Filipino, was not about to disturb or interrupt him and just stood in the doorway of the galley patiently waiting.

Meanwhile on the bridge, Pablo was beginning to panic. His instructions included no engine speed change because it could foul up the one-hundred-foot steel cable towline. It could also break the barge's bridle if the subsequent tightening pressure was too strong. The other option was to temporarily change course. Pablo held his hand on the remote engine controls trying to make a decision. The freighter was obviously not going to give way. *Should he cut the engines?*

As the freighter came up to just thirty yards off the port side of the tug, Ronald finally interrupted, "Captain, should that big ship be out there?"

Captain looked out the porthole and immediately jumped to his feet. Though he was fifty years old, he scrambled up the ladder to the wheelhouse like a teenager. In less than fifteen seconds he was on the bridge. Pablo's hand was on the remote controls to back off the engine and suddenly he felt the large hand of Captain Bill's on top of his. He could now relax. He was under the master's control.

Captain watched closely without making any change as the freighter cut right across the tug's bow with only ten yards of clearance. The flag of the Philippines was flying on its stern. Captain muttered, "You cowboys!" He was tempted to call them on the VHF ship-to-ship radio but decided against it.

After that experience, everyone remained sharper while on the bridge.

◊

Oxygen bottles whizzed across the tugboat's stern deck. As the skies darkened and the winds strengthened, the waves of the South China Sea grew larger and larger.

"Todd, grab a life jacket and come with me," Captain Bill yelled.

Todd Miller, a strong, athletic young man, was on duty in the engine room. As they came out the door to the deck, they were met with a shower of salt spray and a foot of water swirling around their feet.

"Take this line and tie it around your waist," Captain shouted. "It's your lifeline. Go back on the stern deck and tie down the oxygen bottles and gasoline drums that have slipped their lashings."

Todd looked puzzled but followed orders.

The stern deck was rolling, chaotic, and dangerous. Each time the tug rolled to starboard, the water flowed through the scuppers and over the low rails. When the roll changed direction, the water across the deck was well above Todd's knees.

Todd wrestled the rolling tanks and drums from under the water and was finally successful in tying them up in a safer location. He would never forget the experience—he had seen his life flash before his eyes.

◊

Later that night, the crew sleeping in the fo'c'sle woke up with a start. Not only was the tug rolling violently from side to side, it was also rocking from bow to stern at the same time. Torrential rains blew horizontally as the storm reared up with its full might. In addition to the explosive winds and piercing rains, there were mammoth waves, blown high by the storm's wrath. With every revolution the waves crashed against the metal bow with an incredible bang and the whole vessel shuddered.

The smell of vomit became so strong in the fo'c'sle, most of the crew headed up to the mess hall. There it was even worse because a jar of instant coffee had rolled off a counter and smashed all over the floor. The strong coffee odor did not help any who were feeling seasick, and with the severe rocking of the ship, no one was able or willing to clean up the mess. The bathroom seemed to be the safest place in the turbulence, so the men congregated there.

Michael was experiencing its first serious storm, and only a few of the crew were capable of standing their watch. Captain had never seen waves this big in the South China Sea. They were twice the size of those described in the *China Sea Pilot's Handbook.* He later wrote in his logbook:

> The bow plunged down as if to be swallowed by the angry sea. Then the shudder as the steel plates of the tug Michael vibrated from stem to stern. Tons of foamy salt water enveloped the main deck and salt spray obliterated the vision through the wheelhouse windows. It soared completely over the fire fighting turret platform some thirty-five feet above the surface of the sea. It was another mad attempt by the sea to engulf our small vessel.
>
> Then slowly, as one extricated from a watery grave, the ninety-six foot tugboat rose as a proud man-made monument in a wasteland of huge waves with breaking crests and foam strewn slopes . . . It seemed the torrent of mountainous waves was trying to turn us from our goal. I looked aft at the royal blue barge towed a hundred yards astern. Its bow rose skyward until a large portion of her bottom plates was exposed. She teetered for a brief moment on the crest and then plunged violently into the trough. At that moment, I did not know her crew of three had tied themselves to their bunks to avoid being airborne and smashed into the cabin roof . . .
>
> I glanced sideways at the helmsman, his face ashen, the color of the leadened sky above. I wondered how long it would be before he, too, would rush outside and involuntarily lose what he had eaten earlier. His knuckles were white as they gripped the rungs of the mahogany wheel to which he clung for dear life, to avoid being helplessly lifted and slammed into the wheelhouse

walls. Some of the cabin stools were already strewn about. Their flat tops decapitated from their legs as a result of violent collisions with the stout steel bulkheads.

I stood with my legs spread wide apart for balance and labored over the chart table with pressing decisions. Should I reduce speed or change course more to ease the strain on the tug and her tow?

One of my watch team laughed. "Hey, look at the captain!" he shouted to the others over the noise of the sea. My bare feet slid from side to side, first a few inches one way and then a few back on the slippery wheelhouse floor. I hardly noticed, for my mind was filled with the problems facing a captain on a seagoing tugboat towing a two hundred ton barge in stormy seas.[1]

The storm raged for about thirty hours—hours the crew would like to forget. But the time was not without its moments of humor. Some of the crew were seriously seasick. Motion sickness is a product of the inner ear; each person is wired differently as to how he is affected. Chief Engineer Alastair Barr was quite proud that his inner ear was stronger than most. He proved this by going to the galley when relieved from standing several watches in a row. In spite of the horrible coffee odor, he made some good thick Scottish oatmeal for breakfast. Then he climbed up the ladder to talk to Captain Bill through the open door on the port side. Pablo was at the helm and Captain was still sliding back and forth on the wet floor.

"How are things below, Alastair?" he asked.

"Very good, Captain. I stood three watches and now Todd's on duty. He's a little queasy but doin' fine. I've just finished eatin' breakfast," said Alastair proudly.

Captain Bill was surprised. "What did you have to eat?"

At that moment, the tug heaved hard to port, and Alastair also heaved his oatmeal breakfast over the side of the ship.

"I asked you to tell me, not show me," Captain laughed.

Alastair grinned and then a horrified look crossed his face as he felt the front of his mouth. The partial plate of upper front teeth had gone overboard with his breakfast. "I've got a face like a flat tire," he moaned. "I'm away to ma wee bed!" was his parting comment.

When the storm slowly subsided, Keith, Joseph, Jim, and Captain Bill tackled a broken watermelon in the mess hall, seeing who could best project the seeds out the porthole. It tasted great after hours of fasting.

∽∾∿∿∿

In the calm that followed the storm, *Michael* with *Gabriella* in tow, cruised easily up the Lama channel toward Hong Kong Harbor. Pablo checked in on the ship's radio at all the appropriate points as they entered.

At Green Island, two large tugboats arrived to take *Gabriella* to her docking area. It was more complicated undoing the tow cables and passing them over to the large tugs than if *Michael* had just towed her in. Then a pilot boarded the tug. Captain was unaware that a tugboat needed a pilot. He was an elderly Chinese man in a trench coat and light, narrow-brimmed hat.

"Ahhed slow!" came his first command. *Michael* crept across Hong Kong's Western Anchorage and past Stonecutters Island at a snail's pace.

"Stop engine," he ordered when finally approaching the dock at Kowloon's Sham Shi Po port area.

"Ahhed slow! Stop engine! Pot rudda! Slow astern! Stop engine!" The pilot kept giving orders but was obviously confused as he was used to piloting large freighters. Finally he turned to Captain Bill, waved his arms impatiently, and ordered, "You takey to dock!"

Good night! thought Captain. *This guy wastes our time taking all afternoon to get us here and he can't even dock the boat!*

Within minutes, *Michael* was tied up dockside, and half an hour later *Gabriella* was secure behind.

On the dock, in twenty-five shipping containers, one million Chinese Bibles in their one-ton blocks with waterproof packaging were waiting. At long last, everything was coming together and right on schedule.

Just four days left to Pearl.

10

The Needs in China

Chan bounced along on the old, crowded bus. The twelve-hour trip to Anhui was difficult because the driver was forced to swerve repeatedly to miss the local farmers' winnowed rice set out on the road to dry. Also dust swirled up continuously through the holes in the rotting floorboards.

Anhui is just east of Henan Province in central China and is watered by the Yangtze River. Rice, barley, and cotton are important crops for its population—fifty million in 1981. Southern Anhui is mountainous, with thirty peaks nearly a mile high. The capital city, Hefei, is home to the well-known University of Science and Technology.

In 1869 the China Inland Mission (CIM), headed by Hudson Taylor, began Protestant missionary work in the northern part of the province. It was the only missionary agency to work in Anhui for fifteen years. At the turn of the twentieth century, the Boxer Uprising, during which 146 missionaries were killed, sparked great growth in missions work. In 1905, five mission agencies served at twenty-three mission stations, and the number of Protestant Christians was 1,543. By 1920, there were ten agencies with 172 missionaries working at thirty-three mission stations, and the number of believers had more than tripled to 5,000; 67 percent of whom were male.

Sadly, we remember CIM missionaries John and Betty Stam, who were martyred in Anhui on December 8, 1934. In that same decade a mighty revival broke out in Anhui that resulted in a deep-rooted indigenous church, which continues to thrive and mushroom to this day.

When Chan finally arrived, the exhausting ride left him feeling nauseated. He was pleased to see Matthew Lo, who greeted him with a welcoming smile, waiting for him at the bus terminal. Pastor Cho Ling, Matthew and Chan's host for the weekend, was by his side.

Soon they were seated around the pastor's simple kitchen table, with large bowls of rice and steaming cups of tea in front of them. Quickly the three were deep in discussion about Project Pearl deliveries to Anhui Province.

Pastor Cho Ling told of recent trips to visit Christians who met in caves in the southern mountainous areas of his province. "The last cave I visited," he said, "was the actual living quarters for seventy believers. They had only one Bible for all seventy persons, just as they had only one toothbrush that everyone used." The toothbrush comment didn't even raise an eyebrow, but the scarcity of Bibles concerned the men.

"Now that you've told us about the serious Bible shortage, Brother Ling," Chan said as they refilled their teacups, "please tell me the background of your church here."

"Over the past few years, our growing church has suffered the effects of a very repressive environment. But by God's hand of protection, step-by-step, we have managed to grow in the amazing work that He is calling us to undertake.

"Because of the great need for more leaders, we've had one training session after another. One time we had about seventy future leaders in a training session. A member of the TSPM church went off to report this gathering to the PSB. They came to our meeting place, completely surrounding it.

"All the co-workers could do was collect the books, tapes, and teaching materials and pass them over to the police. Following this, security officials came into the meeting place and became violent, beating the believers. Using rope, they tied our fingers together very tightly two-by-two.

"Once outside, we were divided into two groups. One group of forty-two believers was transported to a PSB office, while the other group of twenty-eight was taken to the local police station. The police van made several trips because there were so many people to transfer.

"The brothers and sisters were undeterred. As we sang together to the Lord, a new resilience renewed us through our communal praise. The police were amazed at this and asked us how we could possibly sing such songs when we had just been arrested. We replied by quoting from Romans 8:35–39: *'Who shall separate us from the love of Christ? Shall trouble or hardship or persecution or famine or nakedness or danger or sword? . . . For I am convinced that neither death nor life, . . . nor anything else in all creation, will be able to separate us from the love of God that is in Christ Jesus our Lord.'*

"Then the police captain ordered that we be locked up in an underground prison, the sisters in one area and the brothers in another. They tried to punish us with electric batons. But as they began to strike us, the batons wouldn't work. In their frustration, they used their fists to beat us. The brothers and sisters were brave and we faced this in God's strength. We were willing to be beaten and punished because of the desperate need to spread the gospel. Our suffering was not a great concern in comparison with the cry we have heard for the gospel message.

"They accused us of meeting illegally. We replied that we had done nothing illegal and were simply living the lifestyle of normal believers in a state that proclaims religious freedom. On hearing this, they told us they had every right to punish us, as we had not registered our meeting place.

"The police attempted to negotiate our release with the owners of the home where we were caught. They wanted five hundred yuan each. That's over one year's salary for many farm workers. Our coworkers spoke to the homeowners and urged them not to be coerced into this agreement. The owners decided not to pay off the police, even when these officials continued to reduce their demands to four hundred, three hundred, two hundred, down to ten yuan.

"The police, now with inoperable electric batons, decided to deprive us of our blankets, which we needed at night. We called out to God saying, 'We know You love us and so we'll continue to praise You!' Throughout the night and into the morning we danced, sang, and worshiped. We sang to each other:

We are no longer strangers;

God has already revealed Himself among us. He is here.

We must, therefore, be joyful constantly, exhorting one another.

The Lord is near to us so we must take hold of the vision He has
given us and not stand still.

We have been called to give to others without reserve or worry,
moving from village to village.

Let us stand up together.

No matter how strong the waves or winds are, they will not keep us
from this burden, which drives us on.

Let us take each other's hand and climb this mountain before us.

No matter how high, it will never block the view of our eyes, fixed
on the vision ahead.

We must love one another and soon meet our Lord face-to-face.

"Then the PSB officers decided to starve us. No food was brought to us for two days, until one of them became afraid of the consequences should any of us die of malnutrition. Eventually they told one sister outside to bring us a meal. She brought food and drinks for everyone to enjoy. And again we celebrated together.

"A policemen at the station discovered his sister was one of the believers who had been locked up. On hearing this news, he told her, 'I'm getting you out, and you must go home. What are you doing here, anyway?' His sister explained the circumstances of her arrest and told him she couldn't go home unless everyone was released. Otherwise, she explained, she would stay inside with the others.

"One of the group went to the police station bathroom early in the morning. The police captain was there and asked the man if he was ill. He answered that he indeed had been sick. The police captain asked if he believed in God and whether or not there really was a God. The believer replied that he knew that God is real, and if it were not true, he wouldn't be a Christian.

" 'Where is God?' asked the captain. The brother mentioned the incident when the police officers' electric batons were useless when used

"MICHAEL BEACH" NEAR SHANTOU ON THE COAST OF CHINA

CONSTRUCTING *GABRIELLA* IN THE PHILIPPINES

CREW TRAINING CENTER IN *PARADISE,* PUERTO GALERA, PHILIPPINES

SMALL BOAT TRAINING IN HONG KONG'S SNAKE BAY

PLANNING TEAM SEARCHING FOR A TUGBOAT

TUGBOAT *MICHAEL* FOUND IN SINGAPORE

ONE-TON BLOCKS OF WATERPROOFED BIBLE BOXES

LOADING ONE MILLION BIBLES ONTO *GABRIELLA* IN HONG KONG

"CREW PRACTISING QUICK LAUNCH OF SMALL BOATS

GABRIELLA ON SHORT TOW BEHIND *MICHAEL* IN HONG KONG

CREW DEVOTIONS ON TOP OF BIBLES IN *GABRIELLA*

CREW DEVOTIONS IN TUGBOAT MESS HALL

"CREW PRACTISING HAND DELIVERY OF BIBLE BOXES

INSTALLING THE CRANE

WELL-USED PROJECT PEARL CHINESE BIBLE AFTER TWENTY YEARS

TWENTY HAPPY MEN – MISSION ACCOMPLISHED!

on the believers. He explained this was just one example of God's existence. At the end of the conversation, the brother was set free. In fact the police captain asked him to come back to visit him after he was released.

"There were still many Christian brothers and sisters inside the detention center. The police informed parents and families to come at once to collect their relatives from prison. The only condition was a financial payment, a so-called fine.

"However, the family members claimed this was impossible, as they were all too poor. They told the police they didn't even have ten yuan to spare. And if they did, they'd use it for the work of the gospel.

"Ultimately almost all were finally released. The ones who paid money later regretted that they had not trusted in God's provision and protection. Only two were not released. These two were teachers involved in the training of other Christians. The PSB officials planned to press charges against them and to put them in prison for two to three years.

"A relative of one of these teachers had a good relationship with the head official and went to see him. The PSB chief then changed the charge and decided that the two Christians must pay an 'insurance payment' of two hundred yuan each. If the two teachers continued to teach other believers or preach the gospel, the police would keep the two hundred yuan as a fine. If they discontinued teaching, the money would be returned to them after some time.

" 'But how can we remain silent and not teach or spread the gospel?' the two brothers asked. 'This is our lifestyle—whether at home, on the road, or in jail. We have given our lives to the Lord, for His use and work.'

"They, too, were finally set free and we were all able to meet together to praise, worship, and give glory to God. We believers are now stronger than before. It's as if the more they want to pull down the banner of Christ, the higher it will fly. The more the persecution, the greater the revival."

Chan smiled as he contemplated Cho Ling's conclusions. "In Henan Province," he said slowly, "the believers told me that we

Christians are like bamboo. The more you cut us down, the faster and stronger we grow back again!"

"Amen," replied Cho Ling. "The work here has grown as a result, and we are excited now to see our workers sent out to Xinjiang, Sichuan, Liaoning provinces, and many other places. Most of our missionary work has taken place to the south in Sichuan, where many people have given their lives to Jesus and many have been healed of their illnesses.

"One brother there named Kwan was previously a gang leader of some four hundred hooligans. As soon as he received Jesus, he not only repented but immediately began to spread the word about Jesus. Soon after his conversion, he saw an elderly woman by the side of the road, crying in pain. Brother Kwan asked her what the problem was, and she told him that she had a severe headache.

" 'Let me pray for you and you will be healed,' Kwan said.

" 'No,' she replied, 'I know that after praying you will ask me for money.'

" 'I've changed,' said Kwan. 'I received Jesus. I don't want your money.'

"So the elderly woman knelt by the side of the road while the young man prayed for her healing. Immediately the pain left her and she was healed. Many people had already gathered around them and were amazed. They then raced home and brought their sick to him.

"*Lord, I've only just believed. Should I be doing this?* prayed Kwan silently. But as he prayed for each one of them, God continued to heal them.

"Right at that time, a PSB officer arrived and asked what was going on. Brother Kwan told him that he was a follower of Jesus. So the official took out his handcuffs to arrest him. Kwan prayed silently again, *Lord, You know I'm a new believer. These people will not believe in You if I'm taken away. I ask that You cause this man's handcuffs to jam so that he can't open them.*

"No matter how hard the PSB officer tried, he couldn't open the handcuffs. The people around him asked, 'Why do you want to arrest him, anyway? He's a good man. He prayed for our illnesses and we've all been healed.' The PSB officer finally gave up and sent them on their way, making no arrests."

"You've seen God perform so many miracles," responded Chan. "It shouldn't be difficult for you to believe that He will send you thousands of Bibles."

"Yes," Pastor Cho Ling answered, "and the more Bibles we have, the stronger the missionary vision our co-workers develop. Even now, with very few Bibles among our whole group, they continue to go out as missionaries. As they do, they first say farewell to their parents, brothers, and sisters and then proclaim the words of this song:

Hand in hand, hand in hand, let's follow Jesus together.
Don't be deterred by your surroundings and don't be afraid of the
    road ahead.
Just keep one thing in mind.
Run on ahead and don't look back.
Catch the wind from south to north, ride the waves from west to east,
Open your wings of faith and spread the name of Jesus.
It's time to say farewell to your parents, brothers, and sisters.
I'm willing and ready now to take to this gospel road.
Although it will be tough, I stand up straight and look ahead.
It will be made all the more challenging with the wind, frost, snow,
    and rain.
Because I have already set my sights on the New Jerusalem,
My footsteps grow faster and more determined."

Matthew had been quietly listening to the report without reaction until now. With tears streaming down his cheeks, he turned to Chan. "Can you understand now what drives me and why I am so fulfilled in my ministry?"

⚭

Lili had joined itinerant evangelist Enoch Ma and his wife on a trip to remote Inner Mongolia in the far north of the country. They were staying at the home of Wen Rou, a widow, and her son in Baotou.

The Inner Mongolia Autonomous Region, with its capital in
Hohhot, is the third largest as well as the widest province of China. It
borders Russia and the Republic of Mongolia. Inner Mongolia was
made part of China during the Chinese Revolution of 1911 when
Outer Mongolia declared independence and aligned with Russia. The
majority of the twenty million people in 1981 were of Mongolian eth-
nic background rather than Han Chinese.

In the nineteenth century, European and North American Christian missionaries brought the gospel to Inner Mongolia. A few mission stations were set up with small hospitals and churches. During
the terrors of the Cultural Revolution, Christians suffered great hardships. They were diminished in numbers and almost vanished. But by
1981 the outreach of Chinese evangelists was rewarded with a house
church movement that was growing quickly. Much of the growth was
attributed to Wen Rou, who had been a Christian for only a few years.

"Let's ask Wen Rou to tell us her own faith story," said Enoch
early one morning over breakfast. "She's always so busy serving us and
others, I usually end up sharing her testimony for her."

Wen Rou smiled, handed her stirring spoon to her son, brushed
her hair away from her face, and sat at the table. She poured herself a
hot cup of tea and made sure her guests' cups were topped off.

"After my husband died," she started, "my son and I had a difficult life trying to run the farm. One day I became so sick I was taken
miles away to the doctor. He told me I had an incurable liver disease
and that I should go home to die.

"My son and I used our savings to purchase my burial casket. Like
other families we kept it in the front room for the fateful day. One day
as I lay dying beside my casket, some Christians from the village came
and offered to pray for me. I had very little faith but I accepted their
offer as the last resort.

"After several visits and earnest prayer, I was miraculously healed.
Many villagers were curious to see me when they heard the news.
Sometimes my house was full of visitors, so I used the casket as a pul-
pit and explained that I had been sick and dying, but Jesus Christ,
God's Son, had healed me.

"Dozens of people committed their lives to Christ. So I began a church group right in my home. We now have more than one thousand meeting places in the region, all of which started through God's power."

"Praise the Lord!" Lili interjected in amazement.

Enoch Ma took the opportunity to ask, "Do you have any special needs?"

Wen Rou nodded and took a sip of tea. "We have such a shortage of Bibles and I feel such a lack of understanding of God's Word when I read it. So when I heard about a training center far away in central China, I decided to go there. First, I traveled ten hours in an old bus. Then fifty hours on the train. Nothing could stop me.

"What shocked me most was that the training institute had only one copy of the Bible. To keep it for all the students to use, they fastened a rope around it and tied it to a desk to make sure it didn't disappear. The students were allotted two hours each with the Bible around the clock. Every two months a few women from local house churches spent hours copying pages. During that time, the students got irritated because they couldn't read the Bible. The women copied twenty-four hours a day for a week each time. One of them copied the prophet Isaiah in a week, but mostly they copied the Gospels, Acts, Romans, and Revelation.

"I learned so much there. I was also able to encourage one of the students to come to our area to establish a training center. Now we have more than one thousand young people eager to serve the Lord.

"But we desperately need more Bibles. That's why everyone in leadership here is so excited about your promise to bring us many."

∽∞∾

Mei-ling always preferred to travel alone. While it was a high risk for a beautiful young woman, at the same time it deflected the suspicions of the PSB. Lili sent her to mountainous Zhejiang Province on the east coast of China. In 1981 thirty million people lived in this poor, underdeveloped region.

Zhejiang was not far from her home near Shantou, and it was

strategic because the Bibles bound for Shanghai and farther north would travel through this province. Co-workers would have to be trustworthy—the need for Bibles in Zhejiang alone could swallow up the entire shipment.

The city of Wenzhou was now called the Jerusalem of the East because so many Christians lived there. It was a title that Pyongyang in North Korea had held until 1953, when the peninsula of Korea was divided at the end of the three-year war.

Mei-ling found warm hospitality in the small home of another young believer—Sister Chen. This young woman lived with her widowed father. She talked about the need for Bibles constantly. One night she shared her story.

"I did not own a Bible, even after I began to preach the Word," Sister Chen said. "I copied the New Testament by hand from one my devout grandmother borrowed for me to study. I was born in a Christian family during the pre–Cultural Revolution era, when the severe shortage of Bibles began. My own copied version became the foundation for my personal Bible study and preaching.

"As I became more active in the ministry, the PBS took note of me. One night six officers surrounded my father's house to arrest me. Aware of the possible danger, I was sleeping in the attic of a neighbor's home. My heart filled with terror as I watched the officers close in. Quietly I crept down from the attic and dashed toward the field. I thought I had narrowly escaped, but they heard me and began to come after me. I could see the lights of their motorbikes and cars. With a pounding heart, I ran as fast as I could.

"While rushing through the darkness, a thorny bush cut my arms, legs, and face. I fell into several muddy ponds. I sprained my ankle trying to climb over a fence. Finally, I lay wet, muddy, and bleeding on the ground, unable to go farther. I was ready to renounce my calling and quit the ministry because I didn't know how I could go on.

"My heart almost stopped beating when a tall, dark figure came suddenly toward me. I braced myself for the worst, but to my amazement, the figure identified himself as a local believer. He served the

Lord by offering protection to persecuted pastors. He took me in and tended to my wounds.

"After a simple meal, I lay down exhausted. Then I noticed some writing on the wall, '*Do not be afraid of those who kill the body but cannot kill the soul. Rather be afraid of the One who can destroy both soul and body in hell.*' A pastor who traveled here before must have written it. God touched my heart through this verse and took away all my confusion, fear, and self-pity. I rededicated myself to Him. Now I'm ready to give my life for copies of God's Word."

Mei-ling was so moved, she could not speak. Finally she asked, "Are there others here who have the same commitment?"

"Oh, yes!" Sister Chen exclaimed. "Just recently in a nearby village the police rounded up several Christians, particularly three leaders of the house church who had been very successful in evangelizing.

"Three tables were set up in the middle of a crowd of villagers. A large pile of food and sweets was on two of the tables. On the middle table they placed three bowls of pungent night-soil [sewer] water.

"The police chief was smirking. The three house church pastors had been kept in prison for some time and were now physically weak. 'The choice for you is easy,' the police told them. 'You can renounce your faith simply by having some of the good food and treats we've prepared for you. Or you can ignore the food and return to prison.'

"The crowd pressed in to watch as the police brought out a small pile of Bibles they had confiscated from local believers. 'Regardless of what you choose,' the police chief continued, 'these Bibles will be destroyed. We will burn them all—unless you drink all of the night-soil water.'

"The crowd gasped. Some jeered. The leaders, however, made no sound. There was a brief pause. Then each, in turn, stepped to the table, picked up one of the bowls of night-soil water and drank it down without a word.

"The police stared in amazement. The local believers cried in relief. When the task was done, the three leaders gathered the Bibles into their arms and pressed them into the hands of the Christians.

Angrily, the police watched them, and when they were finished, quickly took them back to jail."

"Did they survive?" asked Mei-ling still in amazement at Sister Chen's story.

"Yes, they were released two years later and are still serving the Lord today."

After her visit, when Mei-ling returned home, she reported to Lili: "The Bible need all over the country is great and everyone is filled with eager anticipation for the arrival of the Pearl Bibles. Many are even willing to sacrifice their lives, if necessary, in distributing them. The networks in Zhejiang and Shanghai are ready and waiting!"

11

The Surprise

Brother Andrew sat straight up in his bed at home in Harderwijk, Holland. It was the middle of the night and he had just experienced a terrifying dream. He describes it in his own words:

> I was riding in a truck, going down a long steep hill in the Alps. As I put my foot on the brake to slow the vehicle, the brakes lost all pressure and the pedal went to the floor. I was careening down the hill, faster and faster, with no way to stop the truck. At the bottom I managed to avoid a huge crash by swerving onto the last gravel escape road, which somehow brought the truck to a stop, leaving me sitting there with my heart pounding.
>
> The dream disturbed me a great deal. What could it mean, if anything? I was too upset to go back to sleep, so I lay there in bed and replayed it in my head over and over, praying that God would reveal its meaning.[2]

Hong Kong
Wednesday, April 15, 1981

At the same time, in Hong Kong, everyone was excitedly getting ready for the big trip. Doug, Keith, Joseph, and Michael Bruce had taken shore leave to stay at a hotel, giving them a landline telephone, so they were able to make personal and business calls. It would appear to outsiders that they were just doing business as usual. Doug was very fond of the Hong Kong Hotel in downtown Kowloon, but because of the secrecy of this mission, he decided to stay at different hotels on each visit. This time he chose the Mandarin Hotel on Victoria Island.

Mother Hickey, along with two crewmates, was also in town buying supplies for the hungry men he had to feed.

On the tug, Jerry, Jim, Cor, and Douglas Junior, using a large crane, were busy loading the one-ton Bible blocks onto the barge. Terry Madison had now joined the crew for the final journey and was taking pictures of the loading activity.

Pablo, Bill Schwartz, and two others were installing new electric winches for stowing and unloading their Boston Whalers on top of *Gabriella's* cabin. Bill was operating the electric welder.

Captain Bill and Alastair worked on the deck generator. The storm had smashed the plywood shelter Alastair and Bill had built in Batangas. Also the salt water had shorted out some of the generator circuits. That meant the ship was again operating only on emergency battery power.

"Wash it out with fresh water and dry it as well as possible. Let's see if we can get it working!" ordered Captain Bill.

Holland

Brother Andrew sat in his office at 6:00 a.m. behind the unique coffee table made from a blacksmith's bellows. Bookshelves with Bibles from all over the world lined the walls around him.

Johan Companjen, Brother Andrew's assistant, had responded to Andrew's middle-of-the-night telephone call and was there bright and early. Andrew told him again about his dream and concluded, "I have a strong feeling the dream is related to Project Pearl. I believe God is sending a warning—perhaps not to call off the project but certainly to wait. Something about the timing is not right. If we proceed, I think some kind of disaster's in store for the crew."

They prayed together and telephoned Dr. Ed Neteland, who was in South Africa. After much discussion they decided there were issues significant enough to call a halt to the project.

Then Brother Andrew called Sealy Yates, chairman of the ODI board. He was not with the crew on *Michael* because he had not been able to make it for the needed crew training. When Brother Andrew explained his concern, Sealy suggested a special meeting of the Open

Doors senior management team and the ODI board with Doug and Dr. Jim in Palm Springs, California.

Next, Andrew telephoned Doug at the Mandarin Hotel in Hong Kong. "Doug," Andrew started after exchanging greetings, "I had a terrifying dream last night. I believe it was the Lord telling us to put a stop on Project Pearl."

"What? You've got to be kidding! We're loading the Bibles right now and we'll be ready to leave Hong Kong tomorrow. We're right on schedule!"

"I'm afraid I'm *not* kidding. I've talked and prayed about it with the team here, as well as with Dr. Ed and Sealy Yates, and we all feel you should halt everything for the time being."

"But what about the ship and crew?" Doug countered. "They're ready to go and not all of them can just wait around indefinitely."

"Captain Bill and the crew should remain in Hong Kong—whatever the cost—and you and Jim Schmook come to Palm Springs Monday," concluded Brother Andrew. "We'll all get together, fast and pray, and discuss this matter there."

Hong Kong
Wednesday, April 15, 1981

At lunch Jim was limping and grimacing with pain as he dragged himself to the mess hall for the noon meal.

"What happened?" asked Captain.

"He was almost smashed," reported Cor.

"The crane operator left one package standing on its end. It fell over and pinned me against another package," said Jim.

"It almost killed him!" shouted Douglas Junior.

"I thought it would flatten him like a pancake, but we were able to lift the package just enough for him to get his leg out from underneath," explained Jerry.

Miraculously, Jim got away with just a very sore leg.

"There's a much bigger problem," Jim interjected. "I think we'll finish the loading late tonight but I don't think there's enough room on the barge for all the blocks. It's like we didn't measure correctly or something. I don't understand it. Please have the crew pray about this tonight during devotion time." With a concerned look, he hobbled outside with Cor, Jerry, and Douglas Junior to finish the loading.

By sunset Alastair had the generator putting out the power needed to run the ship. A fuel barge had stopped by to top off the tanks. Ten crewmen squeezed around the mess hall dinner table to pray with Mama and Papa Kwang's older son, Daniel, about the newest challenge—the barge loading. Daniel came aboard *Michael* specifically for this prayer time. He prayed with a gentle confidence: "Lord, You're able to make the Bibles fit. I'm certain You mean all one million to go to my people."

∞∞∞

"All I can conclude is that it's another miracle," Jim stated the next day at lunchtime. "I kept measuring the barge as we were loading and there was no way all the blocks were going to fit. But we just kept putting them in as tight as we could and by four o'clock in the morning, they were all on board in their place! I still don't understand it."

"When are we planning to leave, Captain?" Pablo asked. "There's a lot more detail work we need to do. I haven't even started radio contact and procedures for the voyage with Dean Keaney back at home base in the Philippines."

"I told Doug we needed forty hours pulling this heavy load to arrive at Michael Beach on time," Captain Bill responded. "So we'll have to leave no later than noon tomorrow—Good Friday."

∞∞∞

Thursday afternoon, the ship-to-shore radio-telephone called out, "Hotel Oscar 5357, Hotel Oscar 5357, come in, please."

Pablo hit the transmit switch and replied, "This is HO5357. Go ahead."

"Pablo, this is Michael. Over."

"Yes, Michael. Go ahead."

"Doug is requesting that you and Jim come to his hotel room as soon as possible this afternoon. He's at the Mandarin Hotel, Room 2155. Do you copy? Over."

"Gotcha. We'll be there as soon as possible. Over and out!"

Jim and Pablo boarded the local water taxi, known in Hong Kong as a *wala-wala* boat. Captain yelled after them, "Please ask Doug to contact me. I need to discuss our departure with him as soon as possible. Meanwhile, I'll have the crew make sure we have all the supplies on board that we'll need for the next week of sailing."

"How's the leg, Jim?" Pablo asked over the roar of the little boat's engine.

"It's still quite sore. Hopefully, it'll improve so I'll be able to stand my watch tomorrow." They commented on the miraculous loading of the Bibles onto the barge as they headed to shore, but then Jim changed the subject.

"I'm concerned we haven't had enough training with the little boats to develop our night vision. Six of us are going to have to operate in total darkness, and I'm not sure we're ready."

"We did about three nights of training in Paradise," Pablo countered. "Captain has assigned Ronald and Todd to operate the smaller Zs with Terry Madison and Douglas Junior assisting them. You and I are assigned to the larger one that will take Doug, Keith, and Joseph to shore first. That night we looked for Captain Bill, when he was out of gas and drifting, certainly was good training, even if we didn't rescue him."

"But you had your running lights on. When we deliver these blocks to shore we can't risk lights."

Pablo shrugged and responded, "I still think we're ready!"

The Mandarin Hotel was an easy walk from the Hong Kong pier. When Pablo and Jim arrived at Doug's hotel room, they found a solemn group waiting for them. Doug's face was ashen, and Joseph, Keith, and Michael looked as though they were in mourning.

Doug wasted no time in explaining the situation. "You guys won't believe this," he began, "but Brother Andrew phoned yesterday and has called off Project Pearl."

For a moment there was silence and then in unison Jim and Pablo asked, "Why?" as they searched for answers in the faces of the four men.

"Oh, he had a bad dream and he thinks it's to do with Pearl. None of us can believe it. I don't know what to do," Doug answered, looking away from Pablo and Jim and letting his gaze rest on the buildings he could see out the window.

"What does he suggest?" Jim asked.

Doug continued, "He thinks Captain and crew should wait here in Hong Kong while you and I, Jim, go to California for a special meeting."

"But we can't just postpone the delivery," Jim replied. "What about the contacts inside? Theirs is a bigger challenge than our having the vessels ready. How long will it take to reset the delivery date?"

"Exactly," Doug agreed.

"That's why I say we should go ahead as originally planned," said Keith. "I say Brother Andrew's mistaken. Doug is the man of faith leading this expedition. We've seen God work so many miracles to bring us to this point. We should *not* stop now!"

Joseph nodded, while Jim and Pablo, with raised eyebrows, still struggled to take everything in.

Obviously Doug was in a terrible dilemma. He liked what Keith was saying, but he also had deep respect for his leader, Brother Andrew. He sat there just shaking his head, unable to make a decision.

"Have you contacted Captain Bill and Mama and Papa Kwang about this?" asked Pablo.

"No," Doug replied softly. "I'm still in shock and disbelief and I don't know what to tell them. I'm still hoping for a last-minute change of heart."

"Tell it like it is," advised Jim. "I don't see that we have much option. If we go ahead with our schedule and disobey Andrew, whether we have a disaster or not, our relationship with Open Doors is finished. We both lose. You'll be starting from scratch again, Doug. But if we obey Andrew, perhaps we can come to a mutual agreement in California about the rescheduling and have a win-win situation."

Doug realized Jim was giving wise counsel, but he just could not bring himself to take the next step and decide whether to stop or keep going.

On Board Ship
Thursday, April 16, 1981

"Hello there, Captain," said the tall Englishman who stepped aboard the tug that afternoon. "I'm the Hong Kong Safety Engineer. Captain Stevens is my name." His proper British accent seemed to make his no-nonsense attitude more apparent. "Do you mind if I inspect your vessels?"

Captain toured him around the tug and barge and explained the construction. Captain Stevens was a stickler for detail. He even disassembled the running lights to see if he approved of the bulbs.

As they walked across the cargo covers, Captain Stevens asked, "By the way what is your cargo?"

Captain Bill whispered a quick prayer and responded loudly, "Literature." Captain Stevens made no more inquiries until he saw the three bunk beds. "You have men living on your barge?" he gasped in disbelief.

"Yes, we have a three-man crew," Captain replied.

"Oh, that will never do. We never allow that here."

"But this barge is registered in the Philippines where it's required that the barge be manned," Captain explained.

"Well, the Philippines, you know . . ." He did not have to finish his sentence. His tone communicated it all. "The truth is you cannot sail from Hong Kong with a man on that barge," he stated emphatically.

As Captain Stevens continued to find many things substandard with the equipment, Captain Bill finally said with a big smile, "Will you give us sailing clearances if I promise to leave and never come back?"

The safety engineer looked down his rather long nose and said, "I hear that from a lot of Filipino boats that come here. Let me do one more check of the barge."

The tide was low at that moment and the barge was well below the level of the wooden pier on which they were standing. Captain Bill climbed down first saying, "Watch your step!"

Captain Stevens reached out to brace himself on the closest tall steel whaler davit. Unfortunately, Bill Schwartz had just finished cutting the winch mount with a torch moments before.

"Oww," he cried as the hot metal seared the flesh of his bare hand. He fell straight down. Bill Schwartz reached out and grabbed him on one side and Captain Bill on the other, preventing him from falling into the water. But that did not stop him from landing astride the steel wire that was the life rail around the stern of the barge. Ouch!

The mishap ended the inspection. Captain Stevens was quite sullen as they broke open the first-aid kit to treat his injured hand. At least he did not find the first-aid kit substandard and he signed the necessary papers for legal departure.

Everything was ready to go and the project was right on time, but Captain heard nothing from Doug or any of the inner circle planning team. The dock supervisors attempted to order the vessels away and were very unhappy when Captain would not leave.

That night Captain Bill had a vivid dream of impending disaster. It revealed that if they should go ahead with the project as scheduled, everyone would end up in the hands of Chinese authorities! Since he had heard nothing from Doug about proceeding, he felt that the dream was God's message to him personally and decided to keep his dream to himself.

⌀〰〰⌀

The next morning, Good Friday, Michael Bruce arrived on the pier. He made no comment whatsoever about departure, decisions, or the project situation. The two tugboats he had ordered arrived to assist in their transfer from the dock to an open anchorage.

Captain spent all day speculating with the crew about what might be wrong. "Your guess is as good as mine!" he said.

⌀〰〰⌀

Saturday evening, just before sunset, a *wala-wala* boat approached the tug in Hong Kong's Western Anchorage. On board the water taxi were Doug, Keith, Joseph, Jim, Pablo, and Michael.

"Call the crew together," Doug told Captain Bill. Doug's face resembled a man who had just come from the funeral of his best friend. Quickly the crew assembled in the mess hall. This gathering soon became known as the Black Saturday meeting.

"I'm afraid I have bad news," Doug began. "The project's been called to a halt. We must make a complete stop."

Seventeen grim-faced men listened as he continued. "We were given this instruction three days ago by Brother Andrew after he had a bad dream, but I've been doing everything possible to try to get a go-ahead, hoping that after three days in the tomb, we, too, would experience the miracle of resurrection. I called Brother Andrew back today, but he has a long list of questions and concerns he wants me to answer.

"I've prayed for hours with Mama and Papa Kwang at their home. They've told me to obey my superiors and do whatever they tell me to do.

"Now it's too late to make the delivery on schedule. We're expected to be at Michael Beach in three hours' time. There'll be a lot more disappointed people there when they realize we're not going to show up. Let's pray for them right now."

Doug poured his heart out to the Lord and to the men. They respected him because, up to this point, he had been one of them in all the ordeals at sea.

"So, tomorrow morning," Doug continued, "Jim, Keith, and I are going to celebrate Easter Sunday with you in a sunrise service here on the boat. Then we'll head to Kai Tak Airport for our flight to Palm Springs, California, for the special meeting. I'm going there to be reconciled with the mission leaders. I'll keep you informed about our progress. I'm expecting most of you will be given two weeks home leave to spend some well-earned time with your families. I appreciate the sacrifices you all have made.

"I have faith this project will still be completed," Doug concluded. "So the need for secrecy and the element of surprise has not changed! I'm holding you all accountable."

As the sun peeped over Victoria Island the next morning, eighteen men sat on top of *Gabriella's* cargo. Terry Madison took one of his well-framed photos for posterity. It was Easter Sunday, a day of great celebration for most Christians. But this group looked as though they thought it was still Good Friday. Their faces showed little hope.

Their mood paralleled the first half of the Easter hymn, "Low in the grave He lay, Jesus my Savior," which begins mournfully. They sang it, but without much feeling, even when it came to the upbeat chorus.

But it *was* Easter Sunday. Chaplain Keith brought the devotional from Romans 6:1-10 before serving communion. Though a somewhat sad day, everyone considered the event another highlight. Imagine the memory of an Easter communion service sitting on top of one million Chinese Bibles in Hong Kong's Western Anchorage!

"What makes me the saddest," concluded Doug, "is that I know our co-workers inside China are suffering over this delay far more than we are!"

China

Lili, Mei-ling, and Chan spent the afternoon of Easter Sunday at Lao Zhao's house in Yuxin. Lili's cheeks were streaked with tears as she shared the events of the night before. "So many came to the beach with eager anticipation," she wept. "I tried to explain that the project was put on hold, but it was hard for them to understand and their mood turned sour. We lost so much face with these friends; I don't think I can ever stand before them again! I was thankful when Pastor Samuel Wu took responsibility and calmed down the crowd before they dispersed."

Mei-ling was also upset and crying. She laid her head on Chan's shoulder without even thinking. His pulse rate quickened and he could not speak. "What makes me sad," she said, "is thinking about Sister Chen. She's willing to give her life for Bibles for her brothers and sisters. How disappointed she will be!"

They sat in silence for some time. Only the sniffles of the weeping women broke the quiet. No one drank the tea. Finally Lao Zhao spoke. "I have served the Lord for many years, and He has never let me down. Yes, there are times I questioned Him and wondered about His timing, but now I can honestly say that God does all things well.

"I don't have an answer as to why nothing happened last night, but I believe the promises of God, that He has a bright future for us in China and He will not leave us alone. He said to Jeremiah that His plans are to prosper us and not to harm us, plans to give us hope and a future.

"Trust Him, young people. Don't be disappointed in the problems of today. God holds your tomorrows in His hand!"

12

The Wait

We must wait . . . wait . . . wait on the Lord.
We must wait . . . wait . . . wait on the Lord.
And learn our lessons well . . .
In His timing He will tell us . . .
What to do . . . where to go . . . what to say![3]

The song from Maranatha Music's *Praise III* cassette blared out of the boom box as the crew members enjoyed a relaxing afternoon in the sun on tugboat *Michael*. Western Anchorage had its moments of beauty and this afternoon was one of them, with the Hong Kong city skyline as a backdrop. The water was a little too polluted in the harbor for good swimming. Five of the crew dived in anyway and made sure they had long, hot, soapy showers after their swim.

Barge *Gabriella* floated beside the tug. The weather was almost perfect. The crew lounging on the foredeck talked over their options for home leave.

"I'm going to tell my wife to visit her parents in northwestern USA," said Cor. "That'll make it easy for her and a shorter flight for me."

"I'm going to suggest that Nancy fly out here to see me instead of my flying home to Phoenix," said Jerry Simmons. "That way y'all will at least have a great cook to feed you when Mother Hickey is away!"

"Aw, c'mon. You guys don't look like you're starving to death," Terry responded. "Anyway, if you give me a hard time, I'll burn your steak tonight!"

"Steak," said Pablo rubbing his stomach. "Did I hear the word *steak*?"

"Yah, they're marinating right now. Captain thought we needed something tasty to lift our spirits."

"Well, I, for one, am lookin' forward to it," spoke up Alastair, "even if I don't have all my teeth to chew it."

"That's right, Alastair," bantered Pablo. "You're not going to get home leave until we find some dental replacements for you here in Hong Kong. I guess I can put you last on the list, eh?"

"Och, and to think I'm the only one goin' home to a girlfriend and not a wife," lamented Alastair with a sly grin.

"But we'll still expect a full and detailed report when you get back, Alastair," called out Todd. You could hear the smile in his tone. Everyone laughed and nodded.

"You're a cheeky lad," Alastair concluded, getting in the last lick.

The crew had bonded and now as brothers they were accepting the disappointment of the delay—even with a touch of humor.

＊＊＊

Easter Sunday night, the wind began to roar and tugboat *Michael* was again dragging anchor. A powerful squall took them by surprise. It succeeded in ripping the cargo covers down the middle for at least sixty feet and drenched everyone with rain.

Captain rounded up a quorum of crew to work with him in untying *Gabriella* from tug-side to try to alleviate the anchor dragging. As he stood on the barge's cargo in the rain giving instructions, a twenty-foot section of two-inch steel pipe was thrown into the air by the billowing cargo cover. The heavy pipe landed right on top of Captain's head, knocking him flat on his face. He grabbed his head expecting to find a gaping wound. Instead there was neither a wound nor pain. To this day, Captain Bill calls it his personal miracle.

The following day strong winds continued blowing at more than thirty knots, with waves to match. Western Anchorage was designed for large freighters with heavier anchors, not small tugboats. Captain had to run the main engines to keep the vessels from dragging anchor again.

In the midst of this, Cor came running to the bridge. "Captain, there's almost two feet of oil in *Gabriella's* bilge," he reported angrily.

"Where did it come from?"

"From the main fuel tanks that you insisted we needed to fill the other day. It's the first time we've had any fuel in the tanks and now this! When the water tanks leaked in Batangas, I said to you, 'What makes you think the oil tanks won't leak?'"

"Well, we can't pump out the fuel into the sea," replied Captain Bill. "So you'd better bail it up into drums."

Cor stomped back to the barge with Jerry and Godfrey following behind. They were slipping and sliding and repeatedly falling onto the oily floor. Oil slicks are just like ice. Cor was so angry when they finished, he slammed the shower room door, "I don't take it anymore! I don't work Sundays from now on! But I'm no Jonah."

⌒◌◌◌◌◌

"This is going to be a challenging time for us all," Captain said to Pablo as they met together on the tug's foredeck. "The day after my dream of disaster, I didn't want to go anywhere. It was all going down! But this morning when I woke up to sunshine and a quiet, peaceful harbor, my first reaction was why don't we just go ahead and make the delivery and be done with it!"

"There's the small matter of having someone there to meet us at the other end," Pablo responded with a grin.

"Yah, I know!" Captain Bill was an emotionally expressive man and usually thought on his feet. "Anyway, let's discuss the crew leaves. I told Doug before he left that I needed at least seven men at any one time to look after these vessels. So who do you recommend to stay with me?"

"Aren't you going to take a break?" asked Pablo. "You've been under tremendous stress since this whole project began!"

"What I want most is Mom to join me here. That'll be the only good thing that's happened to me since we arrived in Hong Kong. And she can cook!"

"Okay, I'll arrange it. Then do you mind if I go home to Manila for three days? I haven't seen my wife and kids for months. We were supposed to be going on summer home leave to Canada in two weeks. Now we'll have to adjust our plans."

"Just remember," said Captain, "Doug is so over the top on secrecy, he doesn't want you going near Union Church or any of your other non–Open Doors friends 'til this is over. He's afraid your new beard and darker tan will raise more questions than you can answer."

Pablo smiled and scratched his growing dark beard in disgust. "Seems to me, it creates more questions and security issues by staying away from those people for so long. They all know I travel a lot, but this long an absence is crazy! I haven't been to an elders' meeting at Union Church for more than three months. Anyway, I'll stay at home for a few days and be right back. I won't talk to anyone outside the family. Even my kids know nothing about this project."

Captain Bill nodded. "Well, Jerry, Ronald, and Douglas Junior have agreed to stay here permanently. Let's have Nancy come to Hong Kong. She'll be good company for Lil too. And Alastair, John, Todd, and Bill Schwartz have already agreed to stay for the first shift. Joseph's getting married in Manila in two weeks, so we'd better excuse him until we sail—whenever that'll be.

"So Terry Hickey, Cor, Michael, Godfrey, and Terry Madison should probably also get the first break. We'll decide the timing for the other four when you get back. Meanwhile, we'll have Alastair's missing teeth replaced at a local dentist, so he can go home to see his girlfriend without embarrassment."

Palm Springs, California
Wednesday, April 22, 1981

The ODI board members and the ODI senior management team settled down around the hotel's long conference room table. Sealy Yates chaired the meeting, since Dr. Ed was not able to make it back from South Africa in time. He felt, however, that the project was right on track and he was not about to back down.

Sealy opened in prayer and asked Brother Andrew to explain the reasons he had decided to request a stop to Project Pearl. Andrew elaborated on the dream and explained that he was very concerned for the safety of the crew. He proceeded to itemize his other specific concerns.

Dr. Jim and Keith had joined Doug for this trip and they all took turns carefully answering Brother Andrew's challenges. They presented the fact that the crew had signed documents, demonstrating that they understood the risks and were willing to go ahead voluntarily. They laid out the series of miracles to this point, which had convinced all on board tugboat *Michael* that God was in this.

Then Dr. Jim explained the full plan with details about the systems, the delivery, the training that had occurred, and the intelligence gathered inside China. He wanted to demonstrate that this was not an off-the-wall idea thrown together by loose cannons. It helped alleviate concerns among some of the board who apparently did not know about the level of planning that had occurred. He was also trying to calm everyone down so that things were not done or said that would torpedo the entire project just because emotions were running high.

Only the dream remained unexplained, unless it meant that there would have been danger on the beach for the crew on the original date. Captain had not yet shared with Doug or Jim the dream he had.

Some of the board were still worried about financial issues. One board member questioned the expense of Doug's repeated use of a helicopter to visit Captain Bill in Paradise earlier in the project. Another challenged the need to include office expansion in New Manila in the project budget.

Patiently Doug explained the time constraints in visiting Puerto Galera and the extra staff needed at the office to help with the expanded ministry caused by Project Pearl.

After hours of discussion, explanations, and prayer, there was finally unity and an agreement to reschedule the project, but still there remained the challenge of fully financing it. And Brother Andrew was concerned that there was not enough prayer backing for the project. Dr. Dale Kietzman volunteered to organize prayer coverage worldwide.

Hong Kong Harbor

Pablo enjoyed the wind racing through his beard and thinning hair. This was the most fun he'd had in years—dodging Star Ferries crossing Victoria Harbor in a Boston Whaler going fifty miles an hour.

The distinctive green and white Star Ferries are double-decker, passenger-only boats. They have been crossing Hong Kong Harbor for more than a century and their five-minute journey is still the most economical way of getting across the water. The fleet is comprised of twelve diesel-electric vessels with air-conditioned upper-deck cabins.

Pablo thought of the dozens of times he had made passage on a Star Ferry, enjoying the scenery of the amazing city skyline with so many boats, barges, and Chinese junks using the channel. Many locals—as well as tourists—consider the crossing a rare moment of quiet and calm amid the constant hubbub and ceaseless energy of Hong Kong. Little did he dream he would be piloting one of those other boats plying the most photographed harbor in the world.

Captain had sent him and Terry Madison on a mission to the marina of the Royal Hong Kong Yacht Club at Causeway Bay to find diving wet suits and to refill the oxygen tanks. Within an hour they were en route back to Western Anchorage. Approaching the anchored tug, they saw Lil waving from the stern deck.

"I just sent Douglas Junior and John to the city for some supplies," she yelled over the idling engine noise. "I forgot to put condiments on the list. We're out of soy sauce, ketchup, and olive oil. Would you try to find them before they catch a *wala-wala* back? In fact maybe you could give them a ride."

"Sure," said Pablo as he pulled back on the remote accelerator arm and roared off toward the Victoria Island piers. Days like this were just plain fun.

It was not easy working around the numerous *wala-wala* boats jostling in and out at the pier. But he finally spotted the men arriving with two huge dolly loads of boxes. John ran back to get the additional condiments for Lil while Douglas Junior helped load the boxes onto the whaler.

"Eighteen guys sure need a lot of food!" Junior panted as he heaved the heavy boxes onto the whaler's deck. "And lots to drink too!" he added laughing.

"You won't believe this, but on our way back from the grocery store, we ran into some teachers who know me from my school, Faith Academy, in Manila. They must be here in Hong Kong on vacation. I was pushin' the dolly loaded with boxes. They saw me and asked, 'What are *you* doing here, Dougie?'"

"What did you say?" Pablo asked with a worried frown.

"I just kept walkin' and said, 'I'm workin' for someone here.'"

As they waited for John, Junior added, "If we have to wait much longer before we make the delivery, I'll be celebrating my birthday here in Hong Kong."

"How old will you be?"

"Eighteen!" Douglas Junior said proudly. He was such a large young man that he looked more like twenty-one.

"What would you like for your birthday?"

"I want a small portable TV."

Since they were in Hong Kong, Pablo made a mental note.

☙❧

"Hello, Captain! How ya doin'?" Doug said softly as the two embraced on the tug's bridge.

"I'm okay, I guess." Captain Bill replied. "It's not been easy. You'll probably hear the crew has a new name for the tug. They call it Prison Ship *Michael*. I guess they figure I'm a little hard on them and a bit of a slave driver. Actually, I consider it a blessing to have this valuable time to upgrade and repair our gear. Next step is completing our oceanography cover. And I still haven't installed the autopilot!"

Captain had kept the crew on a rigid work schedule, beginning at eight o'clock every morning. Most of the guys were desk workers or executives who would obey an order if they agreed with it. If not, they would normally want to discuss it. They were not used to repairing and installing equipment without being involved in the decision making. This caused some grumbling from a number of the crew. Nevertheless they worked hard. Some helped put in a new radar system for the tug while others repaired both of *Michael's* generators. Electric winches were installed for launching the three Z-boats more quickly. Many cosmetic changes and improvements were also added. This necessitated many trips into Hong Kong for tools and supplies.

Doug smiled and said, "I know it's been rough. We've prayed for you every day. You know we were here with you in spirit."

"I'm sure it wasn't easy for you either," Captain replied.

Doug just smiled and shrugged. "Dr. Ed wasn't able to make the meeting as he was in South Africa. After answering a long list of concerns, we finally got a go-ahead with the project whenever things are reset on the inside. Dr. Dale Kietzman is organizing major prayer coverage worldwide for us. Let's talk to the whole crew about it."

The crew quickly assembled in the mess hall.

"I'm going to tell you our actual situation," Doug began. "After continued prayer and many hours of going over every facet of the operation, the ODI board and senior management felt the project could move ahead. But we're going to have a struggle now to prepare for the delivery.

"A huge number of Chinese believers gathered on the beach the night we didn't arrive. You can understand their disappointment when we failed to show. Worse, the young leaders who arranged it all lost face. Now we'll have to wait until they can work out that problem. It may be awhile yet before we can sail.

"But I want to encourage you all with a message from the Lord we received in prayer a few days ago. Pastor Mike MacIntosh from San Diego, and some of his friends, joined us in an extended evening prayer meeting.

In the course of this prayer time, the Lord gave a message through one of our brothers. It was startling. The message was in three parts.

"First, the Lord said, 'Project Pearl is as good as done in My eyes.'

"Second, 'Keep pressing on until it is actually finished.'

"Third, 'When Project Pearl is completed, do not make a golden calf of it.'

"That last instruction was what startled me. We planned that Terry Madison would shoot photos on the delivery night with special—and expensive—infrared film. Now I think we shouldn't do that lest we—or others—are tempted to use them to make a 'sacred cow' of the project."

Everyone nodded, understanding Doug's concern.

"I've been encouraged to hear from Pablo that you all are continuing evening devotions together on the stern deck. Thanks, Todd, for taking the leadership of this.

"Over the next few weeks, I'll send some special people to minister to you. Ernie Coombs from Maranatha Music is in Hong Kong after a courier trip into China. He'll be here on board tonight to lead you in worship and to give a message from the Word. Mama Kwang and her son, Daniel, have also promised to come to share and pray with you.

"Keep up your spirits. God is not finished with us yet!"

ⲟⲙⲱⲟ

"CQ DU1ODP . . . DU1ODP . . . this is TI5TM. Come in DU1ODP . . ."

A voice crackled over the amateur (ham) radio. "This is DU1ODP . . . Hello, tug *Michael*! Is this Pablo?"

"Sure is, Deaner! I'm on night watch duty on the bridge. How was home leave? Over."

"I didn't get any yet. Waiting for you guys to get the job done! Over."

Dean Keaney was development manager for Open Doors Asia and radio officer for project communications at home base in Manila. He and Pablo had worked out a system of coded expressions.

Dean was from the Denver area in the United States and started the Australia base for Open Doors in 1977. He served for four years as the first director there before he and Becky moved to Manila with their growing family. Pablo always enjoyed talking to Dean. He was more than just friendly. *Genuine* would be an appropriate word to describe him.

Captain Bill had arbitrarily chosen the maritime mobile station call signal TI5TM for the ICOM amateur radio on the tug. TI was the call prefix for stations in Costa Rica and TM stood for tugboat *Michael.*

"Looks like you'll be waiting for awhile, Dean. No word of any action yet. Over."

"Bet you'd love to talk to your wife, Pablo. Over."

"Sure would! Over."

"Tomorrow night! Same time, same station. Over and out!"

ᘒᙏᙡ

After a hard day's work on Prison Ship *Michael,* the crew always enjoyed their evening meal together. Over dinner they discussed the day's work and played practical jokes on each other, especially on Mother Hickey.

Most important at dinnertime was any news from home. Thomas, a local Chinese friend who functioned as the ship's agent in Hong Kong, delivered the mail each week. He also paid anchorage fees and provided Pablo with the cash flow needed to operate.

Bachelor Alastair was deeply in love and wrote long letters to his girlfriend. Not having Joseph to tease anymore, the crew picked on Alastair.

"What's the appropriate expression to say at your Scottish wedding, Alastair?" Pablo queried.

"Och, you're all definitely invited to my weddin', whenever it happens," replied Alastair. "And you say, '*Lang may your lum reak.*' It means long may your chimney smoke."

"I could remember it easier if it went, 'Long may your rum leak!' " laughed Terry Hickey.

The men also shared their deepest desires and dreams with each other. Cor had always dreamed of driving an eighteen-wheeler filled with Bibles from his home base in Holland into Romania. Nightly he would outline for the crew just how practical his plan was and how he would achieve it. The crew was convinced that someday Cor would accomplish his dream. They prayed regularly for Cor and his vision.

One night they had a frank discussion about the delay in the project.

"Everything was right on schedule, so why stop it?" Pablo started.

"I think the delay happened because we are not spiritually ready," declared Bill Schwartz. "I think the Lord has more work to do among us, making us more unified in direction and intention."

"I agree," said Cor. "There were so many things that weren't right and needed sorting out. It would have been stupid to go on because we would have dug our own graves."

Ronald added, "Captain says his dream of disaster was all he needed to accept the delay."

☙∞❧

Every evening after dinner, Todd, the acting chaplain, would appoint someone to lead in devotions. Usually they were held outside on the cool stern deck where there was plenty of room for everyone to join in the circle of praise. Most often Bill Schwartz played the guitar and led in praise worship.

One night Bill taught the men some praise choruses set to Israeli music with a lively beat. They got so into the music that they jumped to their feet, and with arms wrapped around the person on either side, began dancing in circles around the deck in time to the music. This lasted half an hour until they had worn themselves out and collapsed on the deck, still singing and smiling.

Then Todd led in a short devotional. He said, "Brothers, I was reading today in my personal time with the Lord from *Our Daily Bread*. The recommended passage was Psalm 107:23–32. Let's read it together.

> *Others went out on the sea in ships;*
> *they were merchants on the mighty waters.*
> *They saw the works of the LORD,*
> *his wonderful deeds in the deep.*

For he spoke and stirred up a tempest
  that lifted high the waves.
They mounted up to the heavens and went down to the depths;
  in their peril their courage melted away.
They reeled and staggered like drunken men;
  they were at their wits' end.
Then they cried out to the LORD in their trouble,
  and he brought them out of their distress.
He stilled the storm to a whisper;
  the waves of the sea were hushed.
They were glad when it grew calm,
  and he guided them to their desired haven.
Let them give thanks to the LORD for his unfailing love
  and his wonderful deeds for men.
Let them exalt him in the assembly of the people
  and praise him in the council of the elders.

"You probably think I'm going to focus on the storm and the quieting of it," Todd continued. "We've certainly lived through that experience together. But I'm focusing tonight on the second half of verse 30: *He guided them to their desired haven.*

"Psalm 107 does tell of those *'who go out on the sea in ships.'* Along their journey at sea, they see God as the One behind the tempestuous storm and the One who calms it.

"In Old Testament times, those who sailed vessels had two great fears. One was of a terrible gale, and the other was of having no wind at all. In doldrums latitudes, the wind dies down and a sailing ship remains stationary. Captain and crew are stuck, with no relief in sight. Eventually, with no wind, their water supply runs out.

"Sometimes, life demands that we weather a storm. At other times, it puts us to the test of tedium. We may feel stuck. What we want most is just out of reach. But whether we find ourselves in a crisis of circumstance or in a place where the spiritual wind has been taken out of our sails, we need to trust God for guidance. The Lord, who is sovereign over changing circumstances, has promised to guide us eventually to our desired haven.

"Interestingly, in the devotional the saying for the day is 'God orders our stops as well as our steps.' Here we are sitting in Hong Kong Harbor wishing we were on the high seas en route to our ultimate destination. Let's thank God together for ordering our stops as well as our steps."

The circle of prayer lasted for an hour with prayers of confession, prayers of forgiveness, and many prayers of thankfulness.

13

Snake Bay

Doug, Captain Bill, Dr. Jim, and Pablo were meeting together on the overhead deck of the bridge. It was May 18, more than a month after the original delivery date. Keith was with Mama and Papa Kwang, who were leaving for China the next day. And Joseph had not yet returned from his honeymoon.

"I can't give you a delivery date yet," Doug said to the others. "Mama and Papa Kwang say it's very difficult inside right now. Things are not ready. They're taking a big risk and going inside themselves to check out the situation."

"How long before we have a cutoff date?" asked Captain.

"I really don't know, Captain," Doug responded. "I only know that I still believe we're to proceed with the mission."

"You promised me during our first planning meetings that we'd be back in the Philippines by the first of June," Captain Bill said. "The typhoon season is almost upon us. By June we can certainly expect the first ones, if not before! I'm the captain and the one responsible for the safety of the men on this vessel. I find it very difficult to knowingly put us in a position of grave danger."

"I know all that," Doug replied. "I believe that we'll make the delivery soon."

"Then my next concern is that we've had no opportunity to continue proper training. What little the men had learned has been lost with the passage of so much time."

"What do you suggest?" Doug asked.

"I suggest we ask permission to move to a more remote place here in the islands of Hong Kong where we can train and practice."

"Yes," Jim agreed, "then we could work on our night vision."

"Okay, you prepare the necessary requests, and we'll ask Thomas to approach the port authorities," Doug concluded.

Before the meeting ended, Pablo reported, "Well there's *some* good news. The crew members have all had their home leave and we're now a full complement of twenty men. Herman Boonstra has joined us from the Open Doors South Africa base, as well as a wonderful brother from Ghana named Faithful. He's a real sailor who previously worked on YWAM's new ship, the *Anastasis*."

"That's good," concluded Doug. "Okay. We'll have a full inner circle team meeting here again in eleven days, unless we hear positive news from inside before then."

Captain just glared, obviously an unhappy man.

෨෴෧

That night Captain Bill wrote in his personal logbook:

The horns of a dilemma! I promised Doug and Keith early in the project that I would complete the task no matter what the circumstances. Now it seems we've gone completely beyond reason.

Captain was tired, despondent, and ready to quit. So he prayed, and as he had done in the beginning, he opened his Bible at random. His eyes fell on 1 Chronicles 28:20 where King David was speaking to his son Solomon:

> *Be strong and courageous, and do the work. Do not be afraid or discouraged, for the LORD God, my God, is with you. He will not fail you or forsake you until all the work for the service of the temple of the LORD is finished.*

Captain Bill reasoned that the Scriptures are for the building up of the Chinese believers. The believer is the temple of the Holy Spirit. The meaning became obvious. God had spoken. He took up his pen again and wrote a note of apology to Doug.

Hong Kong
Friday, May 22, 1981

"You've got approval to move to Tai She Wan, 'Snake Bay,' in the New Territories," Michael announced to Captain with a broad smile.

"Raise the anchors and stand clear of the towline," Captain bellowed in his powered megaphone. He moved the tug slowly ahead.

Bill Schwartz came running to the bridge. "*Gabriella's* towline broke!" he announced in a panic. As they looked out the wheelhouse door, the barge was swinging on a starboard course opposite to the tug's direction. One side of the bridle had let go.

Captain Bill shut down the tug and ordered the towline hauled in. It was one hundred feet of one-inch steel line and three hundred feet of three-inch nylon line. It took many willing hands to retrieve it.

Jerry and Bill replaced the broken shackle on the barge and soon they were on their way. With the tug and barge on the move, nothing could discourage them. It was a beautiful day's tow along the Hong Kong Harbor channel and through the islands.

After the long stay in the city's harbor, Snake Bay was like a vacation resort. It was isolated and quiet. The water was clear and good for swimming and diving.

First Mate Jim announced that there would be time for personal enjoyment, but starting tonight, everyone assigned to the small boats would work on developing good night vision. After dark, the three Z-boats and the two whalers loaded their plankton nets and other oceanography paraphernalia on board, in case they were questioned about their activity. They spent hours cruising slowly in the dark without their running lights on, letting their eyes adjust to the darkness.

Suddenly a large Hong Kong Police patrol boat began heading toward them. Jim made a dash in his Z-boat to shore and buried under the sand the infrared goggles he was trying out. But the patrol boat went right on by and didn't even seem to look their way.

༄

The next day was Saturday, so Captain ordered everyone to enjoy a day of recreation. Both whalers were launched and the water skis and slalom board were dug out of the "oceanography" wares. All day the crew enjoyed water skiing, swimming, scuba diving, and sunning. And of course Terry Madison seemed to be everywhere capturing the highlights on film.

Captain Bill spent the day diving, and found he could make it a useful exercise by also cleaning the tug's propeller while underwater.

In the late afternoon as the activities were ending, both Boston Whalers were being returned to their perch on the top of *Gabriella*. One boat was safely stowed and the group was working on the second. Cor was operating the electric winch, thankful he no longer needed to turn it by hand. The winch lifted the boat out of the water by its two sturdy straps held under the davit. At the same time, other crew members were to turn the whaler into position between the four posts that secured it. The turn was not done fast enough. Pablo tried to compensate by lifting the bow over one of the posts. The heavy whaler slipped from its strapping and fell twenty feet with a sickening thud. It was impaled on one of the steel stanchions that supported the lifeline on the stern of the barge. There it hung precariously.

"How can we get it down?" Pablo asked Captain.

"We'll have to push it over," he replied sadly.

Jerry and Bill worked quickly from *Michael's* lifeboat, dismantling the heavy, powerful outboard engine so it would not be affected. Then the whaler was pushed off the stanchion, ripping an even larger hole in the fiberglass bottom.

The following day, Sunday, Jerry and Captain Bill, the only ones with experience in fiberglass, worked at patching the boat. In short order, the whaler was seaworthy again. But Captain wondered when or if the accidents and breakdowns would ever cease.

That night the small-boat team was out again developing their night vision. They cruised slowly around Snake Bay, approaching the shoreline in different locations as they would on the night of delivery.

From out of nowhere, a bright spotlight shone down on them, and the men recognized the Hong Kong Police patrol boat through the night haze.

Pablo pulled up his whaler alongside the patrol boat.

"What are you guys doing out here in the dark with these fast boats?" queried the police officer.

"We're doing our plankton counts," Pablo replied, showing them the nets in his whaler.

"But why do you have to do it without your running lights?" he asked.

"Because they affect the plankton count! Anyway, we're now done for the evening and you can escort us back to our ship," Pablo concluded.

"We don't want to see you out here like this again," the officer continued. "We have a huge problem in this area with fast boats making money bringing in illegal aliens from China. They also operate with no running lights and drop off close to shore. So if you know what's good for you, knock it off!"

"Yes, sir," was all Pablo could say.

⟗⟑⟗

Friday, May 29, was the first meeting of the six members of the inner circle planning group since they had left the Philippines. Joseph had now returned from his honeymoon and took lots of teasing from the other crew members.

The six men sat on the foredeck of *Michael* looking out over Snake Bay. It was a beautiful day, but the atmosphere in the meeting was heavy.

"We still don't have a go for the delivery, although the Kwangs are in China right now working out the details," Doug reported.

"I have a firm commitment in the United States next month," Dr. Jim announced. "The latest I can stay is June 3. Five of the other crew members also have deadlines that are fast approaching."

"Doug," Captain Bill broke in, "we have to face the facts. The first of June is only a few days ahead. Can we risk the lives of the men pushing into typhoon season like this?"

"Why are you guys giving Doug such a hard time?" Keith asked angrily. "The Lord has given His promise for this project, so why put up all the practical objections? You're just exhibiting a lack of faith."

"Keith," Captain replied softly. "I have lots of faith. The Lord has spoken to me clearly about sticking with the project, but I don't believe in needlessly jeopardizing the crew, cargo, and vessel."

"Okay, guys," Doug concluded. "Let's agree that we must hear a go-ahead from inside by the thirty-first of May—that's two days from now—and make the delivery by June 3 or it's a no go!"

All six nodded their approval.

⟨∞⟩

"Those are pretty fast boats you have there," said the sergeant of the Hong Kong Harbor Police as he climbed aboard the tug early the next morning.

"They sure are," Captain replied cheerfully.

"Why do you need such powerful outboard engines?" he asked warily.

Captain Bill understood his point after the events of a few evenings before and replied, "We do a lot of towing. That's the reason for the high horsepower."

"We don't have anything like those," the sergeant said as he continued to eye the sleek twenty-two-foot boats. The Boston Whaler Outrage is famous among rescue and military teams around the world.

"How would you like to take a ride in one?" Captain asked suddenly.

"I wouldn't want to put you to any bother," he replied, turning to see if Captain was serious.

"No bother. Some of the crew need to go to shore for some supplies anyway."

"I'll take you up on that then. My boat can follow along behind," he replied.

Captain Bill introduced Pablo and Terry Madison to the sergeant. Terry jumped in the back of the police boat. The sergeant climbed aboard whaler number one with Pablo and off they sped. Crossing the rough water of Snake Bay was the whaler's strength. Pablo gave the engine full throttle and left the police boat far behind. After five minutes they rounded a peninsula where the protected cove water suddenly became very calm. Before they reached the pier, the police boat had passed them on the smoother water.

On the way back, after picking up supplies, Pablo and Terry pondered the real meaning of the race.

That night Doug called a meeting of the crew on the bridge.

"On my desk at the office I have a sign that says, 'The good is the enemy of the best,' " he started. "I'm going to have a new sign made: 'The practical is the enemy of faith.' Tomorrow is the last day of May, and we still haven't heard a go-ahead from inside. But I have faith to believe we will and I don't want any practical issues to get in the way of that faith. Believe God with me that our faith will be honored. Don't listen to the practical objections. We will complete this project when God gives the go-ahead, and nothing practical will stand in the way."

Keith stood beside Doug with a big smile.

The other four of the inner circle leadership team just looked at each other with amazement. That was not what they had agreed as a team just the day before.

What happened to the original plan that nothing would be done without complete unity and agreement? wondered Pablo.

⚭

"Here, Captain. Sign this please," demanded the Harbor Department officer the following morning as he displayed the order for returning to Western Anchorage.

"What have we done?" protested Captain Bill.

"I have no idea," lied the officer. "You will have to take it up with the main office."

Captain was sure they were upset with the small-boat night activities. The boat race the day before was probably the final straw.

"Raise the anchor and let's head out," Captain Bill shouted an hour later through his powered megaphone. He gunned the engine because he was afraid of hitting the propeller on the shoreline rocks.

Pablo was stern deck officer at the time. Standing on the port side, he noticed something unusual. The one-inch steel tow cable was caught under a stern deck hatch handle. As the tug moved forward, the cable became taut and slipped out under the handle snapping wildly to the starboard side across the two cable guards that curved over the stern deck. The next thing Pablo saw was two legs straight up in the air somersaulting over into the water.

"Tell Captain to stop! Man overboard!" Pablo screamed to a crew member standing outside the bridge port door. Pablo ran to the opposite side to help the rescuers pull Terry Madison out of the water. Terry was grasping two cameras—his favorite Nikon 35 millimeter in one hand and a Super 8 movie camera in the other. He seemed more concerned about the cameras getting salt water in them than about himself.

As he sat on the stern deck, Terry pulled off his shirt to reveal an ugly bruise across the top of his chest, less than a foot below his neck. It was then everyone realized the gravity of what might have happened.

"I was just taking pictures of the departure," Terry sputtered, "and the next thing I knew, something hit me so powerfully, it upended me right into the ocean."

If that cable had hit Terry a few inches higher, he would have been decapitated. The crew paused to thank God for yet another miracle—the sparing of a life.

14

More than Conquerors

Papa Kwang pulled his Mao cap further down over his eyes as a cadre he recognized boarded the local bus. Mama Kwang was wearing her oldest clothes and a farmer's large straw hat to cover as much of her face as possible.

Though the couple was able to cross the border legally from Hong Kong into China, they realized their safe return depended on not getting into any trouble with the authorities. They'd had plenty of that in their past. Papa had spent ten years in labor camp for his faith, and Mama had been in prison three separate times for preaching. This trip was a huge personal risk. But to them, it was worth it.

As they bounced along in the old bus on the dusty road, Mama suddenly poked Papa's arm and pointed out the window. There in a barbed wire enclosure was the first prison where she had spent time. She shuddered at the memory. As they slowly drove past, she stared at the inmates working in the prison gardens. Papa put his arm around her and drew her to him. "We're close now. We'll be there soon."

From the bus station in Shantou, they took a tricycle to Lili's house in Dahao. They had specifically forbidden anyone to try to meet them at the bus station.

When they arrived, there were tears all around as old friends embraced and rejoiced in the joy of meeting again.

Over cups of tea, Mama reminisced about her ministry in the area. "When we passed that prison earlier today, I remembered the feelings that went through me during my first imprisonment.

"My cell was dark. I couldn't see the faces of my cell mates because the windows were covered with shutters. They were sitting hopelessly on the dirt floor. There was no water supply or sanitation facility.

"The next day I was taken from the cell and told to confess my crimes. 'What crimes?' I asked.

"They said, 'About your faith! Start at the age of eight.'

" 'I believed in Jesus even before the age of eight,' I began. 'The past five generations in my family all believed in Him. They loved the Lord with all their hearts.

" 'When I was young, I had five major illnesses. The doctor said I would surely die and told me to prepare for it. But the Lord healed me and told me to share His gospel with the sick and needy. Jesus is the great physician!'

"I talked on for half the day. They were very touched by what I shared. But at noon they decided I needed another struggle-session because I did not confess clearly enough."

Mama reached for a *baodze* and her tea. "You don't know how much I've missed this." She paused to take a bite. "In Hong Kong, the dumplings have quite a different taste."

Since everyone else was quiet, she continued. "They took out paper and pen to record my confession. So I repeated the last message I had preached about the second coming of Jesus. The Holy Spirit worked in their hearts, and they asked me to also sing the song I had taught.

"The next day, they said, 'Yesterday, you talked about Jesus! Today you must talk about something else. How many co-workers do you have? How many house churches? How did you begin?'

"I replied, 'I began because I know Jesus. He's my Savior and He can be your Savior too. I don't know any other things. My co-workers have not committed any crimes. So I have nothing to confess.'

"They angrily returned me to my cell where I wrote a thirty-seven page document about my confession. I wrote about Jesus' birth, death, resurrection, and His salvation.

"That night they held another struggle-session against me. Four hundred prisoners and cadres listened as they read aloud all thirty-seven pages of my confession. The Holy Spirit worked in many hearts, and a number of prisoners repented in tears and received the Lord.

"The struggle-session went on 'til dawn. The authorities said they planned to hang me up and beat me the following day. But back in my cell, as I was praying, the Lord showed me several visions. In one, He revealed that my sentence would be only thirty days, not twenty years as the authorities threatened.

"The prison cells were indescribably filthy. I asked the guards to give me some water and rags so I could clean them up. Amazingly, they agreed and even assigned some other inmates to help me. We cleaned the cells until they were as clean as our homes. The authorities were so pleased, they opened the window shutters and installed electric lights. The inmates had a clean place to live and, even better, they now had Jesus living in their clean hearts.

"I taught them to sing, 'Where Jesus is, 'tis Heaven there.' We sang while we worked, and that terrible prison did become like heaven to us. The Lord's grace is beyond measure."

"But we didn't come here just to reminisce," Papa Kwang said gently. "What's the status of the project, Lili?"

"Well, to say it's been difficult is an understatement." She brushed away a tear. "Mei-ling and Chan are both traveling today. They're re-visiting their contacts in other provinces. Our friends from far away seem to understand what is happening. They're cooperating well. As some of them said, 'God's timing is perfect.'

"But the local believers in our network are causing the most grief. Perhaps that's because they were the most disappointed when no one came to the beach at Easter. They had been so excited. And now they don't believe it's going to happen. Maybe you can dispel their frustration and disbelief."

Papa Kwang sat up straight and said, "What is the house church venue that holds the most people now in the local network?"

Lili thought for a moment. "The largest is also probably the most secure. Lao Zhao has a niece in Hexi. She and her husband live in a compound with other Christians. It has a large courtyard. As long as we don't sing too loud, we could securely pack in about a thousand people there."

"Perfect," Papa exclaimed. "Please organize a secret meeting of all the brothers and sisters in the area for Friday night in Hexi—especially those you want to be involved in the project. The Lord will give Mama the right message for these people."

Lili nodded. "While you're here, we also need to have a meeting with the five leaders in Chaoyang. Peter Wang has been able to secure two trucks that'll each carry more than four tons for the delivery, as well as an automobile.

"That's exciting!" Mama said, beaming.

"The Bible need is so great," Lili continued. "That's what frustrates me regarding this project. Everyone seems hungry for God's Word in our country right now.

"I gave a small Project Rainbow New Testament to a Christian music teacher who read it through in a few days. One day a very poor woman came crying to the music teacher's house because her husband had left her to marry another woman. No one could comfort her. The music teacher said, 'Don't cry. I have a book for you that will give you comfort. Its words are full of strength and power. Every word in it is very valuable and can save our souls.'

"The poor woman replied, 'Very well, may I borrow it?'

"The teacher said, 'You may borrow it for only one week and no more.'

"The woman began to read and was especially blessed by Philippians 3:7–8. Realizing that she had Christ, who is the most valuable possession of life, she became a joyful believer.

"After one week, the teacher said, 'Please return the Bible.'

"She responded, 'May I please borrow it for another week? It is so precious!'

"The teacher allowed another week. But the day before she was to return it, a sick woman came to the poor woman's home and said, 'I have many diseases that the doctors cannot cure. I'm afraid to die because I have committed many sins. But if I remain alive, I'm like a walking corpse.'

"The poor woman said, 'I have a book that is very precious and can help you but I must return it tomorrow. I can lend it to you for only one day.'

"The sick lady took the book and began to read. When she came to Jesus' statements in Matthew where He said that it's not the healthy who need a doctor but the sick, and that He had come not to call the righteous but sinners to repentance, she knelt down and asked Jesus for forgiveness of her sins. She received peace and her diseases were healed!

"She was so excited, she passed on the Bible to another who then passed it on to another. The music teacher was never able to trace it or get it back."

"Let's pray together that God will provide His much needed Word for China," Papa Kwang concluded.

ᏇᎷᎧ

People were already crowded in the courtyard and yet more were pressing in. It was obvious the entire meeting would be standing room only. Those who arrived early became a little annoyed at the jostling caused by those entering later at the rear.

When Matthew Lo appeared at the front, he encouraged the crowd to sing softly together while they all found their place. "Let's begin with Mama Kwang's chorus, 'Lord, Send a Bible,'" he said. The entire crowd, as though a choir, began to sing:

Lord, send a Bible for that's Your gracious light,
True love and teaching and the Word of God.
We know for sure that Your Word will lead us on,
Brighten the path all through our journey home.

The crowd quietly sang song after song as they waited to hear from the special guests of the evening. After they sang "The Way of the Cross Means Sacrifice," Papa Kwang appeared at last and brought greetings from the Kwang family and the Teochew dialect church in Hong Kong. His youthful grin brought smiles and even tears to the faces of the faithful who were assembled. Then it was Mama's turn to preach.

After her opening greetings to the faithful, she read from Romans 8:35–39.

"The great apostle Paul says that you and I are more than conquerors and that absolutely nothing can ever separate us from the love of God in Jesus," Mama Kwang began.

"Here he talks about four areas of victory. First, we see the *extent* of his victory. It is 'in all these things.' The verses list some of these things. Sometimes we can overcome in little things, but Paul says we can be overcomers even in the great trials and discouragements of life. I know you've had difficult ones lately.

"Second, we see the *dependency* of his victory. He is able to be victorious through 'Him who loved us.' When we depend on ourselves, on wealth, or on reputation, we will fall. But Paul depended on Him who loved us. We know His love for us is the same yesterday, today, and forever. He is the rock of our salvation. He is the Almighty God. With Him, nothing is impossible. Our dependency on Him even takes the fear out of death. We learned a new song in Hong Kong: 'I have no fear of death nor danger because Jesus Christ has delivered me.' Let me sing it for you." Mama broke out into song.

"Third, we see the *depth* of his victory," she continued. "He is *more* than a conqueror. Some people don't believe they can score 100 percent in the game of life. But Paul says we can be even better than that! Three times he was put in prison, but as a result, he saw a jailer's family come to Christ. He witnessed to kings and rulers, and he saw dark prison cells turn into a mission field. Sixteen times in his letter to the Philippians, he mentions rejoicing in the Lord and always having joy. He was happy whenever the gospel was being preached. He became more than a conqueror.

"Fourth, we see the *time* of his victory. Paul says we are *already* more than conquerors. He was a victorious Christian from the day he met his resurrected Lord on the road to Damascus. God can forgive our past. We don't know what will happen to us tomorrow. We just have today and we can rejoice today in already being overcomers.

"Dear brothers and sisters, let us enthrone the resurrected Jesus as the Lord of our lives this day. He was already victorious on the cross. He now wants to live His resurrected life seated on the throne of our hearts and make us victorious too. When that happens, then we, too, will be 'more than conquerors.' And we, too, will want to boldly preach the gospel and bring others to Christ.

"There is a practical way you can help the gospel go forward in this country. Sister Lili needs some help in the next few weeks. And I'm asking you to stay for a few minutes at the end of our meeting to see how you can help her. I want *you* to be an overcomer in all these things. Amen."

☙

"Thank you for your encouraging message, Mama Kwang," said Matthew Lo, as they drank tea in his home in the town of Chaoyang the next day. "After the disappointments of last month, we needed that!"

"We all thank you, Matthew, for how you've taken Chan under your wing and enabled him to see what God is doing in other parts of our country," Mama replied. "I know he's been inspired in evangelism and missions."

Then Papa Kwang thanked Samuel Wu for his help on Easter eve when he quieted the upset crowd on the beach and protected Lili and Mei-ling. Samuel nodded and smiled. Enoch Ma, Peter Wang, and John Chow sat quietly beside him.

"But now we need to know your thinking about a future delivery of the one million Bibles," Papa said boldly. "Our friends from the West are now ready and waiting to make the delivery. It's up to us."

Enoch wiped his brow and began slowly, "Our current problem is not related to Easter weekend. That's all behind us now. What *has* happened is that there's been a robbery in the home of a powerful cadre near the beach in Gezhou. There are PSB officers and PLA patrols combing every inch of this territory right now. It's too high a risk to try a beach delivery at this time."

Everyone sat quietly, pondering the news.

Peter Wang took a long sip of tea and then broke the silence. "We have a good number of local Christian fishermen with sturdy small boats. I think they'd be willing to make a transfer of the cargo at sea in shifts if that could be arranged."

Papa Kwang sat up straight and smiled. "That sounds like a good plan. I'm sure our friends could make that adjustment. Let me talk to them about it."

Hong Kong
Sunday, May 31, 1981

As the sun was setting over Hong Kong's Western Anchorage, a *wala-wala* boat approached tugboat *Michael*. Doug and Joseph jumped onto the stern deck with smiles from ear to ear. On the bridge, they reported to Jim, Pablo, and Captain. "They're almost ready for the delivery!"

"We're all ears," replied Captain Bill.

"Are we prepared to transfer our cargo at sea?"

"No, we're not," came Captain's quick reply.

"I think we should get ready then," Doug said. "There's a possibility of this happening!" Everyone looked stunned for a moment.

"Well, that certainly reduces our personal risk tremendously," said Captain.

"What will you need in the way of gear we don't have?" Doug asked.

"To start with, we'll need a crane, some conveyors, and some cargo nets," answered Captain Bill looking more and more relieved the longer he thought about it.

"Pablo will get these for you and anything else you can think of."

"More crew," said Captain as he thought through the process of off-loading the massive cargo at sea. "I've already lost three crew members due to the delay and, without a sailing date, it looks like we'll lose three more—including my First Mate Jim here. We're going to need a lot more than fourteen guys to accomplish this type of delivery. I've even included you and Keith in that number," he added with a twinkle in his eye.

Jim nodded with a look of *wish I didn't have to go*.

"More crew may not be so easy," Doug commented, half talking to himself. "I'll see what I can do!"

"How much time do you think we have?" Captain Bill asked the inevitable question.

"Maybe two weeks."

"Two weeks!"

"Listen," Doug said impatiently. "If we don't leave by then, we'll unload and store the cargo and head home to the Philippines."

෴

I've anchored my soul in the haven of rest,
I'll sail the wide seas no more;
The tempest may sweep over wild, stormy deep,
In Jesus I'm safe evermore.[4]

As Pablo climbed the port-side ladder to the bridge the next morning, he heard the strumming of the ukulele strings and Captain's strong baritone voice. It was good to hear him singing again out in front of the wheelhouse. Usually, he followed this song with "Softly and Tenderly."

"Don't mean to interrupt, Captain," Pablo interrupted, "but John Kulisich and Terry Hickey are leaving in half an hour for the airport. The rest of the crew are on the stern deck saying their good-byes.

"And by the way, Jim has booked his flight home two days from now. That's going to leave a big gap in our team!"

"I've been thinking about that," said Captain. "I'd like you to take the First Mate position and claim that upper bunk in my chambers that Jim uses now. And I think I'll appoint Bill Schwartz as the Second Mate in your place. He's more than earned it."

"Okay, while we're discussing crew, who's going to replace Mother Hickey in the galley?"

"The Lord has already solved that one," Captain Bill answered. "The other day, when we learned Terry Hickey was planning to go home, Terry Madison came to me and said, 'Since I don't have the experience and training of the others, I'll volunteer to be the cook, if you help me.' I'm thankful for guys like that with a servant's heart!"

"I'm sure his wife, Carole, will be pleased with whatever training you can give him in the galley!" Pablo concluded with a wry smile.

Captain laughed and said, "You just get busy and find us a good crane!"

⟨✤⟩

Michael and Pablo spent four days locating an appropriate five-ton hydraulic crane with a belt conveyor system. It took another four days to get it delivered and installed on the barge.

While shopping in Kowloon, Pablo dropped into Swindon's Book Store and bought a copy of *Murphy's Law and Other Reasons Why Things Go Wrong.* He spent several hours reading aloud to Captain Bill, causing both of them to erupt in gales of laughter.

While the crew members were waiting for the new crane, they moved some of the one-ton Bible blocks up on top of the others to make a space in the center of the barge's deck for the crane to be anchored. This was done with the help of a Chinese *lighter*—a flat-bottomed crane barge. They also welded the underpinnings for the new crane and installed a backup generator.

At the same time, they began a series of exercises in which they handed forty-five-pound boxes of Chinese Bibles daisy-chain style to one another across the tug stern deck. These boxes had been left out for this purpose. It was probable that some of the smaller boats would need to be loaded this way and the crew needed to be prepared.

They had responded to the news of the change with revived enthusiasm. The thought of a land approach at night in a strange and hostile harbor was the toughest phase of the project to imagine. Now that fear, as well as the fear of the barge not living up to expectations, was gone. Everyone worked with a new fervor. The crew's usual sense of humor returned.

The following night the wind whipped through the harbor with an intensity that reminded the crew of Easter Sunday night. Captain sent Pablo and Todd out onto *Gabriella,* which was normally tug-side, to untie her from the tug and let her trail by her short towline. Pablo and Todd didn't even know where to start.

Captain Bill yelled in frustration at them from the bridge, "Do it just like last time!" Pablo looked sheepishly at Todd and said, "But I didn't do it last time!"

"Neither did I," added Todd. The two of them lay down on the Bible blocks and laughed themselves silly. Poor Captain still had to endure an untrained crew.

⟨⟩

The ship-to-shore radio-telephone on *Michael* called out, "Hotel Oscar 5357, Hotel Oscar 5357. Come in, please."

Pablo hit the transmit switch and replied, "This is HO5357. Go ahead."

"You have a call from the Hong Kong Hotel for a Pablo. Over," said the operator.

"This is Pablo. Go ahead."

"Hi, this is Dianne."

Pablo was excited to hear the voice of his wife. "Di, where are you? Over."

"I'm at the Hong Kong Hotel with Melinda for just tonight. Tim and Tanya went ahead of us a week ago on their own. They're with your parents now. Tomorrow, we fly home to Canada. Can you come meet us tonight?"

With big puppy dog eyes, Pablo looked at Captain who was nearby and overheard the conversation. "*Please,* Captain. May I have shore leave just for tonight?"

"Only if you're willing to take the teasing you'll get from the rest of the crew tomorrow when they find out."

Pablo turned back to the radio-phone. "I'll see you at dinnertime, Di. Over and out."

During dinner, eight-year-old Melinda said, "Daddy, you think it's a secret where you're staying, but I know all about it."

Pablo looked at his wife with a puzzled expression. Dianne was surprised too.

"I heard Mommy calling you on the phone," she continued. "You're staying at Hotel Oscar in room five three five seven. Do you have a color TV in your hotel?"

15

Welcome to the Party

The *wala-wala* nudged against the stern of *Michael*. Out stepped three new crew members from New Zealand: Eddie Cairns, the board member who had the original vision of the tugboat; his friend Ivan Scott; and Mark Houghton, the son of the Open Doors New Zealand director.

"Welcome aboard," said Captain Bill. "Things are pretty routine here for the moment. We've been stuck on this tug for nearly two months."

"Good to meet you, Captain," said Eddie with his jolly smile. He was a short, heavyset Santa Claus without the beard. "We're willing to do anything you want us to do," he stated in his upbeat manner and Kiwi accent.

"Then I have a job for you that our crew members hate—cleaning the toilets. And after you finish and wash up, maybe you could give Chef Madison a hand with the dishes in the galley."

The men unloaded their luggage, claimed bunks in the fo'c'sle, and began to work. But it wasn't long before Captain revealed his heart to Eddie. "Until we sail, you'll find you have plenty of time on your hands. I'd like you to take as much time as possible to pray. We need divine intervention as soon as possible if we're going to accomplish this mission."

It didn't take Eddie and Ivan long to scramble onto the Bible barge and pray over every block of books on it. They, along with Keith, became the prayer backbone of the project from that day on.

On June 9, three more new crew members arrived from Australia: Bob Cole, John Everingham, and Art Babbington. None of the men—like most of the original crew—had ever been to sea. John was a farmer and Art a mechanic. Bob was a representative for Open Doors Australia. They worked hard and brought with them a spiritual uplift, like new blood to a tired body. The sounds of "Good on ya, mate!" became common. But as Captain surveyed the gang he now had to train and work with, his private reaction was, *Good grief, Lord! What are You doing?*

꒰꒱

"Now there's a typhoon coming toward us. It's only a few hours out of Hong Kong." Captain Bill was briefing the crew on the stern deck. His voice revealed his inner frustration. "Our anchors can't hold in those winds and we're going to end up on the rocks! Let's prepare everything as best we can."

While the crew busied themselves with Captain's assignments, Eddie and Ivan completed their chores of cleaning toilets and washing dishes. Then they clambered up to their favorite prayer perches on *Gabriella*.

"Lord," Eddie prayed aloud. "You know what our needs are at this time. You know the impending dangers we face. We need you to deliver us!"

Then, as though to mock them, the wind began to whip up into a frenzy. The sky turned an ugly gray. It seemed as if the typhoon was about to unleash its fury.

"Ivan, we've stirred the devil, brother," shouted Eddie. "Let's continue to pray."

They prayed passionately and as quickly as the storm had come, the angry winds dispersed.

Two hours later a weather bulletin on the ship's radio reported that the impending typhoon, which had killed twenty-nine people in the Philippines, had unexpectedly veered off to the northeast and was now heading for Taiwan.

꒰꒱

It was Sunday, June 14, and Doug's two weeks were up. Sheepishly he walked into the wheelhouse to talk to Captain Bill, who had completed all necessary departure clearances two days earlier, except for radio notification of exact embarkation time.

"Bill, we still don't have any news, and I promise today is our last day. If we don't have a go-ahead by tonight, it's over. But would you please come with Keith, Joseph, and me to visit and pray with Mama and Papa Kwang?"

"I'd be happy to get off this tub for awhile," responded Captain. In two months he had been off the ship only for a short trip to town to arrange for equipment purchases and once with some crew members visiting the Cameron Street night market in Mong Kok. He enjoyed Lil's four weeks on board *Michael*, but it seemed like an eternity since he'd even talked to her.

Captain Bill, Doug, Keith, and Joseph spent a memorable day with Mama and Papa Kwang. In the late afternoon, all six were on their knees praying—there had been no call from Lili.

After prayer, Doug motioned to Keith and Bill, "Would you men come outside with me, please?"

Once out of the room, in hushed tones, Doug questioned Captain Bill, "What do you think?"

"It's up to you, Doug," he replied.

"I want to take one last step of faith," Doug said. "You go back to the ship and get ready for a delivery departure. Keith and I will stay here with Joseph and wait for the call from China. If no call comes, we'll unload the cargo tomorrow."

⁕

At nine in the evening, Doug, Joseph, and Keith climbed aboard the tug with a loaf of bread and a bottle. With huge smiles, they yelled, "All hands on the bridge!"

"We received a call from China. They're ready for the delivery," Doug shouted breathlessly, as the crew assembled excitedly in the wheelhouse.

"Is it a sea transfer?" asked Captain.

"No, we have to deliver to the beach! Original plan."

After a long pause, Captain muttered, "Well, at least we're on our way!"

"We've arranged for Thursday night, June 18. There were a whole lot of coded messages to Joseph by phone," Doug reported. "First, Mama Kwang said in Chinese, 'By faith, we are ready to move the patient if the hospital is ready to receive.' Then the answer came back, 'We are ready to receive! Just one thing we would ask of our friends. If the patient dies after the injection, neither of us is to blame the other.'

"What they meant," Joseph interjected, "is that we must all be prepared for any suffering or problems that might take place for Jesus' sake. Both sides now lay down their lives before Him.

"Papa Kwang reminded me of the story about a famous Chinese warlord named Xiang Yu. He was a military hero in China. One time his army of twenty thousand men was not able to make headway in a battle and requested reinforcements. Xiang Yu then led all his remaining troops across the Chang River. He gave orders to his soldiers to sink the boats they had sailed in. They were also to smash the cooking utensils they were carrying after burning down the huts that housed them. He gave every man three days rations and commanded his bewildered soldiers to fight to the death as retreat was now impossible. They fought with great resolve with seemingly superhuman boldness. Deliberately Xiang Yu had sacrificed all for the sake of victory. There was no turning back, and he won a great victory."

"We, too, are at the point of no turning back," said Doug. "Pablo, lead us in that song about not turning back."

The crew sang together from their hearts and the simple chorus took on new meaning for them:

I have decided to follow Jesus.
I have decided to follow Jesus.
I have decided to follow Jesus.
No turning back; no turning back.

Doug continued, "Keith is preparing for the communion we will celebrate together before our life-and-death mission. But before we break bread, if any of you for any reason wishes to leave the boat, there'll be an airline ticket waiting on shore. There will be no hard feelings. Everyone who comes with us tomorrow must clearly understand that there will be no turning back. This will be an extremely dangerous mission."

Doug paused to see if there were any takers. There was complete silence.

He continued, "We will not attempt to escape should we be intercepted. We will carry nothing that can be construed as a physical weapon—not even a pocketknife. Our cargo is God's Word, and we are dependant totally on God to accomplish our delivery. Of course each of you will work very hard in your assignment, which Captain Bill will outline as we sail. Let's go with God!"

As Keith distributed the elements of communion, the mood was solemn. Each one thought of family members who could be left alone. As the Lord had set His face to Calvary, so they were setting their faces toward what could very well be a Calvary experience for them too.

There was no turning back!

⟩◦⟨

The sunrise in Hong Kong Harbor was spectacular on Monday morning, June 15. It was Pablo's thirty-ninth birthday and what a present this day would bring—departure from the long, uncertain wait in Hong Kong!

Before making a final visit to the Kwangs, Doug phoned his wife, Judy, to say that everything was a go. She reported to the other wives and called Brother Andrew in Holland. He sent out an urgent communiqué to every Open Doors base around the world: "Chinese courier team in danger. Please pray for seventy-two hours." Each base in turn notified staff, supporters, and prayer chains. Thousands of people worldwide were soon praying for Project Pearl's delivery.

Captain prepared new watch assignments and engaged in some last-minute training with the new crew members.

Chef Madison marinated steaks in the galley for a special meal on this memorable day.

At four in the afternoon, they weighed anchor, wove their way among the picturesque coastal islands of Hong Kong, steering north to the open sea. With a fully loaded *Gabriella* heading soon into hostile territory, they were traveling at the incredible speed of three knots.

⁂

"CQ DU1OD . . . DU1OD. Come in, please. This is TI5TM calling."

"This is DU1OD. Is that you, Pablo? Over," crackled the voice on *Michael's* ICOM radio.

"Yes, Dean, the weather's beautiful here! What's it like where you are? Over."

"We just had another strong typhoon roll through, and it seems to be headed your way. But you've got a few days before it'll bother you. Over," said Dean Keaney at the home radio base in New Manila.

"Great honk!" exclaimed Doug, as he listened in the background.

"We've got a message for you to phone to Mama Kwang in Hong Kong, Dean. Over," Pablo said.

"Okay, go ahead."

"We're going to have a dinner party. We're expecting so many people that we've arranged twenty-one teacups and cooked eighteen bowls of rice. Over." The numbers *twenty-one* and *eighteen* stood for the hour and date of the delivery—2100 hours on June 18, when there would be high tide and full moon.

"Let me repeat that to be sure I got it all. You're going to have a dinner party with twenty-one cups of tea and eighteen bowls of rice? Over."

"You got it. Over."

"Sure wish I could join that party! Over," Dean responded.

"You're an important part of the team where you are right now, Deaner! Over."

"Okay, I'll be happy to forward the message right away and I'll get back to you tomorrow. Everyone here sends love and greetings. Over and out!"

⁂

There is no more beautiful place to be than on the ocean on a warm, calm, sunny day. Pablo and Terry sat on the bow of *Michael* soaking in the scenic beauty. Porpoises jumped and played along the starboard bow as though they thought they were bodyguards. Flying fish skimmed along the calm water surface, the sun on them reflecting the colors of hummingbirds. And the water of the warm South China Sea was as blue and clean as the crew had ever experienced. The trip out of Hong Kong was considerably different from the trip in!

In the wheelhouse, Captain had temporarily given command to Doug while he worked in his private quarters on the final delivery plan. Instructions for the bridge crew were simple: "Head due north and watch the radar for other vessels!" There were no ships within miles at the moment.

In the afternoon, Captain Bill ordered, "Pablo, call all hands to the bridge! I'll share the delivery plan with them."

The scene in the wheelhouse was quiet. The mood was pensive and the crew were more attentive than usual.

"The day after tomorrow we'll be heading toward Michael Beach," said Captain. "We plan to arrive at 9:00 p.m. because it'll be high tide and we can get *Gabriella* as close to the beach as possible.

"We have eight excellent sets of high-quality walkie-talkies that Jim brought on board for us. We're going to assume that China does not use the same frequencies. So those to whom I assign a set will use channel two—to start—and keep all communication to a necessary minimum," Captain Bill continued.

"Joseph, you'll carry the one for the beach team. Pablo, you'll be in charge of the Z-boat delivery team. Bill Schwartz will carry one and supervise the barge team. I'll have the fourth one on the rear bridge deck and oversee the whole operation. Each Z-boat will have one as well as the barge crew below. Remember, they don't work well when covered in saltwater!

"Joseph, Doug, and Keith will be on the beach team. You'll coordinate all communications and liaison with the local people.

"Bill will be in charge of the actual off-loading of the one-ton packages. Mark, Bob, John, and Art will be his crew. Jerry and Cor will take care of barge operations down below.

"Pablo, you'll command the small-boat detail with Michael, Ronald, Terry, Todd, and Douglas Junior.

"Alastair, as chief engineer, you'll remain with me aboard the tug. That leaves Eddie and Ivan. I want you to be the prayer team and lookouts for me.

"Each of you will be given a body belt with a waterproof bag attached. Keep your passport in that bag. And remember, carry nothing that can be construed as a weapon.

"Here are the instructions I've prepared and written out for delivery day. I'll read them for you now and post them here on the bridge. Please read them over many times:

1. The crew is to stay out of sight as much as possible on the approach.
2. Only six men will be on the bridge during the navigational approach—the inner circle management team and Second Mate Schwartz.
3. Don't act in haste but don't be slow either. Be deliberate and do everything with a purpose. FOLLOW SPECIFIC ORDERS!
4. If approached by strangers or hostile people, do not stop and stare. Continue with your tasks until I call a halt. Be friendly to all under every circumstance.
5. You are not sightseers. Pay little attention to the surroundings beyond what is needed to get the job done. Do your work as if you did it every day.
6. Follow the chain of command. I will communicate with the group leaders. They in turn will manage their responsibilities. DO NOT ANTICIPATE ORDERS. FOLLOW SPECIFIC INSTRUCTIONS.
7. You've been rightly praying as though the outcome of our efforts depends on the Master. Now go and act as though it all depends on you.

"If any of you is hurt or injured, needing serious, immediate medical attention," Captain continued, "you'll be left in the hands of our Chinese brothers. It'll take more than four days to get back to the Philippines."

At twilight, as *Michael* plodded up the coastline, Todd was stunned by what he saw looking out the stern deck. The wake left by the tugboat and the barge in the calm, glassy sea was perfectly straight not curving back and forth. This was his witness of God's presence.

⌀๛๑

Pablo's crew entered the wheelhouse promptly at four in the morning on Wednesday when their next watch was to begin. As was their pattern, the departing crew—under Captain's watch since midnight—prayed for the new crew that was arriving and beginning the new shift.

"This'll be your most boring watch, yet," Captain Bill predicted as he headed toward the bridge door of his private quarters. "Your course is due north for the next four hours and the radar shows no one near us for a hundred miles. But stay alert!"

Pablo ordered, "Ivan, you take the first shift at the helm. Joseph will supervise since you're still a relative novice. Junior, you do general lookout and Ronald will man the radar. I'll keep an eye on the satellite navigator."

Pablo turned his back to the wheelhouse crew to work on the chart table. What he enjoyed most on the ship was marking latitude and longitude on the charts every time a satellite passed over and the position was illuminated on the readout screen. From each fix he could then calculate their true course and speed. Sometimes satellites passed overhead as frequently as every three minutes.

After half an hour, Pablo heard Joseph say casually, "I think you've gone slightly off course, Ivan."

"Maybe," Ivan replied. "I did my training as a helmsman in the daytime and now at night that light on the compass is very dim. I can't see the headings very well."

"Here, let me correct it for you," Joseph said, wanting to help. However, he corrected the heading in exactly the opposite direction needed. Now instead of the ship being ninety degrees off course, it was traveling at one hundred and eighty degrees off course.

Suddenly Pablo heard Douglas Junior shout, "Hey, there's a ship out there!"

Then Ronald chimed in, "That's no ship, that's *Gabriella!*"

Pablo turned around and jumped to the wheel. He could see the green and red running lights of the barge dead ahead about one hundred feet. He grabbed the remote controls for engine speed and backed the engine right off. *Gabriella* had a bridle that already had given them grief when beginning a tow. If he simply turned the tugboat around to the correct heading, the tension of the towline would probably snap the bridle right off and the barge would be floating aimlessly in the dark.

Killing the engine, however, woke everyone up. Captain was on the bridge in a flash, and soon every crew member had climbed the ladder to the wheelhouse to find out why the engine was not pounding. In the absence of normal, loud engine noise, silence can be deafening.

"We almost sank our own barge!" Pablo reported with embarrassment.

⚭

"TI5TM . . . TI5TM . . . DU1OD calling TI5TM," crackled the radio again.

"Hi, Dean. This is Pablo. Over."

"Hey, Pablo, I've got a message back from Mama Kwang for you. Over."

"Go ahead, Dean. We're all ears. Over."

"The message in response to yours is, 'Welcome to the party!' "

16

The Promised Land

The morning of June 18 arrived with a beautiful sun, no wind, and a flat sea that was to get flatter as the day grew older.

After Pablo completed his sunrise watch at eight in the morning, he sat on the bow to read his daily devotional book, *My Living Counselor*. The reading for this day included these words:

> At last we are on our way to the Promised Land. Come with us and we will do you good; for the Lord has given wonderful promises to Israel! . . . Keep a close watch on all you do and think. Stay true to what is right and God will bless you and use you to help others.[5]

Tension mounted as the day wore on, growing like the tightening of a guitar string. As Captain Bill said, "It's certainly not every day that a crew sails uninvited into a Communist seaport to deposit unconsigned cargo—especially into a port that harbors half that country's navy!"

The afternoon seas were as calm as anyone had ever seen. But Captain knew flat, oily waters meant they were in the path of an approaching storm. Right now they were enjoying the proverbial calm that comes before. After double-checking his calculations, Captain Bill said, "Okay, let's do it!" *Michael*, with *Gabriella* in tow, made a hard turn to port in a due westerly direction. They were soon to leave international waters.

"Nine hundred revolutions," said Captain. The slow cruise was over and full power was now required. "Raise the Chinese flag on the foremast and turn on the running lights," came the next order. The flag indicated they were aware of being in China's sovereign waters. Now there was no turning back for sure.

The sun was low over the western horizon above the city of Shantou. The pale full moon could already be seen hanging lazily in the sky above the glassy smooth ocean.

The six men on the bridge were all busy with some aspect of navigation. Joseph was at the helm, since he was Asian and would look natural there to any curious onlookers. Over his full black beard, Pablo held a powerful set of binoculars to his eyes. "I can see several gunboats in the distance plying back and forth across the entrance to the harbor ahead," he announced.

"They must be the blips I see on the radar screen," added Bill Schwartz.

Pablo's bass voice suddenly went tense as he continued the report, "And one of those gunboats is now heading straight for us!"

"All you white-faced guys sit on the floor," Captain Bill commanded sharply, as the destroyer-shaped gunboat headed east. "Pablo, man the VHF ship-to-ship radio in case of a communications call," he added.

The gunboat approached quickly. Joseph tightened his grip on the helm. "O Lord, O Lord," he prayed aloud. The ship came close enough on *Michael's* port side so that the heavy machine guns on the fore and stern decks could be seen clearly. It was a seventy-five-footer with lots of speed, and now so near the crew could throw a soda can at it.

Captain looked straight ahead and softly said, "I won't look at you if you don't look at me!"

With a tenseness they had never experienced before, the crew waited breathlessly for the gunship to pass. Pablo stood by for a radio query. But as quickly and quietly as it had come into view, the gunboat glided past them into the gray dusk heading out to open sea. The crew later assessed that either it didn't see them, or they looked perfectly normal.

"Praise the Lord," whispered multiple voices throughout the ship.

Twilight turned to darkness. Captain spotted the white signal of the lighthouse atop Good Hope Cape that juts out and marks the southern limit of the Shantou port entry. *Strange,* he thought, *there are other vessels anchored far out into the bay.* It was stranger still to see they were Chinese navy troop ships. *Michael* passed close by them, since it was still on the normal course into the harbor of Shantou and Captain didn't want to raise any suspicions.

"Is that a submarine?" asked Bill as he motioned out into the darkness on the port side. He saw a dark mass, low in the water with a slim spire projecting up its center. There were tense moments again until they concluded it must be offshore rocks not marked on the broad-scaled chart. The night can play strange tricks on the eyes.

Several ships and fishing boats moved past them in the darkness, identified only by their colored running lights.

Then it was time. "Turn off the running lights," commanded Captain. He altered to a southwesterly course straining to see any sign of the cove, which they had dubbed Michael Beach. Bill Schwartz took the wheel as Joseph went to the lookout post. He was the only one who had been on the beach before.

Right where he expected it, Captain Bill saw the white blinking light that marked the north side of the cove entrance. "Shorten the towline," he called to Pablo. It was part of the prearranged plan. He reduced speed slowly as the crew went to work hauling in the longer, heavy nylon towline, leaving the barge on the shorter, steel wire tow.

"All done, Captain," reported Pablo.

"Lower the big Z," Captain ordered. It was the largest inflatable rubber boat, which would take the beach team to shore.

As a flashlight beam signaled three flashes from the beach area, Joseph shouted, "There it is, Captain! That's our beach!"

"I see it!" said Captain.

Bill Schwartz beamed three flashes back to the beach.

"There it is, Doug! There it is!" Joseph kept shouting.

"There it is, Captain!" Doug repeated. They both sounded worried Captain might miss it.

"If you guys don't shut up, I'll have to ask you to leave the bridge!"

he yelled back. He was under great stress, as they had veered from the main channel and were approaching the shallow water in the small cove. The sea charts showed many underwater obstructions in the area—rocks, reefs, and even a submerged shipwreck.

The full moon shone down on the cove like a torch. It was nine o'clock. High tide. Michael Bruce started the engine on the largest Z-boat. Soon Doug, Keith, and Joseph were en route to shore with fifty pairs of shears for the local believers to cut off the waterproof wrapping of the 232 Bible blocks.

Lord, I need your help now, Captain Bill prayed silently. When he calculated the distance was about right, he started the tug into a slow turn. It was to swing the barge through an arc and place it behind and close to the beach.

"Let the anchor go!" he called to Alastair and the crew standing by on the tug's bow. With a horrible, grating screech, the anchor chain rattled down the steel hawsehole into the water. With everyone trying to be quiet, it sounded so very loud.

"Cor, drop your anchor! *Now!*" Captain shouted into the walkie-talkie. The barge came to a slow stop right behind the tug. Captain gave a sigh of relief.

Pablo noticed that the Chinese fishermen sitting on the rocks at the mouth of the cove when they arrived had gone to the beach. They were now talking to the people milling around.

From a small Chinese bamboo raft on the water, came Doug's voice. "Captain, they want you to move farther south and closer to the shore."

"Doug, it's going to be difficult to move now," protested Captain.

"I'm sorry, but they insist you must come closer," he replied. There was no time for discussing pros and cons.

"Alastair, pull the anchor up!" shouted Captain. Again the grating screech pierced the silence.

"*Gabriella! Gabriella!*" Captain Bill shouted into his walkie-talkie.

"This is *Gabriella*. Go ahead," came Cor's voice over the small speaker.

"Cut your anchor line! Just cut it off and stand by to drop the spare." Fortunately, they had brought a backup anchor.

Captain edged *Michael* farther into the shallow water as far as he dared.

"Let her go, Alastair!" he ordered. The metallic clanking erupted in the silence again, as the ship's anchor chain played out through the hawsehole.

I might as well blow a siren with all this noise we're making, thought Captain.

"Drop your anchor, Cor!" Captain radioed again. The whole operation took only five minutes but it seemed like an eternity. Quickly the barge was snubbed up close to the stern of the tug. The barge crew scrambled up *Gabriella's* hanging bow ladder and over onto the barge deck. Two of the men wore foam rubber wet suits, more for safety than for warmth.

The three Z-boats were now idling at the side of the barge, awaiting their towing instructions.

"Flood the port side," Captain Bill radioed to Jerry in the belly of the barge. It was necessary to flood only one side because they had installed the crane in the center of the deck. If the entire barge were flooded as originally planned, it would drown the crane's electric pump motor. The crane was now to be used to help hook the packages on the high side and drag them off the deck into the water.

From the beach came Joseph's voice on the walkie-talkie. "Okay, Captain, they say you can bring the Bibles in now."

Then Doug's reprimanding voice came through clearly. "Joseph, watch your language! Someone might be listening!"

"Okay, Captain," came Joseph's voice again. "You can bring the bread in now."

The small-boat crew members were laughing hysterically while listening to all this, and then there were blocks of Bibles in the water from the sunken port side of *Gabriella.* As practiced, they wound the lines around their tow bars and slowly headed toward the beach with a chain of one-ton blocks slowly trailing behind.

The Chinese men came out into the water up to their necks. Pablo recognized some of the local fishermen they had seen on arrival.

As the small boats approached shore, the Z crew member not driving threw the lines connecting the blocks to the Chinese men. Several men pulled the blocks up onto the sand. With shears, they cut open the waterproof wrapping and handed the cardboard boxes of Bibles along a line, daisy-chain style, up the beach to the tree line.

"Captain," came a voice over the walkie-talkie, "this is Bill. The crane is jammed."

"What's the problem?" asked Captain.

"I don't know. It's too hard to see in the dark."

"Well, do the best you can." Captain Bill watched as the other barge crew members literally pushed the packages into the water by hand. Their progress was painfully slow.

Suddenly Eddie, the watchman, yelled, "Looks like a boat is coming, Captain." One of the several boats passing by toward Shantou harbor, did look a little close.

Captain hit his transmit button and ordered, "All Z-boats. Close in and hide behind the barge." It took several calls before all three were safely out of sight.

"All clear, all clear. Resume your tow," he transmitted a few minutes later after the ship had passed by in the darkness.

"There's thousands of people here," came Doug's voice over the radio. "Keep the bread coming!"

Captain Bill spoke into his walkie-talkie again. Half the cargo was unloaded. This time he called to Jerry down in the belly of the barge. "Pump out the port side and sink the starboard side."

Then a voice on Captain's walkie-talkie said, "Bill here. The door won't open."

"What do you mean, it won't open?"

"It seems to be stuck."

"Well, there are some steel pipes on the bow. Get them and open that door." The walkie-talkie went silent. The door referred to was the starboard side door—one of two that enclosed the cargo deck. Each door was sixty-four feet long and weighed three tons.

"Schwartz, how's it comin'?" Captain called in a few minutes. No answer.

"Schwartz!" he called again.

After another three minutes of silence, Captain yelled into the walkie-talkie, "Schwartz, where are you?" Still no answer. Captain continued calling, but there was only silence in response.

Then a few minutes later, Bill Schwartz was on the walkie-talkie. "Hello, Captain."

"Where've you been, Schwartz?" Captain asked in an exasperated tone.

"I've been working on the door, Captain. Couldn't do that with a radio in my hand. It's down now!" Whenever there was work to do, Bill Schwartz could be counted on to drop everything and dig in. Cargo began spilling out the starboard side into the sea and all annoyance was forgotten.

"Captain, this is Ronald. Our Z's got engine trouble," came the next voice and problem.

"Are you in danger?" Captain Bill asked.

"No, we're okay." The packages were now accumulating faster than the little boats could get them to the beach.

"Captain, this is Ronald again. We're underway!" Terry Madison, Ronald's partner in the Z-boat, just happened to have a rubber band in his pocket. They used it to fix their outboard engine shifter control.

Again, from behind Captain came Eddie's voice, "Here comes a boat straight for us, Captain." Bill's nerves were now stretched to the breaking point.

"Don't tell me. I don't want to know," replied Captain Bill. Blocks of Bibles were floating everywhere by this time. Again the unknown vessel sailed quietly past toward Shantou harbor.

"Captain, this is Doug again. The people here on the beach are getting very nervous. They'd like us to leave now."

"Standby for a few minutes, Doug. "We're almost done here, but there's a lot of towing to do yet."

"They say don't worry about the floaters," came Doug's voice again. "They have their own small boats ready to tow them in."

"Okay, Michael will bring you back in his Z, and we should be just about done when you get here," replied Captain. At that moment, he was actually watching the barge crew heave the last packages into the water.

"Schwartz, close the barge doors," called Captain. "And Jerry, get the pump started on that starboard compartment."

"Captain, this is Bill. The cable is broken on the port door."

"Good night nurse! Break out the chain blocks and close it! We can't be seen pulling a barge with that silly door hanging open."

"Captain, this is Doug again. We're on our way out to the boat, and the people are insisting that we leave now."

"We'll leave as soon as possible!" replied Captain not telling him about the crew's problem working the noisy chain block in their attempt to close the big barge door.

"We've got it all wrapped up now," reported Bill Schwartz on his walkie-talkie a few minutes later. "We're coming aboard." Captain could already see some of the barge crew scrambling down the ladder from the barge.

"All Z-boats come in. We're going home," called Captain on the walkie-talkies.

"But Captain, we've got more to tow to the beach," countered Pablo.

"Never mind, they can handle it," Captain Bill replied.

"This is Ronald, Captain. Please can I make one more run to the beach?"

"I said, all Z-boats in now," Captain spoke sharply into the radio. The Z-boat drivers headed reluctantly back to the tug.

"This is Jerry, Captain. We can't get any suction on the barge's starboard side."

"What's the problem, Jerry?"

"We don't know. We've tried everything."

"Well, keep on trying."

"Why couldn't we finish towing in the packages?" asked a somewhat irate Pablo, when he faced Captain on the bridge.

"I'm just following orders too," said Captain Bill, understanding the unspoken feelings. *After all this time, why couldn't we just stay a few more minutes and clean it up?*

"Haul up the anchor, Alastair!" Captain yelled.

"What are we going to do about the barge?" asked Bill Schwartz as he looked back at the half sunken vessel.

"We're going to tow it out of here!"

"*Gabriella,* tug *Michael,*" Captain called on the CB intercom.

"Tug *Michael,* this is *Gabriella,*" replied Jerry.

"Jerry, tell Cor to cut the anchor line. And how are you doing on that pump? Over!"

"No luck, but we're still working on it."

"Well, guys, here goes nothing," muttered Captain Bill as he began to give power to the tug's engine. He looked back and his heart sank. The half-submerged barge was veering off in a wide arc. The starboard side deep in the water acted like a rudder. When the barge was quite far out on the port side, the power of the tug would pull her forcibly around. She then began her radical turn to starboard. The cycle repeated itself every minute. Anyone watching these antics would certainly be suspicious.

◇◇◇◇◇

"Captain," said Eddie, "We're going to have a praise meeting down in the mess hall." It was 11:30 p.m., just a little more than two hours since they had arrived at Michael Beach and begun to unload.

"You guys go ahead," said Captain. "I've got my hands full with this crazy barge. It'll be more than two hours before we're safely into international waters. Bill will stay on the bridge with me." *Thank you, Lord. And please get us out of here!*

For a half hour the crew thanked God for his help and protection and prayed for Captain Bill and especially the two crew members still in the belly of *Gabriella.*

After midnight, Doug smiled at Eddie and said, "Didn't you tell me something about a cake that your wife, Betty, made just for this occasion?"

"Hang on. I'll go get it," said Eddie as he dashed for the ladder down to the fo'c'sle. It was a beautiful homemade fruitcake. A friend had decorated it with a pearl and the words, *He has done all things well.*

The hungry crew ripped off pieces with their hands according to the size of their appetite and massacred the cake. Captain and Bill Schwartz got to enjoy the final broken pieces.

While eating fruitcake, the men asked the beach team about their experiences. "There had to be more than two thousand people on the beach at the height of the delivery," started Keith. "At first, a thousand or more people were hiding behind the trees. But then when the packages were opened and bodies needed to handle the boxes, they began literally to come out of the woodwork!"

"Lili, Mei-ling, and Chan were so excited to meet everyone," said Joseph. "They gave Doug and Keith big hugs, which is definitely not Chinese culture. They even practiced some English. I heard them say, 'Welcome to China, Uncles. Praise the Lord!'"

Doug quickly picked up the reporting. "I'll never forget the moment the first packages came to shore. They opened the boxes with 'Oooohs' and 'Aaaahs.' They wanted to keep touching the books. The joy on their faces will be with me forever!"

"My question is," spoke up Terry Madison, "who was that guy with the little flat bamboo raft, Doug?"

"Chan called him Daniel in English. He actually wanted to come aboard the barge and help throw the packages off, so I distracted him by making him my water chauffeur."

"But he did come aboard the barge later, Doug," said John Everingham. "His mouth was wide with amazement as he literally hugged one of the Bible blocks."

"What about those fishermen?" asked Pablo.

"Well," Doug continued, "apparently when we arrived, the fishermen didn't know what to do. So Chan talked them into helping. That's why you probably saw some guys deep in the water with miner's hats on and others with cigarettes hanging from their mouths. They saw your beards and asked if you were Russians!"

Everyone chuckled at that.

"I couldn't help myself," chimed in Ronald. "The first time into the shore with a line of the blocks, I jumped out of the Z-boat into the knee-deep water to help a Chinese believer pull them up on the sand. Our eyes met and we hugged each other just briefly before I had to jump back into the boat."

"It was exciting to talk with elderly Samuel Wu," Doug continued, "and hear his appreciation for our efforts."

Joseph picked up the story. "Samuel Wu said to Doug, 'Tonight Jehovah has appeared to us on this beach and reigned as King!' "

"I think my most exciting moment," said Keith, "was when Sister Lili told me about a lady who'd been coming to this beach every day for two years to pray that God would send His Word to the Chinese church. How neat to see her faith and faithfulness being rewarded on this very night!"

"Hey, Doug, I was just calculating," said Joseph with excitement in his voice. "We left two hundred thirty-two one-ton blocks of Chinese Bibles with our contacts in two hours—eleven thousand one hundred, thirty-six boxes. That works out to nearly two tons a minute, using nothing but human strength, a few small boats, and the awesome power of God."

By 1:30 in the morning, Captain Bill gave a sigh of relief. Radar showed there were no other ships anywhere nearby. *Michael,* towing the erratic barge, was probably now in international waters. The crew burst into hoots and hollers of praise. They sensed that, through it all, they had been spectators as much as participants.

Pablo climbed the foremast and took down the flag of China.

17

The Wet Bibles

Lili was panting. An hour of steadily handing 45-pound boxes of Bibles to the person behind makes the heart race. She breathed a sigh of relief as she saw the two trucks moving out again beyond the tree line with a second full load of Bible boxes. Chan's team was right on schedule. They had a six-ton German-built truck and a Japanese four-ton truck, as well as one sedan automobile.

In front of her, Daniel was commanding a group of small dinghies and rafts that were pushing the last floating one-ton blocks onto the shore.

Mei-ling was supervising the beach volunteers. They were cleaning up the leftover waterproof wrapping materials. When they were finished, no one should be able to tell that anything had happened there that night.

God! You are so good! Lili whispered. In spite of the party like mood, her co-workers were so disciplined. *But where did those fishermen disappear to?* She hadn't seen them for the past hour. It worried her because she had earlier seen a PLA patrol on Hi Bean Road when she was approaching the beach at dusk that day. They had been helping the PSB investigate a burglary at the home of a sister named Huang in Gezhou. She was a deaconess and church treasurer. Her family's hard-earned money had been kept together with the church's money. Yet only her family's funds were stolen, while the church's money remained intact.

When the tugboat and barge left, one third of the delivery load had already been transferred safely to depositories. Now another third was soon to be cleared from the beach. But it was the final third that worried her.

Everyone worked hard and fast so that by three o'clock in the morning all the boxes were under the trees and the beach was clean. Mei-ling's team had accomplished their goal. Not a trace of any packaging was left anywhere on the beach.

"Mei-ling, I'm going to the city to call Mama Kwang and give her our report," said Lili. "I'll leave you in charge of clearing out the final boxes." Soon Lili was pedaling her bicycle up Hi Bean Road.

൭ഝൖ

"What went wrong?" asked Lao Zhao.

"The non-Christian fishermen reported us," Lili replied after a big sigh. Mei-ling and Chan were with her, hiding in the little hut. "Everyone in Dahao and nearby Gezhou has been interrogated—especially my family," she continued. "I'm worried about the believers who took boxes of Bibles to their homes!"

"So, tell me what happened," said Lao Zhao almost impatiently.

"At three o'clock in the morning, a large group of PSB came to the beach," Mei-ling picked up the account. "They arrested everyone they saw and then began to try to confiscate all the boxes that were still under the trees. While all this was happening, we watched from another hiding place nearby. Some of our friends were still boldly carrying boxes safely away right in front of the PSB. It was amazing.

"The police put the boxes they had collected in a big pile on the upper part of the beach and poured kerosene and coal oil all over them trying to set them on fire. The boxes just wouldn't burn. In frustration they emptied the boxes onto the sand and threw the Bibles by the hundreds into the water. They floated with their white pages up. The bay looked like *congee* [rice porridge]. We decided it was time to leave."

Chan chimed in, "At least we know more than two thirds of the Bibles were taken safely to our depositories before the PSB ever arrived."

"But we also know they're looking for all the ringleaders," Lili added. "I don't know how long we'll be able to avoid arrest. I'm especially worried about Samuel Wu and his two daughters. I haven't been able to warn them."

⌒〰〰〰〰⌒

Ming Seng-kee had kept the book in his pocket all night long. Now he knew it was called a Bible. He wanted to read it but he did not want anyone to know he had it. Seng-kee could not forget the memory of hundreds and hundreds of people last night on the beach who were willing to go to jail for the sake of this book. He thought to himself, *This must be some book!* As a fisherman, he would never value one book that highly.

He took out the Bible and settled down to read. He opened the black vinyl cover and started at page one. *"In the beginning, God created the heavens and the earth."*

Seng-kee thought, *No wonder the police were sent to destroy this book! Our government teaches us that God does not exist. They've told me that the world was not created, but it simply happened. The Bible tells a story they do not want us to read.* That day Seng-kee read in secret for the first time about the seven days of creation, Adam and Eve, and the fall of humankind.

Before drifting off to sleep that night, he thought about what he had read. A spiritual part of him was in harmony with what the Bible said. Seng-kee remembered from his reading that when God finished creating the world, He said, *"It is very good."* As he thought about what he had read in the Bible, he echoed the words of God, "It is very good."

On Board Ship

Michael began to roll like a drunken sailor. "There's a storm ahead!" announced Captain Bill to his small crew on the bridge as they started their watch. Typhoon season had begun with a vengeance. "This is the one Dean Keaney promised us!"

Moving unabated across the South China Sea, the storm grew in intensity, exuding a devastating force of wind.

"Keep your back firm against this pole," said Ivan to Eddie as he took a turn on the helm. "If you don't put pressure on it and hang on, you'll be thrown out the door!"

For four days, the seas raged. At times, it was almost impossible to see empty *Gabriella* following along behind. Fortunately, Jerry and Cor had been able to pump the water out of her tanks and she righted herself to normal. Those two men were safely on board the tug.

But in the storm, most of the crew were so sick they could not leave their bunks. Some suffered from severe dehydration. John, unable to sleep in his rolling bunk, would hang over the railing, just waiting for the next heave. In between, he would yell, "Hallelujah! Praise the Lord!"

Chef Madison found few wanting to eat anything because of the turbulence, so he abandoned the galley, allowing those who could to attend to themselves.

Chaoyang, China

Pastor John Chow was just leaving his house in Chaoyang when a member of his congregation came up to him on the street and said quietly, "Have you heard the news?"

"What news?" John asked.

"Last night hundreds of thousands of Bibles landed on a beach— the whole town is buzzing about it." His informant added, "The civic authorities are furious. They are determined to trace every Bible and jail every person that handles one."

Pastor John didn't say anything but he knew he had a problem. He had ten thousand of those Bibles in his house, which, if discovered, could land him in jail for many years. After all, this was no ordinary operation. The scale was too grand. The authorities were embarrassed. And he could not solve the problem by distributing the Bibles quickly to his flock.

He reasoned, *I took the risk on their behalf. If I give them the Bibles, I'll just be spreading the risk, and they'll be liable to receive the same punishment as I.*

After a quick prayer, he talked to an old farmer friend. Together with the help of a few others, they buried the Bibles underneath a barn in plastic bags to make sure they would not rot or be spoiled. When all the commotion died down, they planned to dig them up again.

But when would things quiet down? The newspapers carried many stories claiming the entire consignment had been burned. Pastor John said, "We didn't believe these reports, of course, but it did signal to us that the authorities were very angry and taking the whole episode very seriously." It was not long before they were on his doorstep.

Pastor John was taken to the local police station and asked to account for his whereabouts on the night of June 18. John later recalled, "I got a real surprise to see my four interrogators were not local men but special investigators flown in especially from Beijing." It was an ominous sign that a nationwide effort was underway to track down the Project Pearl ringleaders.

Giving precise details of his movements on June 18 proved tricky for John. He had been preaching at a house church that evening, and though the congregation was his alibi, they could well suffer for admitting to attending an illegal gathering. However, he had stayed chatting to the owners of the home, and they came forward to clear him.

It made no difference. The investigators were convinced John was a key organizer of Project Pearl. He said, "They rested their case on logic not evidence. I was a prominent leader of house churches—the group for whom the Bibles were destined. I lived in the Shantou area—the place where the Bibles landed."

Pastor John refused to answer any more questions, knowing that to speak was futile. The minds of the investigators were already closed. Their case was far from closed, however. They needed names, more names, to piece together how the project was mounted. Their goal was to find all the Bibles and destroy them. So John was pressured to reveal the names of all the house church people he knew who distributed Bibles that came from abroad.

He still refused to talk. He said, "To be quite honest, I had gone through similar problems during the Cultural Revolution, and I knew how to handle this kind of interrogation. You just shut your eyes and pray."

John's serenity under the pressure of interrogation had not gone unnoticed by the investigators, who by this time were becoming increasingly desperate. Beatings would not help either. He was a frail, elderly man, and quite unafraid of dying.

He was taken into a courtyard in the prison and made to stand upright on a tall wooden box. The box was about four feet high and very narrow. In fact there was room on the top of it for only his feet. A noose was put around his neck and tightened. The rope was fixed to a wooden beam above him.

His interrogators said, "We've given up on you. The moment you sway violently or when your legs collapse from tiredness, you will hang yourself." They added, self-righteously, "It's a just penalty for your stubbornness."

Two policemen were assigned to watch John's last moments. He looked down at them. They hardly glanced at him. Bored, they played some gambling games. Suddenly John felt a surge of power in his body. He said, "I felt like Christ on the cross. He must have looked down and felt the same when He saw the soldiers casting lots for His clothes, utterly indifferent to His agonies."

Knowing his end was not far away, John began to witness to the two policemen. He told them of Jesus and he said he was not afraid of death because of what Jesus had done. But one of the policemen merely replied, "Old man, when I get to be seventy and look as unhealthy as you, I won't be so afraid of death either." The two men laughed.

The hours dragged on, yet John had to remain still. His body cried for sleep, but he must not give in. When God wanted to take him, he was ready, but he refused to let his death look like suicide. His legs developed terrible cramps, and in shaking them, he nearly hanged himself. Soon he felt nothing in his legs, though they had swelled to twice their normal size, as the blood began to collect there.

His only relief was the rain that washed his perspiring body. He stuck his thickened tongue out to collect a few drops of moisture.

Days passed. Still John had not toppled over. Word was getting around the prison. No man could survive that long. He had been standing all that time. No food. No water. No rest. It was impossible for him still to be alive.

Finally, a huge thunderstorm struck. The sky went black, rain pelted down. His resistance was over. Through his delirium, he vaguely heard the crash of thunder, a crack of lightning, and he pitched forward. The noose tightened. Oblivion.

But he was being revived in frantic fashion. Someone was splashing water over his cracked, puffy lips. Someone else was rubbing his wrists. His legs had been propped up on a chair, and the blood was running back into his torso and arms. He could do nothing but cry from the pain.

Presently, he became aware of who was working on him—the two policemen. *Why were they suddenly so interested in reviving an old man whom they had mocked when his death seemed imminent? Why had he not been strangled by the rope? Where was . . .* but the two policemen were shaking him urgently.

"Please!" they were shouting, "Don't die, please!" John managed to clear his brain for a moment and concentrate.

"Why?" he simply asked them.

"Because we want to know your Savior, Jesus," they replied. He noticed they were trembling.

"But why?" he asked again.

"Because He saved you! A flash of lightning cut the rope above your head just as you fell. Don't tell us that's a coincidence!"

They believed. John later recalled, "Not only did I feel like the Lord during this experience, I also felt like the apostle Paul when his jailer witnessed his Lord's miraculous deliverance and believed."

Pastor John was later released, more out of indecision than anything else. The story had spread around the prison, and the other prisoners held him in awe. The investigators had no stomach to interrogate him again, so they let him go.

Pastor John Chow recalls that there was a strange disappointment when he was released. "I had looked forward to death. I was ready for it and quite happy just to go to heaven. I thank Him, however, for the miracle and especially for saving those two men through it all. But still, it's got to be harder to live down here than in heaven, and I had so looked forward to being in heaven with Jesus."

On Board Ship

The storm gradually lost its power as the rain and winds faded to a light squall. Then it died as quickly as it had arisen. The sun shone on the blue expanse of the South China Sea, as the tug and barge resumed normal speed toward their final destination.

Most of the crew were on the bow, watching a number of whales with their young calves accompanying them as they approached the Philippine Islands. The whales were no more than twenty feet to the port side. The calves would rise up on their mothers' backs and then slip back into the water as they majestically slid through the ocean alongside the tug.

While the majority of the crew members were occupied with this spectacle, Doug walked into the wheelhouse where Captain was duty officer and Pablo was at the helm.

"This morning when we passed Subic Bay," Doug said to Captain, "three jet planes from the U.S. naval base passed above us. They each made a victory roll when they were overhead. I believe they were watching us by satellite the whole time."

"Well, we shouldn't take any credit," replied Captain Bill. "It wasn't me, it wasn't you, and it wasn't the crew; it was God who did it. And He did it in spite of us!"

"I just want to thank you, Bill, for what you *did* do!" Doug said gently.

Captain was a little embarrassed. His soft gaze rested on his long-time friend and finally he responded, "Well, Doug, it's all in a day's work!"

China

Chan was still breathing quickly as he ducked into Peter Wang's home in Chaoyang. He looked behind, suspecting the PSB might be on his trail. He had heard they had already arrested Lili and Mei-ling. It pained him to think of what the young women might be going through this very minute. And what bothered him most was that he had not been able to bring himself to publicly declare his love for Mei-ling. Now she would probably spend time in prison without the awareness of the love in his heart for her.

Peter Wang was the least known by the police of all the secret church leaders, and from him Chan could find out what else was happening in the community. First, while gasping for breath, Chan told Peter what he knew.

"They also have John Chow in prison. Everyone in the area knows about the delivery," Peter said. "Fishermen plucked the wet Bibles out of the water in the cove following the delivery. Then they put them on the roofs of their houses to dry. Every traveler and visitor to the city is asking questions about where all these books came from.

"Now the fishermen are selling the dry Bibles to anyone who has an interest in them. They still have to do it quietly because the PSB has threatened to arrest anyone who is found with one."

"But there are too many people now with one of the Pearl Bibles to arrest everyone!" Chan exclaimed. "Even the entire PLA wouldn't have enough men to achieve that goal!"

"Yes, I agree," Peter said. "But there is just far too much talk about Bibles around here these days. I'm afraid many innocent people will be in trouble. Yesterday, I attended the local TSPM Church in Shantou to see if there would be any comment. And of course the Bible delivery dominated the sermon preached by the pastor who is also a cadre.

"He said, 'The Bible is sacred, but smuggling is dirty! Smuggling is an illegal and sinful activity. Bible smuggling doesn't honor the Bible; it disgraces it. Therefore, all we Chinese Christians who love and treasure the Bible stand up and criticize such a sinful act, which harms the sacredness of the Bible.'

"He concluded, 'Jesus said, "He who does not enter the sheepfold by the door but climbs in by another way, that man is a thief and a robber. The thief comes only to steal and kill and destroy." The Bible smuggler's aim can only be to destroy—to destroy the reputation of China, to destroy the Protestant Three-Self Patriotic Movement in China, and to spoil the good intentions of kind, foreign Christians simultaneously. We Chinese Christians firmly condemn and oppose such a sinful act. Anyway, most of the Bibles were washed away into the sea by the waves of the rising tide.' "

As Peter repeated the Sunday sermon, Chan broke into a sardonic smile. "The irony is that a majority of those people listening probably had one of those smuggled Pearl Bibles secretly tucked away in their pocket."

"Let's pray," concluded Peter, "that just as the high tide washed those Scriptures ashore, so God will continue to wash His church in China."

18

More Precious than Gold

In Shantou Daniel Ng is ecstatic. After praying for years for Bibles, he has boxes of them now hidden in his home. *Lord, You are so good!*

Daniel was able to rescue eight boxes of the Pearl Bibles during all the confusion when the PSB were trying to burn the books on the beach. One by one he carried them from under the trees to his home nearby, trying not to draw attention to himself. Now he was overwhelmed that he actually had in his possession more than seven hundred Bibles. *Who do you want me to give them to, Lord?*

∽∞∾

The candle flickers as it begins to burn out in a small room in Inner Mongolia. Sister Grace is up late reading her Pearl Bible. No longer is it necessary for her to copy from a borrowed Bible. Now she finally has one of her own!

∽∞∾

Brother Lee is riding his bicycle quickly down the rutted path in central Henan Province. He's made the twenty-kilometer trip many times before. He used to borrow Pastor Goh's Bible to prepare his messages. On this trip Pastor Goh gave him his own personal Pearl Bible. As his legs pump tirelessly, he prays, "Lord, thank you for answering my prayer of three years. I now have my own Bible. Thank You! Thank You! Thank You!"

On arrival home, Brother Lee opens to page 1 and begins to read. He reads the entire Bible through in one week. The second week, he reads it through a second time. The third week, he reads it through a third time.

My people don't know this wonderful message, he thinks. He quits his job and becomes an itinerant evangelist working in the countryside.

〇〜〜〜〇

In the ancient capital city of Sian, where the eastern end of the Silk Road originates, a young pastor is on his knees. His lips are moving, but no sound comes out. Soon his tears flow and he has to stop his prayer to wipe his wet face.

"Are you praying for Bibles again, Wang?" asks his wife.

"No, my dear," replies Wang, continuing to wipe away the tears. "I'm thanking God for the Pearl Bibles and asking Him to guide me as I deliver thousands of them to brothers and sisters as far away as the mountains of Qinghai Province."

〇〜〜〜〇

In central China, Sister Ling works as a young evangelist, commissioned by her house church to this ministry. She was sent out with a one-way ticket and two weeks' worth of rice. She loves her work but it bothers her that believers lack Bibles.

She overhears that a woman only four miles away received wet Pearl Bibles from the beach and carefully dried the pages one by one in the sunlight.

Ling approaches the woman and requests a Bible. The old lady says, "No, no. These Bibles are very valuable, and I don't even know if you're a true believer!"

Ling persists in her pleading but cannot convince the woman to give up even one Bible. Finally the old woman says, "If you can recite the Lord's Prayer without a single mistake, I'll give you one."

Ling knows an elderly believer in a nearby village, so she goes there to borrow his Bible. She is amazed to discover it is totally hand-copied, and the brother cherishes it with a holy reverence. Reading this laborious work of love gives Ling a new appreciation for God's Word.

On her way back to the old woman, Ling worries that she may not have memorized the Lord's Prayer correctly. *What if he made a mistake in copying?* But she says the prayer perfectly.

The old woman is still not convinced. She makes Ling pray out loud to be assured of her sincerity. Then she asks her question after question about how she came to faith in Christ and what her ministry is accomplishing.

Finally the interrogation ends, and the old woman kneels down with Ling, hugs the Pearl Bible, and presents it to her. "I'm sorry for being so cautious," says the old woman. "After our brothers collected these Bibles from the shore, they began to distribute them all over China. It was very dangerous, and some paid with their lives. Remembering their sacrifice, I treasure these Bibles even more."

Ling leaves with her Pearl Bible, some of the pages still rippled from when it was wet. She reads it with tears in her eyes.

⁊⫴⫴⫴⫴⫴⫴⫴

Chan carries a three-foot-tall bag of Pearl Bibles by train and bus from southern China to Sinjiang Province in the far northwest. That trip takes five hours by airplane.

On arrival, when he opens the bag, the house church leaders can't believe what they see. They ask Chan, "Are you sure these are all for us?"

When he nods, they circle the bag of Bibles. Then taking one copy in their hands, they begin to pray and give thanks. They can't stop their tears. One by one they pray, giving thanks and embracing the Bible, holding it close to their faces. When the Bible is returned to Chan, it is wet with tears! Many more tears flow when he hands out personal copies to all the brothers and sisters present.

⁊⫴⫴⫴⫴⫴⫴⫴

Peter Xu is the leader of the Born-Again Movement—the largest house church network in China. They place a lot of emphasis on repentance of sin, and when people repent, they weep. As the years have gone by, weeping has become the symbol of repentance among them. If people cry, they are seen as saved.

In 1979 they began their outreach ministry, and many people experienced healing. Now they have a following of two million people and are one of the more stable networks. They are the top group in China for children's ministry and have twenty thousand Sunday school teachers across the country. The Born-Again Movement closed their doors to outsiders and foreigners with just a few exceptions.

After Pearl Bibles were stored in depositories in southern China in 1981, Peter Xu sent three men every month by bus to these depository contacts. They were to bring back a thousand Pearl Bibles per trip for their growing house church movement.

They did this repeatedly, but one month the PSB discovered the three men with their Bible load while they waited for the night bus home. The police threw the one thousand Pearl Bibles into the cesspool of the public latrine. The three men were interrogated and jailed for the weekend.

On Monday afternoon they were released and commanded to go straight home and never return. Instead, they waited inside the latrine until darkness fell. Then they climbed down into the filthy cesspool of human waste, carefully retrieving each of the foul-smelling books. They washed them off under the local water tap and carried them home in their bags. There they dried them out, sprayed them with perfume, and circulated them through the network. These books became known as the "Perfume Bibles" and were gratefully received. Such was the hunger and importance of every copy of God's Word.

☙❧

Another network leader, who also calls himself Peter, says, "In June 1981, Open Doors delivered one million Bibles to China in one night. I was not there on the shore to receive these Bibles, but I have a Project Pearl Bible that was reeled in by fishermen. Some brothers and sisters bought it from the fishermen and gave it to my church network. This Bible was very precious to us. We hid it at a meeting place by digging a hole, putting it in, and covering it with a rock. I used it for ten years, until it was discovered and confiscated. The revival of the

Chinese church came hand-in-hand with those co-workers overseas, and the Lord knows that we are so thankful!"

New Manila
September 1981

Doug was seated in the comfortable oversized chair in his office on a late September day. "What's the latest word on Lili, Mei-ling, and Chan, Joseph?" he asked, as his program manager walked into the room for the post-project meeting.

"Sadly," Joseph began, "all three are now in prison. Lili and Mei-ling are in a women's penitentiary with a three-year sentence. Chan's situation is worse because he was caught by the PSB distributing Pearl Bibles in Henan Province. He's now serving a ten-year sentence."

"Let's stop right now and pray for them," Doug said with deep emotion. "Lord, we pray for your special presence with our sisters and brother wherever they are today. Thank you that they were always willing for this to be the outcome of their involvement in Pearl. Yet we ask in the powerful name of Jesus for their release, literally and spiritually. May they sense freedom of spirit this very day! Give them many opportunities to share your love with other needy prisoners and meet their every need."

After the circle of prayer, Doug continued to ask Joseph about the Bible distribution status.

"It's much better than we thought at first, Doug." Joseph began. "When the first phone call came from Mama Kwang, we thought that maybe one-third of the delivery had been confiscated or destroyed. But the call today indicated that they can account for 80 percent, and the number is increasing every day as they meet more local Christians. It's a challenge to account for them all because many individuals took boxes from under the trees to their homes. Even non-Christians did this with the purpose of selling them. I think in another month, we'll find the number accounted for even higher."

"What impresses me, Doug," Pablo interjected, "is a recent report that the TSPM have announced they're now going to print significant quantities of Bibles inside China. It sure seems we've met our overall goals for the project."

"Are you working on the press release, Terry?" Doug asked.

"Sure am," Terry Madison replied. "Also, I'm putting together a photo album for each of the guys involved. It'll make a great keepsake, as well as another way to say thank you for their valuable involvement."

"That's great, Terry. What do you hear about Project Pearl in the Christian community, Dean?"

"There's still a lot of criticism from other ministries, Doug. Just today a donor sent me a copy of a letter from a Hong Kong–based ministry that has always been critical of us. Here are just a few lines of what they're writing to their constituency right now." Dean began to read:

> Open Doors chartered a freighter and shipped Bibles to the coastal port city of Shantou in South China. There they were met by Christian fishermen in their boats. The government got wind of what was about to take place, intercepted the fishing boats, refused to allow the Bibles to be taken ashore; whereupon, they were dumped into the sea in plastic bags. The fact is, many of them did float ashore or towards the shore. Many of them were picked up by police boats or by soldiers waiting on the beach. Eyewitnesses said that the government burned Bibles that were confiscated for three days and three nights. Estimates vary widely as to how great the loss was. But obviously, it was a very significant percentage.

"What bothers me most," Doug commented with disgust, "is that these so-called brothers in the faith didn't even try to contact us and find out what really happened—or even our point of view—before publishing and reporting." He sat back in his chair, rubbing his eyes, and then said, "I wish this were the only negative report.

"Just this morning I got a phone call from Brother Andrew because the full report you read from, Dean, has already been published in Christian newspapers in Scandinavia. I also received calls from

Japan and Australia, reporting that disinformation about the project is being circulated. I'm going to call my good friends David Aikman and Bing Wong at *Time* magazine. We need the truth to be told. Pablo, tomorrow you and I will go to Hong Kong and visit Bing. We'll take Terry's press release with us." (See *Time* article in Appendix.)

Washington, D.C.
May 6, 1989
Brother Andrew was speaking at a fundraising mega banquet in Washington for Open Doors. As he spoke, a note was passed to him from one of the tables:

> Brother Andrew,
> Several months ago, I came to America from mainland China. This morning I heard about this banquet from a Christian brother. I come here in order to say thanks to Brother Andrew. In 1982, I carried Bibles from Sian to Qinghai. Those Bibles were carried to Sian from Canton. The ones Brother Andrew shipped to Swatow from Philippines.
> Thank you, Brother Andrew. Many house churches in China know you and pray for you.
> Wang, from mainland China

Sao Paulo, Brazil
January 1994
The office door opened and a beautiful Chinese young lady, about twenty-five years old, entered, holding her baby in her arms. She introduced herself to the Open Doors staff as Lina and explained that she was a house church Christian from China.

In the 1970s Brazil experienced a large influx of business people and shopkeepers from Taiwan. Then in the 1990s a second wave of immigrants began to arrive from Mainland China. Ninety percent of these Chinese immigrants are concentrated in the Sao Paulo area—Brazil's largest city with nineteen million people. Lina was not one of them. She had come to Brazil as the wife of a YWAM missionary.

They had met in China and were soon planning to return to her country to be a gospel witness.

Lina and her family spent all day long at the office. They prayed with the Open Doors Brazil team. The staff listened very carefully to her words of witness.

She spoke about China's itinerant preachers, the wrong doctrines that develop because of a lack of Bibles, and the fast and huge growth in membership experienced by the house church movement in China.

The team felt as though they were in a movie and transported to China. The reports they had read or heard earlier were now brought to life. Lina could clearly testify to how God's power had been manifested to our Chinese brothers and sisters.

When she held up her Chinese Bible, the staff began to cry with joy. It was a Project Pearl Bible. So much time had elapsed, but the fruit remained. They praised the Lord many times that day for Lina and other recipients of the Bibles from Project Pearl.

꧁꧂

Open Doors Australia Director, Gary, tells of visiting with some house church leaders who were medical doctors in southwest China. He asked them, "Have you seen many miracles in China?"

The senior leader, a surgeon, responded immediately, "We see many miracles; however the biggest was a secret shipment of Bibles from the West one night in 1981. These Bibles arrived when we had very few Christian books and at a time when the revival was flourishing.

"The majority of these Bibles were received safely by unregistered house church leaders on a beach near Shantou. But a percentage were confiscated by the PSB, loaded onto trucks, and taken to Beijing under police escort. These Bibles were stored under strict security for some time.

"Then a meeting was called by the leadership, and senior cadres were required to attend. They were scolded for allowing the Bibles to be 'smuggled in' and were told that the book is an enemy of the state. Every effort must be made in the future to ensure that Bibles do not come into China again."

Then the doctor started to laugh and said, "Praise the Lord," before relating the rest of the story.

"After the cadres were scolded for this failure in security, the leader of the meeting said, 'I'm going to give each one of you senior officers a copy of this Bible. I want you to read it from beginning to end and understand why this is such a threat to Communism.' They all left the meeting with a Project Pearl Bible."

The surgeon concluded with a smile, "Today (fifteen years later) at least 15 percent of the Communist Party members are now Christians because of Project Pearl!"

❦

Fifteen years after Project Pearl, an Open Doors worker met itinerant evangelist, Brother Lee, in Henan Province. She was surprised to discover that Brother Lee, who started out on his own, now pastors a network of house churches that has grown to more than four hundred thousand members. His network of churches continues to need more than twenty thousand Bibles a month, just for new believers.

Brother Lee still had his first Bible—from Project Pearl—because he could not bear to part with it. By now, it had masking tape holding it together, and the pages were worn. Like many others, he said, "This gift was more precious than gold!"

❦

House church leaders in the Shantou area were undeterred by the authorities and their threats of imprisonment. The leaders even began requesting more deliveries of Bibles. Enoch Ma, who had managed to evade the authorities, wrote, "In order to continue the work, please prepare two million pieces for us and send them in. Every group is waiting for the goods."

Matthew Lo expressed his thanks this way: "Thank you so much for your concern for the Chinese Christian brothers and sisters. Your act has really encouraged us. You love the Chinese so much that we feel we should love our own countrymen more. We will always remember you in our prayers. But you have already received your reward—the smiling faces and thankful tears from hundreds of thousands of Christians in China."

⚬⚬⚬⚬

By the mid-1980s the accounting of Project Pearl Bibles had reached 98 percent. An extra twenty thousand Chinese Bibles were taken in by suitcase couriers to complete the request for one million. Pearl Bibles have been spotted repeatedly in every province of China, other than Tibet. Most of the largest house church networks of China have reported the positive impact of the Pearl Bibles, including the report from the most public figure of China's house church movement, the "Heavenly Man." [6]

One of the Gezhou local church participants in the project concluded:

"The Bible incident caused a number of brothers and sisters to go through a time of testing, but with the critical shortage of Bibles at that time, those disciples who hungered and thirsted after righteousness were able to receive spiritual provisions. At the same time, God also used this tiny church to accomplish a big thing that shocked the whole world."

⚬⚬⚬⚬

Many Christian ministries to China had been outspokenly negative immediately after Project Pearl, and even more so after the *Time* article, but their response has ameliorated over the ensuing years. Yet it is amazing to read disinformation about Project Pearl more than twenty-five years later.

For example, in a recent book titled *Hearts of Fire,* which tells the complete story of Sister Ling (mentioned in the prologue and in this chapter), there is a reference to the project. Sister Ling heard about the old woman nearby who had Bibles available and the story proceeds: "It turned out the woman had a few *Bibles that had washed ashore after members of a Christian mission group had been forced to throw them overboard while attempting to smuggle them into China at night*" (emphasis mine). [7]

Project Pearl did have a significant impact on the future printing of Bibles inside China, which continues today. Shortly after the project was completed, China's TSPM announced the first official printing of Bibles inside the country.

Todd Miller became the Hong Kong director for Open Doors Asia in early 1982, following Project Pearl. Todd remembers visiting the United Bible Society office in Hong Kong that year with Doug and Michael to talk about the new request for two million Bibles. The director, an old acquaintance of Doug's from Manila, informed them that the TSPM in China had really put the heat on their international headquarters and Hong Kong office for giving Open Doors the plates to print the one million Pearl Bibles. He also questioned the success of the delivery and distribution.

The conversation came to a crucial point when Doug mentioned the immediate need for two million Bibles. The director said he was willing to wait, however long it might take, for official permission from the Chinese government before going ahead to print Bibles, regardless of the urgent need inside. He would wait ten, twenty, one hundred years and longer if necessary. The three men sat in stunned silence at such lack of compassion for the needs of Chinese believers.

A few years later, the TSPM announced a plan to print one million Bibles. By 1987 the Amity Printing Company was founded cooperatively in Nanjing—with the help of the United Bible Society—and began printing Bibles. From 1988 to mid-2007 Amity Press has printed more than fifty-five million Chinese Bibles and New Testaments, which are available to Christians in the major cities who can afford to buy them.[8]

Doug Sutphen recalls meeting Han Wenzao in 1996, then the chairman of the China Christian Council (under the TSPM) and head of Amity Press. Han admitted to him, "Project Pearl meant we had to build Amity Press. It put so much pressure on us, we could not go on with small printings."[9]

During the China Consultation (an initiative of the Forum of Bible Agencies) in New York in April 2000, Dr. James Hudson Taylor III reportedly commented, "Project Pearl was used to put pressure on the Chinese Government to officially allow a Bible printing press. Otherwise, projects like Pearl would happen again because of the tremendous demand for Bibles in China."

In 2003, noted author and China watcher, David Aikman, wrote in his significant book, *Jesus in Beijing*, "[Project] Pearl had a major long-term impact on the overall availability of Bibles in China."[10]

This is the reason there was never another Project Pearl, though many people, from Bing Wong at *Time* in Hong Kong to Pastor John Chow in Shantou, asked many times, "Why didn't you do it again?"

After his imprisonment, Pastor John was asked if Project Pearl was worth all the trials it had brought him. He replied, "I was surprised twice over the whole affair. First of all, that Christians actually had the courage and the vision to mount something this big. They did well. I was surprised again when it was never repeated. We need more 'Pearls.' There are millions of us still needing Scriptures. We must be prepared to take the risks again and again."

In China today it is still estimated that approximately one third of all believers do not have a personal Bible.

19

High Tide at Nine

No one else was walking on Hi Bean Road as Lili turned and headed east toward the sea. She stood for a long time on sandy Michael Beach looking out at the water. Then she sat on the sand for an hour or more, watching the fishermen working from the breakwater rocks at the mouth of the cove.

Though it was now eight years since the night of the Project Pearl delivery, her mind clearly relived the scenes on this beach. She visualized thousands of believers moving thousands of boxes of Chinese Bibles quickly across the sand, through the tree line, and out to depositories.

Her pulse quickened at the memory of the army patrol. She could still picture them trying to arrest people at the same time they were collecting and piling up the boxes they found under the trees. Lili recalled that she had just come back from sending Mama Kwang a coded message from a telephone center in the city and was watching the activity from behind some trees.

She laughed out loud as she recalled Ming Seng-kee running away repeatedly with boxes of Bibles—one box at a time! On that night, he didn't even know the Lord. He really had no idea what he was risking his life for. Now as a result of reading one of those Pearl Bibles, he was an elder in a new house church in his village.

She would never forget the anger of the PSB as they tried unsuccessfully to burn the boxes of books. Then they threw individual Bibles into the water. Meanwhile, anyone who came anywhere near the PSB officers was arrested and dragged off to the city for interrogation.

The PSB also took pictures of the many Bibles floating in the bay for propaganda purposes.

Lili smiled, remembering the hundreds of small houses in the Shantou area where Pearl Bibles dried on the roofs for days.

But the smile faded as she thought of Pastor John Chow and his harrowing prison experience. *Thank you, Lord, for the miracle in saving John's life.*

She recalled a great crisis that arose in the church in Gezhou. Members who were linked to the incident were also investigated by the PSB and even detained. They were relentlessly interrogated. Many felt that there must have been a "Judas" among the church members who had already reported everything to the relevant authorities.

Then Lili relived the night she visited Mei-ling at her home in Queshi. They were praying together for the safety of Chan as well as Pastor Samuel Wu and his two daughters. Suddenly the PSB broke into the house. They grabbed Lili and Mei-ling by the hair and dragged them outside to the worn-out police car.

At the police station they were interrogated separately for three days. They were repeatedly asked to confess their crimes and reveal the names of their superiors and co-workers. Lili had learned from Pastor John Chow that the best course of action was to say nothing and close your eyes and pray.

She recalled eighteen rounds of interrogation. Once the PSB were so furious they beat her twice on the hands, kicked her in the thigh, and abused her with vulgar language. Her mind resisted reliving any more of that experience, but she did think about the prison. Because of the seriousness of her crime, she was sentenced to three years in a maximum-security prison with six thousand other women.

Again she smiled as she remembered a prisoner named Sister Hu from Henan Province. They became close friends after they realized they were both followers of Jesus. Sister Hu was imprisoned with a six-month sentence for public preaching. Her gift of personal evangelism was so strong, she led eight hundred women prisoners to faith in Jesus during her six months there.

Lili was left to do the discipling of all these new believers. Her three years seemed to fly by.

When she returned to her home in Dahao near the city of Shantou, she began teaching again in her house church fellowship. She was surprised to find that in three years, the network of churches begun by Mama Kwang had grown so quickly. Two hundred churches had expanded to six hundred, and they were still short of Bibles for every believer.

She looked out at the water as darkness closed in and the moon shone down on the cove. She could still visualize *Michael* and *Gabriella* anchored there.

Lord, she prayed silently, *the first time I prayed on this beach, you performed a million miracles. What do you want me to do now? I'm available!*

⊙〰〰〰〰〰〰〰⊙

Ten years later, three shadows stretched on the sand of Michael Beach, caused by the setting sun. The young family approached a log washed up on the shore. The man and the woman sat down on the log. The seven-year-old boy found a flat stone and skipped it out across the calm water of the cove.

"Caleb, come sit down. I want to tell you a story," said the man.

"But, Dad, can't I throw some stones first?"

"Okay. But come back and sit down with Mom and me in a few minutes."

"How do you feel, coming back here?" the man asked his wife.

"There were days when I thought I'd never live to see this beach again. But my feeling tonight is just one of awe. I'm amazed that God used us to help so many brothers and sisters receive a copy of His Word," said Mei-ling. "How do you feel?"

Chan smiled and hesitated. After a long pause, he replied, "I'm anxious to tell our Caleb how we met and what a great God we serve."

Caleb walked slowly toward the log and sat between his parents. Taking turns, they told him the story in detail of a million miracles.

They explained how, from this very beach, they helped with organizing Pearl Bible deliveries. They told Caleb the impact the Bibles had on the growing house church movement in their country. They mentioned the long difficult years they spent in prison and later their engagement and marriage.

Then Mei-ling reached into her bag and pulled out a colorful children's Bible. "This is what we're helping to distribute now. This is your copy, Caleb. And in a few years when you're a teenager, there'll be Chinese youth Bibles for you to share with your friends."

By the time they finished talking and praying together, the water was lapping near the edge of their log. They left Michael Beach at 9:00 p.m. It was high tide.

20

China Today

China has changed dramatically since the era of Project Pearl described in this story. In late 1978 Deng Xiaoping announced the official launch of the Four Modernizations, formally marking the beginning of the reform era. The Four Modernizations were in the fields of agriculture, industry, science and technology, and national defense. The reform program, essentially stressing economic self-reliance, was designed to make China a great economic power by the early twenty-first century. The Four Modernizations have changed the landscape on many levels. Ostensibly China is now a prosperous, modern, and fast-changing society.

CHURCH GROWTH

Perhaps the most interesting change is the extremely rapid growth of the church since the modernization period began in 1979. At the time of the revolution in 1949, there were fewer than one million Protestant Christians—of all stripes—in China. During the decade of the Cultural Revolution (1965–1975), there was no way for outsiders to know whether the church was growing or declining in numbers.

By 1980 it was clear that significant growth had occurred. When the one-million-Bibles request was received, Open Doors research indicated there were at least ten million Christians in China and possibly as many as thirty million—this after thirty years of incredible oppression.

Of course the first to deny this growth was the TSPM. If they acknowledged that there were this many believers, their responsibility and requirements to provide Scriptures would be staggering. Initially they declared the church numbered only two million. Even today, they still acknowledge fewer than twenty million Protestant Christians.

In 1983, Dr. Jonathan Chao of the Chinese Church Research Centre in Hong Kong announced there were fifty million Christians in China. His numbers were based on extrapolation, since no one—even now—has access to accurate data or head counts of the actual number of believers in the country. Therefore, his statistics came under fire from many sources.

Today, twenty-five years later, even those China church statisticians who will count only the heads they know about personally come close to the late Dr. Chao's claim. Others, still given to extrapolating the unknown from the known, estimate the church in China is more than one hundred million. Leading house church pastors inside the country—such as Samuel Lamb—also use this figure.

Open Doors believes it is fair to say that the church in China numbers between sixty and eighty million people, though the actual number could be higher.[11] Most of this phenomenal church growth has occurred in the unregistered house church movement. This is the longest-lasting revival movement in all of church history.

REVIVAL MOVEMENTS

The mass movement to follow Jesus Christ began among the peasants in the countryside, but today it includes many urban intellectuals as well. This trend began soon after the Tiananmen Square massacre in mid-1989. A British academic has found that Christian fellowships are now active in most Chinese universities, resulting in a Christian explosion that has "reshaped the religious landscape." Edmund Tang from the University of Birmingham recently documented that this university house church movement is now an "open secret."[12]

In the past two decades a new urban house church movement has mushroomed which is intentionally nondenominational and nonconfrontational with the government. It is neither part of the state church nor the traditional "underground" church in the rural areas, though there is plenty of overlap. A significant number of the urban church members are also Communist Party members. "Professors, doctors, lawyers, and business owners are now seeking more freedom as Christians, while also hoping to openly influence society with the values of the gospel."[13]

Among this growing group of Christian intellectuals is a segment known as "Cultural Christians." They do not identify with any church and do not attend church, but they promote Christian ideas and values. Their goal is to make their understanding of Christianity a visible force in China's search for a new order.

The China revival has brought as many burdens as blessings—even for the TSPM church. Their ratio of believers to pastors is about 3,000 to 1. There are too few Christian leaders to disciple the fast growth of new believers. One major house church network numbers more than 500,000. They have the daunting task of discipling an average of 543 new converts per day.

Let me compare this to a church in the West where I live. I attend a church of one hundred members, and we meet in a building with a maximum seating capacity of two hundred. If something like the China revival were to come to my home church, every Sunday one hundred new seekers would show up, wanting to follow Jesus. One month later there would be four hundred new believers. Two hundred of these share their faith and bring their families to church, and many more turn to the Lord. In three months we would have approximately twelve thousand people wanting to worship and be discipled each week.

If a church in the West with all of its resources finds this a challenge, what about the church in China? The first and most basic challenge for Chinese church leaders is securing a Bible for every new convert.

BIBLE AVAILABILITY

In the large cities, Bible availability may not be a significant problem, because the TSPM churches do sell the Bibles printed on the Amity Press at reasonable prices. But in unregistered house churches in the rural areas, the availability of Bibles in adequate numbers is still a huge problem.

Every year Open Doors delivers Bibles free of charge to many Christians in the rural house church movement. Each year since Project Pearl, the number of Bibles provided to the church in China has increased. In 2006 Open Doors distributed in China more than five million pieces of literature, including Chinese Bibles, study Bibles, children's Bibles, spiritual-training materials, and other Christian books.

LEADERSHIP TRAINING

A second concern for the house church movement is the training of leaders to provide discipleship for new believers. Our Open Doors coworkers in China estimate the number of house churches throughout the country is now approximately one million. A great majority of these house churches are pastored by young leaders with little or no formal training. Training sessions are greatly appreciated by leaders, young and old. Again in 2006, Open Doors provided secret training sessions in China that impacted more than twenty thousand church leaders. Some of our Chinese colleagues have even suggested that part two of Project Pearl should be the training of "one million" house church leaders.

MISSIONARY EVANGELISM

Revival in China has brought a passion for evangelism that is unrivaled anywhere in the world. Young people by the score commit themselves to full-time missionary service. One group even call themselves, "Kamikazes for Jesus!" Their first commitment has been to the many unreached people inside China's borders.

The "Back to Jerusalem" movement, which actually began decades ago, has now come to the point of believing God for two hundred thousand trained Chinese missionaries to trek through the Muslim world, ultimately taking the gospel back to Jerusalem where it all began—on the day of Pentecost. For those following the vision, it is a "no turning back" commitment. Though currently there are nowhere near the two hundred thousand recruits, they have begun their work, and our colleagues have met some of these Chinese missionaries in Yemen and Afghanistan.

PERSECUTION

China remains a land full of paradoxes that appear baffling to the outsider. No topic is more paradoxical than that of persecution. While some Chinese Christian leaders languish in jail, others travel the world talking of religious freedom. Part of this is due to varying conditions throughout the country. China watchers often say, "Everything you hear about China is probably true—somewhere. And may be false somewhere else!"

While some deny significant levels of persecution at all, the majority of Christians outside the state-approved churches find the monitoring by government bodies invasive and controlling. Evangelism, outside the registered church walls, is illegal. Even though China's government does not have a national law that explicitly prohibits the teaching of religion to anyone less than eighteen years old, internal regulations exist to forbid baptism of minors and restrict children's programs. Sunday school teachers face the likelihood of detention, fines, or imprisonment of up to three years if caught. House church leaders are still jailed and beaten for what in Western society would be regarded as the free expression of their faith.

While some may exaggerate the levels of persecution, it's true that the average believer constantly faces discrimination and harassment. The Christian church in China may not have as many martyrs as in Colombia or face as many restrictions as their brothers and sisters in Saudi Arabia or fight as many extremist mobs as believers in Indonesia, but the millions of Christians in China remain the world's largest persecuted community today.

OPPORTUNITIES

This does not negate the overall progress China is making. In addition to economic growth and modernization, remarkable opportunities for service exist for Christian English teachers, medical workers, social workers, and many other Christian professionals. These opportunities are likely to increase in the future. Discerning groups should continue to take advantage of this open door as long as they acknowledge the risks and remain aware of the levels of government corruption involved.

In his October 2006 e-mail newsletter, noted China watcher Tony Lambert reported the first case of a Chinese house church Christian appealing in court against the local government and winning. Li Huimin held an Easter service in March 2006 at the home of seventy-one-year-old Ma Wenqing in Henan Province. Local police raided and Li was arrested and beaten. On April 26 he was sent to a reeducation-through-labor camp. After filing a lawsuit, Li's sentence was revoked (although the original meeting was still considered illegal). It is hoped this precedent will be widely known within China and push forward the boundaries for greater freedom for house church believers, who have so often experienced harassment.[14]

David Aikman's controversial work of 2003, *Jesus in Beijing: How Christianity Is Transforming China and Changing the Global Balance of Power*, postulates a thesis of continued Christian growth that will ultimately gain political influence in China. At the same time that this book was published, a California-based China ministry released a DVD titled *The Cross: Jesus in China*. It documents the growth of Christianity in the house church movement with excellently produced interviews and reports.[15]

The Aikman book and the DVD woke up top Chinese government officials to the fact that the reports they had previously received from the Religious Affairs Bureau on the Christian population and their activities in China were understated. The government feels threatened.

Furthermore, the government is well informed of the large number of foreign organizations and individuals planning to take advantage of the Olympic Games in Beijing in August 2008 for the purpose of accelerating Christian impact in China. This also makes them nervous.

CURRENT CRACKDOWN

To secure its own control, the Chinese government has reportedly established an anti-infiltration department. Its purpose is to take counteractions against overseas Christian ministry initiatives in China. It is implementing an ironhanded policy that surpasses all previous government actions in its severity. The government has started strict monitoring of foreign Christians working in the country and plans extra efforts in controlling religious activities through the Beijing Olympics.

BIBLE NEED

In March 2007 Compass Direct News Service spoke with several house church leaders in Kunming, and these leaders reported an acute lack of Bibles—in a city where Bibles previously were readily available from TSPM churches. Bibles have also reportedly been deliberately withheld from house church pastors.

Both house church and TSPM pastors reported a shortage of Bibles and other Christian materials in the northwest, the northeast, Beijing, and the southwest. Church growth in tribal areas has also created an urgent need for Bibles in minority languages.[16]

China expects more than half a million visitors for the Olympic Games in August 2008. The country is determined to put on its best face for everyone—even Christians.

Ironically, Liu Bainian, a representative of the Chinese People's Political Consultative Conference and vice president of the China Patriotic Catholic Association, stated in writing that China should cater to the spiritual needs of its foreign visitors who are religious by placing Bibles in hotel rooms. Members of the Chinese Patriotic Catholic Association (which is endorsed by the Beijing government) will be asked to collect Bibles for use in hotels during the Games. Then they will be returned to the donors.[17]

While this gesture, reported in *China Daily,* demonstrates some positive attitudes toward religion in China, it also reinforces some religious limitations. Even though these Bibles will be in hotels for the

Olympics, they are only on loan and only meant for foreigners.

Bible distribution is a positive step in creating an environment that is supportive of religious freedom, but the greater question remains: What will China's policies be toward Christians after the Olympic Games are over?

Our hope and prayer is that they will be positive and all house churches will be given complete freedom to worship without having to register with the government. Pray that China will be more open to Christian expression and witness in all areas of the country.

Epilogue:
Faith Steps to Accomplish the Impossible

Project Pearl was definitely a miracle, but it was not just one big miracle. It was actually a series of smaller ones, as each step and each incident seemed to involve a supernatural act. But after the project was accomplished, we look back and call it a "big" miracle.

I've written this story for a number of reasons. Not only did I want to document the background details and miracles of Project Pearl but also to share the spiritual principles this story embodies.

In case you missed some of the nuances as you read, let me outline what I think are the spiritual highlights: seven faith steps to accomplish the impossible.

1. PREPARE TO OVERCOME OBSTACLES

It is obvious that Doug Sutphen was a man of strong faith. When God spoke to him, he took the message at face value and believed God would bring it to pass. This faith was not blind. Doug studied the Bible to find examples and principles. He was especially impressed with the story of Nehemiah in the Old Testament. Nehemiah received a vision and calling from his times of prayer. He did his research and then acted with authority.

Obstacles, however, are the challenges to faith. Nehemiah had many detractors and critics, yet he kept his focus on God's promise and the task at hand. The apostle Paul also faced many adversaries. He told King Agrippa that he *"was not disobedient to the vision from heaven"* (Acts 26:19), even though his preaching about it was the reason his enemies tried to kill him.

An Open Doors co-worker was visiting a Cuban pastor who was experiencing severe hardship and difficulties. He asked him, "With all these problems, don't you ever want to give up?" The pastor smiled and simply replied, "If there were no battles, there would be no victory!" Someone else once said, "Whatever does not kill me, strengthens me."

We live and work in the midst of a spiritual battle—the kingdom of light versus the kingdom of darkness. Our adversary, Satan, wants to trip us up, but our task is to throw off those things that hinder us and *"run with perseverance the race marked out for us"* (Hebrews 12:1b). We have the whole armor of God to help us. Therefore we run, walk, or stand by *faith* and not by sight.

2. ACCEPT THAT YOU MAY LOOK FOOLISH

Sometimes walking by faith can look very foolish to others. Think of Noah and the ark, which took him more than a hundred years to build at a time when it had never rained on the earth. He must have looked very foolish in the eyes of his contemporaries.

Then there was Gideon. God reduced his fighting troops to just three hundred to stand up against a massive enemy army. Any human military general would have called this sheer folly. King Saul's son, Jonathan, told his armor-bearer: *"Nothing can hinder the LORD from saving, whether by many or by few"* (1 Samuel 14:6b).

Missionary Hudson Taylor, who founded the CIM, is credited with the statement, "Without an element of risk in ministry, there is no need for faith."

Often, because of our pride, we refuse to obey God in situations that might make us look foolish. Captain Bill Tinsley, the unsung hero of Project Pearl, says, "Years ago I learned to pocket pride and when I did, I found a real internal power. Project Pearl wouldn't have succeeded if we had exercised pride in the situations we faced. We would never have reached the goal."

There are times when what may seem foolish has been clearly communicated by the Lord in prayer. Brother Willis's prediction of China's opening up after the Love China conference in 1975 is a good example. "Get ready," he told Doug at the border of China. In three years China opened her doors, and six years later Project Pearl was realized.

3. DISCOVER THE FACTS

Walking by faith does not negate the need to do our homework and do it well. In this story I did not bore you with the hours of research, in-depth planning, and fact-finding trips made in preparation for Project Pearl. Be assured these steps were taken and taken with intense seriousness. Dr. Jim Schmook was a stickler for detail and he kept us sharp in making sure every aspect of the plan was researched and studied beforehand.

Wise Solomon said, *"Plans fail for lack of counsel, but with many advisers they succeed"* (Proverbs 15:22). Later he also indicates that plans must be committed to the Lord and only then will they succeed, because the Lord's purposes always win out in the end (see Proverbs 16:3; 19:2). So there is constant tension between our human effort and God's providential blessing. Nevertheless, we must always do our best to learn the facts and make good plans.

4. EXPECT JEALOUSY AND ENMITY
TO COME FROM WITHIN

Though we may be prepared for adversaries, we are often taken by surprise when opposition comes from within our own circle of colleagues or acquaintances. Often Satan uses our own Christian brothers and sisters against us to try to weaken our faith, as well as destroy the unity that keeps us strong. Many times this opposition develops merely from misperceptions when we do not make the effort to discover the facts of the case made against us or the case we are making against others.

For example, in Joshua 22 the nine and a half tribes of Israel that settled in the Promised Land of Canaan took up arms against their brothers, the two and a half tribes that settled west of the Jordan River. The easterners thought the westerners had built an altar in rebellion against God. In fact the altar was a memorial for their descendants to prove Israelis on both sides of the river served the *same* God.

If the easterners had checked out their perception before sharpening their swords, the whole misunderstanding could have been avoided. It is only right that Christians confront one another with kindness in an honest desire to dispel rumor and misperception. This is the road to true unity.

5. Participate in the Power of Unity

Throughout the Scriptures there are insights into the power of unity. Even human rulers understand this. In his early years Mao Zedong is often shown in Chinese movies demonstrating to the peasants how it is easy to break one chopstick, while it is almost impossible to break many chopsticks together. There is power in unity.

The wisest man who ever lived said, "*Though one may be overpowered, two can defend themselves. A cord of three strands is not quickly broken*" (Ecclesiastes 4:12).

One of the lessons of Project Pearl is this power of unity—unity with God in purpose, unity of teamwork, unity of actions. When the Project Pearl "inner circle" management team was convinced of God's direction, their unity in the planning and execution of the plans provided great strength and morale building.

6. Experience Peace in Perseverance

A frail sister in China who was severely persecuted said, "A ship cannot stop just because there is a storm. It just has to make sure it stays on the right course. Without times like these, we may not know how to serve the Lord."

For me there was nothing more enjoyable than being on tugboat *Michael* during good weather. I will never forget the warm wind blowing my beard and the fresh ocean smell while standing on the bow early in the morning as the sun rose over the eastern horizon. The porpoises playfully led the way and multitudes of flying fish skimmed on the surface of the deep blue ocean that was as calm and smooth as a mirror.

There was also nothing more terrifying for me than being "stuck" on tugboat *Michael* in what seemed to be the middle of nowhere during a terrible, long storm. There was nowhere to go to avoid its effects as the ship noisily crashed into huge waves and rolled madly from side to side. There was no way to get off the boat. We just had to pray and ride it out.

Life is like that. During those terrible storms, all you can do is lash yourself to the helm and hold fast to your confidence in God's faithfulness and His everlasting love in Christ Jesus.

Perseverance is active not passive. Hebrews 10:19–39 is a great passage to study on this topic. The key verse for me is verse 36: "*You need to persevere so that when you have done the will of God, you will receive what he has promised.*" The interesting thing to note is that this verse stands in the context of suffering insults, persecution, imprisonment, and property confiscation.

7. Focus Your Human Effort to Glorify God

Early in his teachings Jesus told his followers to do their good works in a way that others would see them and glorify God (see Matthew 5:16). Often, though, pride gets in the way, and in our human efforts, we want the glory. A true follower of Jesus will be humble enough to show that God is the one who should receive all the honor.

The warning of not making a "golden calf" out of Project Pearl is a good example. Even those not immediately involved can become so full of pride over the success of a massive project they forget who should receive the glory. This is the reason there are no photos of the actual delivery of Project Pearl's one million Chinese Bibles. Validation of the project is a matter of trust—trust in those who made the effort as well as trust in the reports of those who received the Bibles.

Every person involved in the project in any way—large or small—will tell you that it happened because of God. He is, therefore, the only one who should receive any of the glory.

Look for God's supernatural acts in the small things of life. Walk in unity and perseverance by faith, and you too may experience one of God's big miracles.

Acknowledgments

You may have figured out by now that I am "Pablo" in this story. Ever since my family's arrival in the Philippines in 1971, close friends and colleagues have called me by this Spanish nickname. I chose to use the name in this book to remain more of a background player and to highlight the unsung heroes of Project Pearl, rather than develop a narrative only from a first-person point of view.

To the best of my knowledge, research, and memory, this story is written truthfully. Obviously, some dialogue has been reconstructed because of fading memory banks. The stories of what happened inside China are all true but composite stories, each one documented in Open Doors research and reporting since the early 1980s. The Chinese names are generic pseudonyms and the personalities are sometimes composite also. In this way, I hope to protect our Chinese colleagues and still allow you to enter into the real world in which these brothers and sisters operated.

The very best news is that all the co-workers inside China who were imprisoned because of their involvement in Project Pearl have long since been released and have returned to their homes and ministries.

Both *Michael* and *Gabriella* were "parked" in Paradise after the project. Later they were both sold locally. *Gabriella* is being used as a scaffold barge for bridge painters on the Pasig River in Manila, and *Michael* joined the fleet of the Philippines' Captain Bella.

In early February 1982, Captain Bill Tinsley experienced his own imprisonment on false charges when President Marcos of the Philippines ordered his arrest. The newspaper accounts blazed the story of his involvement in Project Pearl. He has written a moving account of his two-week prison experience and what God taught him there. This account has been added to his book, *Seadog*.

The key stories from inside China (i.e., travels in Henan Province and Pastor John's prison miracle) were originally written by my highly respected colleague and friend, Ron Boyd-MacMillan. Ron also provided much good advice during the process of writing this manuscript.

I have based a significant amount of this volume on previously produced accounts of Project Pearl. The most notable and helpful is the excellent self-published autobiography of Captain Bill Tinsley titled *Seadog*.[18] Without this volume, I would have been less accurate in recounting events and situations. See the footnote for how you can acquire a copy of this amazing, larger-than-life story. It includes an insert explaining Captain Bill's subsequent arrest and lessons learned in prison.

Brother Andrew has also written two detailed chapters from his perspective about Project Pearl in his challenging book *God's Call*.[19] Earlier editions of this book were titled *The Calling* and *For the Love of My Brothers*.

Reference has already been made to Brother David's excellent biographical volume, *God's Smuggler to China*, coauthored by Dan Wooding and Sara Bruce.[20] It gives a good account of the early growth of China's house church movement. And, of course, the last chapter is another account of June 18, the night of the delivery of Project Pearl Bibles.

After Brother David's death, his autobiography was published with the title *Project Pearl*.[21] Because Mr. Hattaway, the writer, was not involved in the project in any way and did not consult the captain or the planners, the many inaccuracies are somewhat understandable.

Finally, Eddie Cairns, the Kiwi prayer warrior who had the vision of the tug and prayed away the typhoon, has an autobiography, also written by Dan Wooding, titled *To Catch the Wind*.[22] This gives Eddie's detailed account of his own personal involvement in the project.

I am most grateful for the help of the men who made up the final crew of tugboat *Michael,* as well as the crew who came in the beginning but could not stay. Other key players also helped with details.

Dr. Ed Netland died on December 3, 2006, after a fall at his California home. Doug Sutphen died May 8, 2007, at seventy years of age, after twelve years of defying doctors' predictions, and Keith Ritter passed away in Japan on August 28, 2007.

As of this writing the rest of the crew are all still living and involved in an amazing variety of Christian ministries literally around the world—some still very secret. Thus a few of them have asked for their pseudonyms to be used. Several of them have given my memory a good jog and have contributed valuable anecdotal details to make the story more interesting and accurate. Thank you, my brothers. I highly value your friendship.

Special thanks also to Mary Suggs for her editing help, to Jeannie Stephenson for her many helpful suggestions, and to Al Janssen for valuable input in structuring the story.

Paul Estabrooks
March 31, 2008

Appendix

From the pages of

Risky Rendezvous at Swatow
Bold Expedition Smuggles
1 Million Bibles into Mainland China

The beach near the mainland village of Gezhou, code named "Mike" looked deserted in the moonlight. Just offshore, in a glassy South China Sea, a crew member on the seagoing tugboat *Michael* signaled inland with three sharp flashes of a handheld light. Almost immediately, three answering flashes came from the shadowy trees at the edge of the 300-yd. beach. Suddenly, hundreds of figures swarmed silently down to the water's edge, where they had a brief and emotional rendezvous with their foreign visitors. The long awaited and highly covert task that evening: unloading and distributing more than 1 million contraband Chinese-language Bibles. The 232-ton cargo of books had been printed in the U.S. and was smuggled 200 miles up the Chinese coast from Hong Kong in the largest operation of its kind in the history of China.

Time has learned that the remarkable mission, dubbed Project Pearl and executed with military precision last June, was engineered by Open Doors with Brother Andrew International, a nondenominational, evangelical missionary organization based in Ermelo, The Netherlands. The group has specialized in smuggling Bibles mostly into Communist countries for some two decades. The purpose of Project Pearl was to bring badly needed copies of the Scriptures to 5 million Chinese Protestants, who worship under the watchful eye of the Peking government in an estimated 50,000 "house churches." Many of these churches were formed after the Cultural Revolution of the late '60s, when Chinese Christians were persecuted and their regular places of worship closed. Now even the more tolerant regime of Vice

Chairman Deng Xiaoping and Premier Zhao Zhang has begun to bristle at the swift expansion of the house church movement, and is hardly likely to countenance the Bible smuggling effort. Says an American ex-Marine who led Project Pearl: "Between obedience to God and obedience to men, we choose obedience to God."

Project Pearl, a name inspired by *Matthew 13:45* ("the kingdom of heaven is like unto a merchant man, seeking goodly pearls"), had its beginnings in late 1979, when Open Doors was approached secretly by a house church leader, who urgently requested Old and New Testaments. Under the guidance of Open Doors President, Anne van der Bijl, 53, staffers began raising money for the mission in the U.S. through dinners, direct mail and TV spots. The aim of the campaign was disclosed but not the way the mission would be accomplished. Cost of the venture: $6 million, of which $3.5 million came from the U.S. and Canada and $2.5 million from abroad.

Simultaneously, local operatives in the Southeast China port of Swatow, the city near the planned landing, made hundreds of area photographs and closely monitored local Chinese security forces. The plan, completed last December, called for a sturdy tug to tow a partly submersible barge loaded with 232 one-ton blocks, each packed with 48 waterproof boxes containing 90 Bibles.

Thomas Nelson Publishers of Nashville, Tenn., a religious house, agreed to produce the million copies. Photographic plates of a Union version Bible, first translated into Chinese in 1919, were forwarded to the U.S. from Hong Kong. The printing bill for the leather-bound, 629-page volumes of the complete Scriptures was $1.4 million. The Bibles were transported last spring to Hong Kong in a container ship.

A special chosen 20-member international crew began to practice dry runs on the secluded Mindoro Island in the Philippines. A special 100-ft. barge was built, and, for $480,000, the tug *Michael* was bought in Singapore. Finally, the assault party sailed for Hong Kong to pick up its illicit cargo. At the last moment, a planned Easter Sunday landing at Swatow was scrubbed by Van der Bijl because of concern that Chinese authorities might be alerted to the plan. Two months later, the crew sent a cryptic message to agents in Swatow:

"We are going to have a dinner party, expecting so many people that we have arranged 21 teacups and cooked 18 bowls of rice." D-day, in other words, would take place at 2100 hours, June 18.

The show was on. The *Michael* weighed anchor, feigned a southward course toward Manila, then swung north up the Chinese coast. At one point, a typhoon threatened to engulf the frail expedition, but fortunately, the storm veered out to sea. Entering the harbor at Swatow, the crew had another bad moment when a Chinese gunboat approached, only to pass by harmlessly. The unloading process went smoothly as villagers snipped packets of Bibles from the submerged barge with rope cutters supplied by the smugglers, then carried them to waiting bikes, buses and trucks (Open Doors clandestinely had supplied $75,000 to hire the vehicles). But about four hours after the departure of the *Michael,* an army patrol turned up unexpectedly in Gezhou village. The patrol stormed the beach, arresting hundreds who were still at work carting off the Bibles. Subsequently, according to Hong Kong reports, most of the prisoners were released.

Open Doors now estimates that some 60% to 80% of the Bibles wound up in the possession of house church groups, some as far away as Heilongjiang and Xinjiang provinces. So far, Peking has remained silent, but the illegal distribution of Bibles is certain to rankle the hierarchy of Peking's official religious establishment, the Chinese Three-Self Patriotic Church. It has attempted to bring the house churches under closer control by printing its own Bibles, although it has delivered only 135,000 copies since 1979.

Project Pearl, meanwhile, already has inspired calls from potential donors willing to finance massive new Bible-smuggling ventures to China or behind the Iron Curtain.

By Russ Hoyle
Reported by Bing W. Wong/Hong Kong
Time Magazine, October 19, 1981, p. 109

Notes

1. William K. Tinsley, *Seadog* (Taipei, Taiwan: Living Stone Press, 1984), 227–29. Available for $15.00 from the author at 3945 Eden Valley Rd., Port Angeles, WA 98363 USA.
2. Brother Andrew with Verne Becker, *God's Call* (Grand Rapids, MI: Baker, 2002), 122.
3. Randy Thomas, *Wait on the Lord* (Maranatha Music/CCCM Music, 1979). Used by permission.
4. Henry L. Gilmour, *The Haven of Rest* (1890).
5. *My Living Counselor: Daily Readings from the Living Bible* (Wheaton, Illinois: Harold Shaw Publishers, 1976) pp. June 18.
6. Paul Hattaway, *The Heavenly Man: The Remarkable True Story of Chinese Christian Brother Yun* (Grand Rapids, MI: Monarch Books, 2002), 58.
7. Voice of the Martyrs, *Hearts of Fire* (Nashville: Thomas Nelson, 2003), 204.
8. http://www.amityprinting.com/englishweb/blbles.htm
9. Ron Boyd-MacMillan, *Faith That Endures* (Grand Rapids, MI: Revell, 2006), 272.
10. David Aikman, *Jesus in Beijing* (Washington, DC: Regnery, 2003), 270.
11. David Barrett in the *World Christian Encyclopedia* estimates the church in China at eighty-seven million. David Aikman in his *Jesus in Beijing* estimates eighty-two million Christian believers. In its May 2008 issue, *Christianity Today* reported that Ye Xiaowen, the head of China's State Administration of Religious Affairs, used the figure of 130 million Christians at two government briefings in 2006. Bob Fu of China Aid Association has also cited 130 million as a credible estimate.
12. Edmund Tang, ed., *China Study Journal* (University of Birmingham and CTBI, Bastille Court, 2 Paris Garden, London SE1 8ND, UK, March, 2007), 1-2.

13. Rob Moll, "Great Leap Forward," *Christianity Today*, May 2008, 26-27.

14. Tony Lambert, e-mail newsletter, (October 2006).

15. *The Cross: Jesus in China* (China Soul for Christ Foundation, PO Box 450, Petaluma, CA 94953, www.chinasoul.org, 2003).

16. Sarah Page, "China Cracks Down on Rights Ahead of Beijing Olympics," Compass Direct News at http://www.compass direct.org/en/display.php, posted Friday, July 13, 2007.

17. "Hotels Told to Stock Bibles for Olympic Visitors," *China Daily*, http://english.people.com.cn/200703/10/eng 20070310_356251.html, (March 10, 2007).

18. William K. Tinsley, *Seadog* (Taipei, Taiwan: Living Stone Press, 1984). Available for $15.00 from the author at 3945 Eden Valley Rd., Port Angeles, WA 98363, USA.

19. Brother Andrew with Verne Becker, *God's Call* (Grand Rapids, MI: Revell, 2002).

20. Brother David with Dan Wooding and Sara Bruce, *God's Smuggler to China* (London: Hodder & Stoughton, 1981).

21. Brother David with Paul Hattaway, *Project Pearl* (Oxford: Monarch Books, 2007).

22. Eddie Cairns and Dan Wooding, *To Catch the Wind* (Orange, CA: D/W Publishing, 1992).

Get Involved!

Project Pearl is the story of a miracle: a miracle prompted by the longing of God's people to read His Word and the determination of His servants to meet the need. That's why Project Pearl reveals the heart of the story of Open Doors.

Open Doors started in 1955 when a Dutch missionary discovered that Christians in Communist countries were desperately longing for supplies of the Bible—and so he began to take Christian literature behind the Iron Curtain. He became known as Brother Andrew – 'God's Smuggler'—and the founder of a ministry still rooted in a passion to follow God's call and release His Word into the lives of believers in the world's most difficult areas.

More than fifty years later Open Doors continues to serve persecuted Christians in around fifty countries, whether the oppression comes in the name of Communism, Buddhism, Hinduism or Islam. Where the people of God are under pressure, Open Doors stands with them, responding to their cries for help and shaping its response under their guidance.

They still ask for Bibles. In China itself there is still a need for Bibles, and Open Doors is committed to meeting that need. But the Church in China is also asking for Bibles adapted and prepared for children and young people, who are growing up in a very different and rapidly-changing China, one in which the Word of God needs to be presented in a relevant and engaging way.

So the work represented by the story of Project Pearl is ongoing; there are still miracles of God's Word transforming people's lives by His Spirit.

What's more, you can become part of that miracle. Prayerful involvement with Open Doors is a great way to strengthen the Persecuted Church, not just to face the onslaught of pressure, but to continue to reach out with the Gospel of Jesus Christ.

Right now Open Doors is ready to give you information for your prayers—the authentic voice of the Persecuted Church brought to you in print, by email, on the web, so that your prayers are timely, informed and effective weapons in the spiritual battle.

Right now Open Doors can channel your gifts to where they will make a significant difference to our sisters and brothers in the Persecuted Church, not least in providing the Bibles and other Christian literature they have requested. You will be helping to train pastors and congregations so that they can stand strong through the storm, to strengthen the Church in its commitment to mission, to make sure that those who have lost so much can receive material help and spiritual encouragement.

Many Christians around the world also volunteer to bring the Persecuted Church into the life of their own church family, sharing news for prayer and exploring the lessons to be learned from our sisters and brothers.

Perhaps you would allow Open Doors to become your link to the Persecuted Church, so that together we can all play our part in God's great plan and purpose for His world? For further information, simply contact the national office listed below – and discover more of the miracles that come in obedience to God's call.

Open Doors
PO Box 6237
French Forest NSW 2086
AUSTRALIA
www.opendoors.org.au

Missão Portas Abertas
CP 55055
Cep 04733-970
São Paulo—SP
BRAZIL
www.portasabertas.org.br

Open Doors
30-5155 Spectrum Way
Mississauga, ON
L4W 5A1
CANADA
www.opendoorsca.org

Åbne Døre Danmark
PO Box 1062
DK-7500 Holstebro
DENMARK
www.forfulgt.dk

Portes Ouvertes France
BP 139
F-67833 Tanneries
Cedex (Lingolsheim)
FRANCE
www.portesouvertes.fr

Open Doors Germany
Postfach 1142
DE-65761 Kelkheim
GERMANY
www.opendoors-de.org

Porte Aperte
CP 45
37063 Isola Della Scala, VR
ITALY
www.porteaperteitalia.org

Open Doors
32-22 Sang-do
2 Dong Dong Jag-Gu
Seoul 156-831
REPUBLIC OF
SOUTH KOREA
www.opendoors.or.kr

Open Doors
PO Box 47
3850 AA Ermelo
THE NETHERLANDS
www.opendoors.nl

Open Doors
PO Box 27630
Mt Roskill
Auckland 1440
NEW ZEALAND
www.opendoors.org.nz

Åpne Dører
Barstølveien 50 F
4636 Kristiansand
NORWAY
www.opendoors.no

Open Doors
PO Box 1573
QCCPO
1155 Quezon City
PHILIPPINES
http://ph.od.org/index.php

Open Doors
8 Sin Ming Road
#02-06 Sin Ming Centre
Singapore 575628
REPUBLIC
OF SINGAPORE
www.opendoors.org/ODS/

Open Doors
PO Box 1771
Cresta
Gautang, 2118
SOUTH AFRICA
www.opendoors.org.za

Puertas Abiertas
Apdo 49
18100 Armilla (Granada)
SPAIN
www.puertasabiertas.org/

Open Doors
PO Box 48
701 40 Orebro
SWEDEN
www.open-doors.se

Portes Ouvertes
Case Postale 147
CH-1032 Romanel,
s/Lausanne
SWITZERLAND
www.portesouvertes.ch
www.opendoors.ch

Open Doors
UK & Ireland
PO Box 6
Witney
Oxon 0X29 6WG
UNITED KINGDOM
www.opendoorsuk.org

Open Doors
PO Box 27001
Santa Ana, CA 92799
USA
www.odusa.org